Young
Workers

Young Workers
Varieties of Experience

EDITED BY

Julian Barling
E. Kevin Kelloway

American Psychological Association
WASHINGTON, DC

Published by
American Psychological Association
750 First Street, NE
Washington, DC 20002

Copies may be ordered from
APA Order Department
P.O. Box 92984
Washington, DC 20090-2984

In the United Kingdom, Europe, Africa, and the Middle East, copies may be ordered from
American Psychological Association
3 Henrietta Street
Covent Garden
London WC2E 8LU
England

Typeset in Minion by EPS Group Inc., Easton, MD

Printer: Automated Graphic Systems, Inc., White Plains, MD
Jacket designer: Minker Design, Bethesda, MD
Technical/production editors: Valerie Montenegro and Anne Woodworth

Library of Congress Cataloging-in-Publication Data
Young workers : varieties of experience / edited by Julian Barling and E. Kevin
  Kelloway.
      p.   cm.
    Includes bibliographical references and index.
    ISBN 1-55798-563-4 (cloth : acid-free paper)
    1. Youth—Employment—United States. 2. Part-time employment—United
States. 3. School-to-work transition—United States. 4. Youth—Employment—
United States—Psychological aspects. 5. Youth—United States—
Attitudes. 6. Youth—Employment—Canada. 7. Part-time employment—
Canada. 8. School-to-work transition—Canada. 9. Youth—Employment—
Canada—Psychological aspects. 10. Youth—Canada—Attitudes. I. Barling,
Julian. II. Kelloway, E. Kevin.
HD6273.Y615   1998
331.3'4'0973—dc21
                                                      98-37411
                                                         CIP

British Library Cataloguing-in-Publication Data
A CIP record is available from the British Library.

Printed in the United States of America
First edition

Contents

Contributors

Julian Barling, School of Business, Queen's University, Kingston, Ontario, Canada

Joanne Carrubba, Graduate School of Social Service, Fordham University, New York, NY

Dawn N. Castillo, Division of Safety Research, National Institute for Occupational Safety and Health, Centers for Disease Control and Prevention, Morgantown, WV

James Curtis, Department of Sociology, University of Waterloo, Ontario, Canada

Serge Desmarais, University of Guelph, Ontario, Canada

Michael R. Frone, Research Institute on Addictions, Buffalo, NY

Daniel G. Gallagher, Department of Management, James Madison University, Harrisonburg, VA

Steve Harvey, Bishop's University, Lennoxville, Quebec, Canada

E. Kevin Kelloway, University of Guelph, Ontario, Canada

Harvey Krahn, Department of Sociology, University of Alberta, Edmonton, Alberta, Canada

Catherine Loughlin, School of Business, Queen's University, Kingston, Ontario, Canada

Graham S. Lowe, Department of Sociology, University of Alberta, Edmonton, Alberta, Canada

Chaya S. Piotrkowski, Graduate School of Social Service, Fordham University, New York, NY

Preface

Several years ago, one of us took a bicycle in to be repaired. The clerk at the repair shop was amazingly knowledgeable about bicycles and clearly highly involved in his job. He was also 14 years old.

In discussion, it became clear to both of us that this boy's experience stood in stark contrast to the research evidence. At the time, most of the research on youth employment focused on the adverse impact of such employment on school performance, family relationships, and substance use.[1] The extent to which the pervasive assumption was that teenagers' part-time employment would be negative can be ascertained from the title of Greenberger and Steinberg's 1986 book, *When Teenagers Work: The Psychological and Social Costs of Adolescent Employment.* Moreover, in contrast with the research literature on adult employment, research on youth employment (at the time) focused primarily on issues such as employment status or the number of hours worked and excluded considerations such as the quality of employment.[2]

From this initial interest, two research themes emerged. First, what are the parameters of youth employment? That is, what are the relative roles of employment quality, quantity, and status in predicting out-

---

[1] See *When Teenagers Work: The Psychological and Social Costs of Adolescent Employment* by E. Greenberger and L. Steinberg, 1986, New York: Basic Books; "Negative Correlates of Part-Time Employment During Adolescence: Replication and Elaboration" by L. D. Steinberg and S. M. Dornbusch, 1991, *Developmental Psychology, 27,* 304–313.

[2] Subsequent research has begun to rectify this omission, for example, "Some Effects of Teenagers' Part-Time Employment: The Quantity and Quality of Work Makes the Difference" by J. Barling, K. A. Rogers, and E. K. Kelloway, 1995, *Journal of Organizational Behavior, 16,* 143–154; "Teenagers' Part-Time Employment and Their Work-Related Attitudes and Aspirations" by C. A. Loughlin and J. Barling, 1998, *Journal of Organizational Behavior, 19,* 197–207; *Work, Family and Personality: Transition to Adulthood* by J. T. Mortimer, J. Lorence, and D. S. Kumka, 1986, Norwood, NJ: Ablex; "Quality of Students' Work Experience and Orientation to Work" by D. Stern, J. R. Stone, C. Hopkins, and M. MacMillion, 1990, *Youth and Society, 22,* 263–282.

comes? Second, what is the role of youth employment? Although substantial evidence links youth employment to immediate outcomes, there is also evidence that such employment is an important formative experience. Early employment may well shape future employment experiences and expectations. Thus, the nature of the experience of youth employment may have important implications for more distal outcomes.

The intent of this book is to address both themes by examining diverse aspects of youth employment. Given our disciplinary interests, our focus is on understanding the psychological experience of youth employment, although related perspectives are also addressed. In addition to examining well-researched areas such as the effects of youth employment or youth unemployment, we also expand the boundaries of current research by highlighting overlooked but crucial areas such as child labor and the roles of health and safety and organized labor in youth employment.

As with all such works, this book could not have happened without the cooperation of a number of people. The contributors to the volume were unfailingly prompt and responsive, and we thank them again for their cooperation. Judy Nemes at APA Books helped us initiate this project and shepherded it through the publication process. The anonymous reviewers provided helpful and detailed commentary that contributed to the work. Finally, the realms of work and family intersect and overlap, and thanks are also due to Debra, Janice, Monique, and Seth for their support.

Young
Workers

1

Introduction

Julian Barling and E. Kevin Kelloway

Society (including both parents and children, Furnham & Thomas, 1984; Greenberger & Steinberg, 1986) generally believes that having its young people employed is a desirable outcome. Young people are thought to learn responsibility and independence through such employment. Although child labor is universally decried, the child who opens a lemonade stand or does yard work in the neighborhood is held up as a role model for his or her peers. Young people who combine their studies with part-time employment are applauded for their industry.

Those who espouse this view might be heartened by statistics indicating that the move toward employment of youth is particularly true for teenagers (and younger children, too) who often devote considerable amounts of time to part-time employment. Just over a decade ago, Greenberger and Steinberg (1986) showed that approximately 50% of full-time high school students are employed simultaneously on a part-time basis. In addition, by the time teenagers graduate from high school, 80% will have held a part-time job at some time during the high school year. The intensity of their employment is also noteworthy: The average high school student works 20 hours per week, with 10% holding the equivalent of a full-time job by virtue of the number of hours worked (i.e., 35 hours or more per week). These data are not peculiar to the United States, as Sunter (1992) has shown more recently in a Canadian sample that 25% of 17- to 19-year-olds were employed more than 20 hours per week.

Greenberger and Steinberg (1986) noted at the same time that it is likely that the number of teenagers employed part-time will increase for several reasons. First, there are increased opportunities for part-time employment in general, a trend that has been amplified in the years since they made that observation (see Barling & Gallagher, 1996). Second, teenage allowances have probably not risen sufficiently to permit discretionary purchases, making part-time employment even more attractive (Waldman & Springen, 1992).

Yet, the popular press is voicing increasing concern that the effects of young people's employment may be negative. Waldman and Springen's (1992) article in *Newsweek* entitled "Too Old, Too Fast?" expresses such concerns. Some of the jobs typically performed by young workers (e.g., fast food service, factory, and farm work) can be physically dangerous, and even fatal. Particularly for young people, employment may involve highly routinized, low-quality jobs that offer little security and even less hope of advancement. These jobs often require teenagers to work at times that jeopardize other activities such as school and sports (Waldman & Springen, 1992). Because much of this employment is in the "informal" labor market or service industries, young workers frequently lack the regulatory (i.e., labor law) and other (e.g., union) protections afforded to older workers. Moreover, there is considerable evidence that exposure to these conditions may result in a host of adverse consequences for young people.

This is the paradox of youth employment: Such employment is valued by society despite extensive data suggesting that it can be associated with adverse and extreme consequences. To some extent, the paradox emerges from the mixed—and frequently contradictory—set of beliefs we hold about work and employment among adults, the view of work as both a source of human growth and fulfillment and a "curse" or burden imposed on humans as a punishment for original sin

(Kelloway & Harvey, 1998). Resolution of this paradox emerges from the recognition that the terms *youth* and *employment* are poor descriptors of the phenomena of interest. That is, the youth participating in the labor market are not a homogenous group, and the experience of employment may vary dramatically with the demographic and socioeconomic characteristics of the individual. Similarly, employment is not a homogenous experience. Both the quantity and the quality of employment vary dramatically in the labor market, and these characteristics interact with individual factors to determine (a) the experience of employment and (b) the consequences of such employment.

Clearly, early work experiences may take many different forms and have different meanings for young people. A goal of this volume is to more clearly distinguish the varieties of work experiences covered by the rubric "youth employment." That the psychological implications of young people's work have only recently been given attention in the literature is surprising, considering that early employment occurs during the "impressionable years" (Krosnick & Alwin, 1989) during which youngsters may be most susceptible to external social influences. Further, as we have seen, youth employment is now so prevalent that it can no longer merely be considered a "social address" (cf. Barling, 1990). Instead, it is now considered as the fourth socializing force that children encounter, the first three being the family, school, and peers (Greenberger & Steinberg, 1981, 1986). Finally, although research on some aspects of young people's employment (e.g., its effects on school performance and social behaviors) has proceeded substantially, other areas (e.g., health and safety issues, young people's knowledge of and exposure to organized labor) are less well understood. Implicit in the notion of youth employment as a major socializing force is that it has a significant effect on young people, and if this is indeed the case, we benefit from a deeper understanding of this issue. Based on the contributions to this book and the existing research literature, we suggest that two conclusions would enhance this understanding: Researchers should recognize that (a) youth are not a homogenous group, and that (b) employment is not a homogenous experience.

YOUNG PEOPLE ARE NOT A
HOMOGENOUS GROUP

Young people participating in the labor market differ in a variety of characteristics. Demographic differences such as age and gender as well as other individual differences (e.g., socioeconomic class, the voluntary nature of employment) may dramatically affect the individual's experience of employment.

Age

As will be apparent throughout this book, research and policy have typically used the term *youth* to refer to individuals between the ages of 15 and 24; less frequently the ages of 16 and 24 are used to define *youth* (Lowe & Krahn, chap. 8, this volume). However necessary such a distinction is for policy formation, defining *youth* by such an age range (a) excludes labor force participants from consideration (children younger than 15 years old are in the labor force), (b) obscures differences between individuals in the category, and (c) creates differences between individuals where differences might not otherwise exist.

As mentioned above, such a definition excludes individuals by failing to recognize that children as young as 12 years old are active participants in paid employment (Mortimer, Finch, Owens, & Shanahan, 1990). Ferman (1990) gives another example in his study of Detroit households, finding children as young as 8 years old participating in economic activity. Excluding youth under 15 years old from the definition of *youth* in these studies places these very young workers at risk for adverse consequences. Take for example, yard work, which is regularly done by children under 15 years old and may involve the use of power tools (e.g., lawn mowers, hedge trimmers, and mulchers) that are designed primarily for adult use. As Castillo (chap. 7, this volume) notes, "children are not simply little adults." Exposure to chemicals and work processes that may be "safe" for adults may not necessarily be "safe" for children who are still developing.

Differences among young people are also obscured by researchers failing to recognize that there are different subgroups within the youth

6

population. For example, some individuals within the 15–24 age bracket are full-time students who engage in part-time employment. Data suggest that over 60% of North American high school students hold a part-time job (chap. 4, this volume). Such employment is typically viewed as temporary and as motivated purely by financial incentives. As a result, such employment experiences may have little influence on the individual's perceptions of work (Loughlin & Barling, 1998) and developing attitude toward work. This is not to say that part-time work for high school students is innocuous (indeed the data suggest quite a different conclusion, see chap. 5, this volume).

However, the category "youth" also includes school leavers who are holding (or hoping to hold) full-time employment. For these individuals, the motivation for employment may be more complex: Employment for school leavers is more likely to be seen as the start of a career. Unlike full-time students, school leavers see employment as long term, of no fixed duration, and motivated by a variety of factors, including —but not limited to—financial gain.

Finally, reliance on the category of "youth" for either research or policy formation may lead to an artificial distinction between "youth" and "non-youth." It is difficult to sustain the argument that employment conditions for 25-year-olds are qualitatively different than those for their 24-year-old counterparts. Perhaps more to the point, several authors (e.g., Frone, chap. 5; Loughlin & Barling, chap. 2) in this volume have pointed to the problem of ignoring the vast amount of data that has accumulated regarding adult employment in attempt to understand youth employment. Indeed the data for young people suggest, as for adults, that employment outcomes are directly related to the quality of the employment. To the extent that young people are engaged in high-quality employment, adverse consequences are minimized and beneficial outcomes are realized.

Gender

As noted by Desmarais and Curtis (chap. 4, this volume), the sex-based segregation of the workforce begins at a very early age. Girls are more likely to hold "domestic" jobs such as baby-sitting, whereas boys are more likely to engage in male-stereotyped tasks. Moreover, girls are more likely than boys to be employed in informal employment arrangements. Correspondingly, gender-based wage differentials are prevalent, with females typically receiving 70–75% of the male wage despite only minor, insignificant differences in the hours worked per week.

If, as Desmarais and Curtis hold, "experience shapes expectation," these early—and often informal—employment experiences have consequences for future employment. Certainly, the available data suggest that future salary expectations are shaped by this wage differentiation, thereby beginning an inequitable process that may continue over the working life.

Socioeconomic Factors

In addition to these demographic characteristics, young people also differ in their expectations of and motivations for employment, and both are related to socioeconomic status. Kelloway and Harvey (chap. 3, this volume) have argued for the notion that children acquire both an understanding and expectations of employment prior to their entry into the workforce (the available data seem to support this notion). In particular, children's expectations of employment are primarily shaped by the employment experiences of the family members and parents with whom they have the most contact. Perhaps not surprisingly, there is consistent evidence that young people's expectations, vocational preferences (Gottfredson, 1981), and understanding of work varies by socioeconomic class (see, e.g., Emler & Dickinson, 1985).

Socioeconomic factors also influence young people's motivations for seeking employment. There is quite a difference between seeking employment to support yourself and your family and seeking employment to afford the latest CD. Research on part-time employment has highlighted the importance of voluntariness (i.e., whether part-time workers chose or had to settle for part-time hours). To a similar extent, young people differ in the extent to which their employment is voluntary or a result of their impoverished status. The individual's reasons for working and expectations of paid employment might reasonably affect the experience of employment.

EMPLOYMENT IS NOT A HOMOGENOUS EXPERIENCE

Research on the consequences of youth employment has been based largely on refining the independent variable. Questions about employment status have generally given way to questions about the effects of employment quantity, that is, the number of hours worked. More recently, questions about the quality of employment have received empirical attention, and several authors in this volume have called for a continuation and expansion of this trend. Just as organizational researchers have recognized considerable diversity in adult employment, youth employment varies along a number of dimensions, including the context of employment and the quality of the job.

The Context of Employment

Although typically not reflected in youth employment statistics, a great deal of youth employment occurs in what Ferman (1990) refers to as the "social" and "irregular" economies. In contrast to the "regular" economy, which is characterized by both the use of money as a medium of exchange and inclusion in the economic measures of society, the social economy is neither enumerated nor based on money as an exchange. The young person who works in a family-owned business or on a family-owned farm, for example, is an active participant in the social economy. Although the individual may not receive a salary as direct payment for her or his labor, other characteristics of the job (i.e., the tasks performed, the hours worked, the equipment or tools used) may parallel those found in "regular" employment. Similarly, the irregular economy comprises those jobs that are based on a monetary exchange but are largely unenumerated by economic measures. Mowing the neighbor's lawn, performing other forms of yard work and home maintenance, and baby-sitting a neighbor's children are all activities that fall into the irregular economy.

In one of the few empirical studies of the subject, Ferman (1990) points to several defining features of the informal economy (the informal economy includes both the social and irregular economies) based on his survey of Detroit households. First, small business units dominate in the informal economy. Keeping activities small and simple are primary values, and business units would rarely exceed six employees. Second, activities in the informal economy are characterized by low capital investment and a virtual absence of regulation. Third, such activities are highly flexible with low degrees of hierarchical control, relative ease of entry, and relatively little concern for training or skill development. Finally, the rewards associated with participation in the informal economy are equally flexible. Hours of work and rates of pay may vary with the nature of the task or the particulars of an individual "contract."

Ferman's study suggests that participation in the informal economy is characteristic of young workers. For example, he found that children between the ages of 8 and 15 years old actively participated in activities such as gardening, baby-sitting, and the manufacture and door-to-door sale of jewelry. School leavers and others considered to be new labor market entrants were also frequent participants in the informal economy. The ease of entry into such economic activity and the lack of regulation or certification may make such activities particularly attractive to school leavers who have not obtained professional training or certification.

The very characteristics of the informal economy that facilitate the participation of young workers may also pose some risk for them. The lack of regulation and certification implies that specific tasks may be completed in a nonstandard fashion with whatever tools are available at the time. Moreover, work in the informal economy may not be structured in the same way as in the formal economy. Put simply, there are no set hours of work or work schedules in the informal economy. Rather, participants work when the work is available, and for as long as it is available.

The Quality of Employment

Whether youth employment occurs in the formal or the informal economy, the quality of that employment appears to be a central determinant of the consequences of employment. Opportunities for learning, social interaction, and exercising initiative (Greenberger, Steinberg, & Ruggiero, 1982) appear to be as important for youth employment as they are for adult employment.

Indeed, one might argue that high-quality employment is even more important for young employees. There are at least two reasons for this suggestion. First, young people can be viewed as a vulnerable subpopulation of the workforce. Given that a vast amount of data has accumulated on the negative effects of low-quality adult employment, it is reasonable to expect that these effects would be magnified among younger workers. Second, the development of work expectations and attitudes early in the career may carry over to later career stages. That is, young people's employment experiences in their teens and early 20s may be occurring during a critical period for their formation of work attitudes and behaviors. Although this suggestion is subject to empirical verification, early evidence supports the proposition and suggests that the provision of high-quality employment to young people should concern society in general.

OVERVIEW OF THIS VOLUME

The first issue that must be confronted is what constitutes youth employment. Focusing on this issue, Loughlin and Barling (see chap. 2, this volume) note that employment has typically been conceptualized in terms of quantity or quality. Earlier research was far more likely to focus on the quantity of employment, that is, the number of hours worked per week. Subsequent research is more likely to include a focus on the quality of employment. Loughlin and Barling also point out that most of the research has focused on teenagers who are employed part-time while attending school on a full-time basis. The extent to which these two foci have dominated the research will become apparent from virtually all the issues discussed throughout this book (e.g., see chaps. 3 and 5, this volume).

How people learn to work has long been of concern, and just what young people learn about employment from their first experiences is discussed by Kelloway and Harvey (see chap. 3, this volume). However, they go further, showing that children come into contact with the world of work vicariously long before their first experiential contact with work (Piotrkowski & Stark, 1987). This point is critical because personal accounts often report these vicarious contacts to be influential (Hamper, 1991).

A major feature of adults' experience of work is the extent to which work is gendered, that is, segregated along lines of gender. Until relatively recently, scant attention was paid to the possibility that youth employment is also gendered. Desmarais and Curtis (see chap. 4, this volume) show that the experience of employment for youth, particularly the experience of income, is gendered as well, creating critical implications for young people's view of the world of work: If experience does indeed shape expectations, as Desmarais and Curtis argue, such that young women are learning first-hand that discrimination does indeed exist in the workplace, exactly what lessons youth learn from their employment would be of critical importance.

As mentioned previously, most of the research on the effects of youth employment has addressed issues of school performance and social behaviors. Frone extensively reviews the wider issue of the developmental consequences of youth employment (see chap. 5, this volume) and persuasively shows that there are both positive and negative outcomes attached to youth employment, often depending on whether we focus on the quantity of hours worked or the quality of their employment.

Perhaps of all the issues raised within the rubric of youth employment, none is as emotional as child labor and exploitation. Despite this, little research exists on any psychological consequences of child labor and exploitation. Piotrkowski and Carrubba (see chap. 6, this volume) attempt to correct this situation, integrating what is already known from different areas. In trying to set the stage for future research, they also point to the sexual exploitation of child laborers, questioning whether our knowledge of childhood sexual abuse may provide a platform from which we can understand some of the psychological effects of child labor and exploitation.

One of the key themes that integrates the chapters on child labor and exploitation and occupational health and safety, is how young children in the workplace have very few protections. Castillo echoes this notion, showing how the issue of occupational health and safety has generally been neglected for adults, and all but ignored for youth. Of course, this would be of no consequence whatsoever if young people were not at risk in the workplace, but as Castillo points out, they certainly are. Piotrkowski and Carrubba concur, noting that one of the key consequences for children in the labor force is their exposure to risk. Perhaps the central element in understanding this similarity is to extend Castillo's observation that children are not "little adults," and to note as well that workplaces are made by adults for adults.

Unemployment has been a major issue of concern for most of the 20th century, and the subject of considerable research (see Jahoda, 1982). But youth unemployment has been overlooked all too often. Just why this would occur may not be surprising: If youth employment in general, and teenage employment in particular, are thought to exert negative effects, then presumably youth unemployment would not be seen as negative, and would generate little interest or empirical scrutiny. Yet ignoring youth unemployment is dangerous, given the fact that it is invariably higher than general unemployment levels within the same area, and youth unemployment occurs during the "impressionable years" (Krosnick & Alwin, 1989). In chapter 8, Lowe and Krahn draw on their own substantial research in the area, as well as on findings from the literature, to point to the consequences of youth unemployment, noting how this is also a gendered experience.

Until recently, the question of whether unions would focus new organizing efforts on youth has not received much attention, but this situation is changing. Gallagher raises the complementary question of the extent to which youth might turn to unions for protection, and there is evidence that this is beginning to occur both in the United States (see Belkin, 1996) and Canada (Kidd, 1994; Robinson, 1994). If indeed child laborers and youth are deprived of the normal protections of the workplace, this question of the extent to which they may turn to unions for protection becomes especially relevant. To date, there is very little research on this issue, but Gallagher makes a start by drawing on the adult literature on unionization (see chap. 9, this volume).

Finally, in the Afterword, we reiterate several themes with the potential to affect both research and policy formation and call for longitudinal studies that can truly identify the long-term benefits and costs of the different forms of youth employment.

Clearly, the study of youth and employment raises many complex issues, and addressing these issues is increasingly important for society. We hope that this volume contributes to this goal by identifying and elaborating on some of the central issues relating to youth and employment.

REFERENCES

Barling, J. (1990). *Employment, stress and family functioning.* Chichester, England: Wiley.

Barling, J., Dupre, K. E., & Hepburn, C. G. (1998). Effects of parents' job insecurity on children's work beliefs and attitudes. *Journal of Applied Psychology, 83,* 112–118.

Barling, J., & Gallagher, D. G. (1996). Part-time employment. In C. L. Cooper & I. T. Robertson (Eds.), *International review of industrial and organizational psychology* (Vol. 11, pp. 243–278). New York: Wiley.

Barling, J., Rogers, K. A., & Kelloway, E. K. (1995). Some effects of teenagers' part-time employment: The quantity and the quality of work makes the difference. *Journal of Organizational Behavior, 16,* 143–154.

Belkin, L. (1996, January 21). Showdown at Yazoo industries: Representing the last best chance for labor, the union kids come to town. *The New York Times Magazine,* 26–31, 38, 62, 64, 67, 69.

Emler, N., & Dickinson, J. (1985). Children's representation of economic inequalities: The effects of social class. *British Journal of Development Psychology, 3,* 191–198.

Ferman, L. A. (1990). Participation in the irregular economy. In K. Erikson & S. P. Vallas (Eds.), *The nature of work: Sociological perspectives* (pp. 119–149). New Haven, CT: Yale University Press.

Furnham, A., & Thomas, P. (1984). Adult's perceptions of the economic socialization of children. *Journal of Adolescence, 7,* 217–231.

14

Gottfredson, L. S. (1981). Circumscription and compromise: A developmental theory of occupational aspirations. *Journal of Counseling Psychology, 28,* 545–579.

Greenberger, E., & Steinberg, L. D. (1981). The workplace as a context for the socialization of youth. *Journal of Youth and Adolescence, 10,* 185–210.

Greenberger, E., & Steinberg, L. D. (1986). *When teen-agers work: The psychological and social costs of adolescent employment.* New York: Basic Books.

Greenberger, E., Steinberg, L. D., & Ruggiero, M. (1982). A job is a job . . . or is it? *Work and Occupations, 9,* 79–96.

Hamper, B. (1991). *Rivethead: Tales from the assembly line.* New York: Warner Books.

Jahoda, M. (1982). *Employment and unemployment: A social psychological analysis.* New York: Cambridge University Press.

Kelloway, E. K., & Harvey, S. (1998). *Work beliefs and work values.* Thousand Oaks, CA: Sage. Manuscript in preparation.

Kidd, K. (1994, June). Big Mac meets the McUnion Kid. *Report on Business,* 46–50, 52–53.

Krosnick, J. A., & Alwin, D. F. (1989). Aging and susceptibility to attitude change. *Journal of Personality and Social Psychology, 57,* 416–425.

Loughlin, C. A., & Barling, J. (1998). Teenagers' part-time employment and their work-related attitudes and aspirations. *Journal of Organizational Behavior, 19,* 197–207.

Mortimer, J. T., Finch, M. D., Owens, T. J., & Shanahan, M. J. (1990). Gender and work in adolescence. *Youth and Society, 22,* 201–224.

Robinson, R. (1994, June/July). Big Mac's counter attack. *Our Times,* 29–30.

Piotrkowski, C. S., & Stark, E. (1987). Children and adolescents look at their parents' jobs. In J. H. Lewko (Ed.), *How children and adolescents view the world of work* (pp. 3–19). San Francisco, CA: Jossey-Bass.

Sunter, D. (1992). Juggling school and work. *Perspectives on Labour and Income, 4,* 15–21.

Waldman, S., & Springen, K. (1992, November 16). Too old, too fast? *Newsweek,* 80–82, 87, 88.

2

The Nature of Youth Employment

Catherine Loughlin and Julian Barling

The quality of young people's jobs is necessarily tied to the quality of jobs available in society as a whole. However, given that education, work experience, and acquiring a skill base are inversely related to age, young workers tend to hold a disproportionate number of society's least attractive jobs. Little attention has typically been paid to the quality of young people's work. Even among young workers who are also full-time students, the primary concern has been with the quantity of their employment; working many hours a week is believed to negatively affect school and personal outcomes (Greenberger & Steinberg, 1986). This lack of concern for the quality of young people's jobs likely arises from the belief that these jobs are transitory, and will teach young people valuable work-related skills before they enter the adult workforce (e.g., punctuality, responsibility). The assumption is that these are not the types of jobs that young people will be doing as adults. However, many of these entry-level jobs are now becoming permanent for young people (e.g., Krahn, 1991), and possibly due to this realization, some

Preparation of this chapter was supported by grants from the Social Sciences and Humanities Research Council of Canada to Catherine Loughlin and Julian Barling.

researchers are beginning to question the quality of young people's work.

A number of issues concerning the nature or quality of youth employment are addressed in this chapter: We begin by giving a brief overview of the current situation. Next, we consider how the quantity and quality of young people's employment affects them. We then consider how the adult employment situation compares to that of young workers. Subsequently, the relationship between employment quality and young people's work-related attitudes and behaviors is examined. Finally, we conclude with a brief discussion of underemployment among youth, as well as how this relates to education and training versus current labor market conditions.

DISTINGUISHING FEATURES OF YOUNG WORKERS

In this section we define *young workers*, discuss the types of jobs they typically occupy, and consider the different trends for full- and part-time work among youth in the paid labor force.

Young workers are typically defined as individuals between the ages of 15 and 24 years who are employed in the paid labor force. This includes groups as diverse as high school dropouts who could have been in the workforce for close to a decade, as well as part-time student workers who are combining education with paid labor force participation (about half of all students aged 17–19 are also employed in the paid labor force; see Sunter, 1992). As will become apparent, these demographic differences may be important, and whether the findings generated from one group generalize to the other remains to be demonstrated. Nonetheless, for the purpose of this chapter we follow this convention and examine employment trends among workers in the 15- to 24-year-old age group.

In terms of the kind of jobs young people do, there are some clear trends. Since the 1980s, most jobs for young people in North America are found in the lower level service industries. These industries include retail sales and other consumer services (e.g., food and beverage services, cashiers, sales clerks, and janitorial jobs). These jobs tend to be part time, require few skills, pay poorly, and offer little career potential (e.g., Economic Council of Canada, 1990; Greenberger, Steinberg, & Ruggiero, 1982; Krahn, 1991). There has also been a decline of youth employment in the goods sector and in public administration, health, social services, and education. These changes in the nature of youth employment are troubling for at least two reasons: First, for previous generations of young people, these industries typically offered good entry-level career opportunities. Second, even full-time jobs in the service sector do not typically pay well enough to allow young people to become independent of their parents. Although this may not present a particular problem for students employed on a part-time basis for supplementary income, it is likely to be a problem for young people who are attempting to enter permanent labor force participation.

Finally, a distinction must be made between youth employment in general, and the part-time employment of youth. Across North America, employment trends for young workers diverge depending on which of these categories we are discussing. For example, in Canada, employment trends for young workers in general over the past quarter century have been generally driven by demographics (e.g., Betcherman & Morissette, 1994): Employment in the 15–24 year age group grew rapidly in the late 1960s and the 1970s (along with increased absolute numbers in this age group), followed by no absolute growth, or declines in employment share during the 1980s (along with a sharp drop in the absolute numbers in this age group). Although the number of young people in this age group has been stable in this decade, with the recent recession, youth employment as a share of the total working population has continued to decline.

In contrast, the part-time employment of young people has increased significantly since the 1980s both in relative and absolute terms. Further, in Canada, there was an important "involuntary component to youth part-time employment growth over the 1989–92 period, with the involuntary share increasing from 17.6 per cent to 26.1 per cent" (Betcherman & Morissette, 1994, p. 3). Given that part-time employment has been associated with underemployment, the higher representation of young workers among the part-time employed (both voluntarily and involuntarily) may be of concern, and we return to this issue later in this chapter. Arguably, in the future, part-time employment for youth will increase, given the current move toward part-time and contingent work in general (Tetrick & Barling, 1995).

QUANTITY VERSUS QUALITY OF YOUTH EMPLOYMENT

Much of the debate surrounding the issue of young workers has focused on the quantity of hours they work. One probable reason for this is that so much research in this area has been done with students who are working part-time while attending high school or pursuing postsecondary studies. At the same time, the issue of the quality of their employment has largely been ignored.

Researchers contrasting employed and nonemployed students have typically found few employment-related differences between these individuals (e.g., Greenberger, Steinberg, Vaux, & McAuliffe, 1980; Gottfredson, 1985). However, studies that focus on differences within groups of part-time students have been less conclusive. For example, some research indicates that increased part-time work has a positive effect on future employment outcomes (e.g., Carr, Wright, & Brody, 1996). Some findings indicate that increased work hours lead to negative outcomes such as alcohol and cigarette use, problem behavior in school, and minor delinquent acts (see chap. 5, this volume). Finally, the relationship between hours of employment and school grades is inconclusive. Despite these somewhat mixed findings, Steinberg, Fegley, and Dornbusch (1993) consider there to be a "consensus" in the literature "that it is long hours of employment, rather than employment status, that are potentially injurious" to youth (p. 172). Although this assertion may seem overstated, other authors have recently echoed this conclusion:

> Hence the issue of part-time work is not working per se, but how much work is involved . . . long hours (more than 15–20 hours per week) of employment are associated with . . . lower marks, higher (school) absenteeism rates, a lower level of in-

volvement in homework and extra-curricular activities ...
higher dropout rates ... (and) more frequent use of alcohol
and drugs. (Cheng, 1995)

The number of hours worked in part-time employment can be
substantial: High school students work an average of 20 hours per week,
and 10% work the equivalent of a full-time job (> 35 hours per week;
see chap. 4, this volume, for a further discussion of this issue). In one
Canadian sample, 25% of 17- to 19-year-olds worked more than 20
hours per week (Sunter, 1992). These figures are critical, because it is
argued that 20 hours a week is the threshold beyond which negative
outcomes are assumed to emerge (e.g., D'Amico, 1984; Greenberger &
Steinberg, 1986; Steinberg & Dornbusch, 1991). However, limiting the
focus of research to employment quantity may well be premature and
shortsighted. In fact, the focus on the number of hours young people
work is peculiar, because the adult employment literature suggests that
it is not the absolute number of hours one works that is critical in
determining personal outcomes, but an individual's subjective experience of those hours that is most important (e.g., Barling, 1990; Hackman & Oldham, 1980; O'Brien & Feather, 1990; Warr, 1987; Winefield,
Winefield, Tiggemann, & Goldney, 1991). Although Greenberger, Steinberg, and Ruggiero (1982) acknowledged some time ago that not all
jobs for youth are equivalent in terms of their quality, this realization
has not been captured sufficiently in subsequent research. Most existing
research on teenagers' part-time employment continues to focus primarily on personal outcomes (e.g., self-esteem, use of drugs) or school
performance (e.g., grades, cutting class) that are related to the quantity
of employment.

Recently, some researchers have gone beyond the issue of quantity
and proposed that the quality of students' employment experiences may
play an essential role in explaining the effects of part-time work on
their development (e.g., Barling, Rogers, & Kelloway, 1995; Loughlin &
Barling, 1998; Mortimer, Finch, Shanahan, & Ryu, 1992). For example,
employed students may benefit from feelings of mastery, the attainment
of job skills, personal happiness, and improved school behavior in some
situations (Mortimer, Finch, Shanahan, & Ryu, 1992; Mortimer & Shan-

ahan, 1991; Yamoor & Mortimer, 1990). Employment quality may also be associated with students' personal well-being and their school performance (Barling et al., 1995).

In a recent study of 349 employed students, Loughlin and Barling (1998) assessed the relationship between employment quantity and quality, on the one hand, and work-related attitudes and aspirations (i.e., work-related motivation, involvement, cynicism, career goals, and career maturity), on the other. They pointed out that most research has accepted the notion of a specific threshold beyond which part-time employment is harmful (e.g., 20 hours per week). This assumes a nonlinear relationship between hours worked per week and any outcome of interest. However, these studies continue to search for linear effects. As a result, Loughlin and Barling tested for both linear and nonlinear effects of employment quantity. Their data showed that neither the linear nor the curvilinear components of employment quantity predicted any of the outcomes. In contrast, support emerged for the role of perceived job quality predictors (e.g., satisfaction with interpersonal relationships at work predicted work-related cynicism; role stressors predicted work-related motivation, career maturity, and cynicism).

Although certainly in need of replication, these findings question the so-called consensus that only intensive work during high school exerts negative effects on teenagers. They also support the importance of employment quality for teenagers as well as adults. Further, these and other findings (e.g., Barling et al., 1995) give us reason to question policy initiatives designed to protect teenage students who are employed part time by simply limiting the quantity of employment legally allowed (Lantos, 1992; Greenberger & Steinberg, 1986; Steinberg & Dornbusch, 1991). It would seem equally important to begin considering the quality of young people's jobs.

Not all jobs for young people are created equal. Although some young people may be gaining valuable experience on the job (e.g., childcare or apprenticeship-type situations), others may be exposed to stressful or even dangerous work conditions (e.g., in the service sector or agriculture). For example, consider the following findings from a recent study conducted by Loughlin and Barling (1997) for the Safe Communities Foundation of Canada: Young part-time workers in Ontario were able to identify numerous health and safety hazards in their jobs (e.g., hot deep fryer grease, toxic chemicals, and handling sharp objects), and 35% of them had either witnessed or knew of someone injured at their own job sites. However, over 70% did not receive any workplace health and safety training, and one third of these young workers were unaware of any health and safety policies and procedures in existence at their workplaces. Because a safe work environment is a fundamental aspect of healthy employment for young people, future research and policy initiatives may be well advised to address the working conditions involved in young people's jobs as well as the sheer quantity of hours worked.

DEFINING QUALITY EMPLOYMENT

Because so little is known about the quality of young people's jobs, a reasonable place to begin framing research is with an understanding of what constitutes healthy work for adults. Findings on adults' employment (e.g., Hackman & Oldham, 1980) indicate that the perceived quality of employment is associated with adult development (Mortimer, Lorence, & Kumka, 1986), productivity (Wall, Corbett, Martin, Clegg, & Jackson, 1990), and family functioning (Barling, 1990). Sauter, Murphy, and Hurrell (1990) list six aspects of work quality most likely to affect workers' mental and physical health (e.g., working conditions associated with potentially hazardous psychological costs such as stress or anxiety). These are career security factors, autonomy (concerning workload or pace), work scheduling, role stressors, interpersonal relationships at work, and job content. Interestingly, Greenberger, Steinberg, and Ruggiero (1982) suggested three dimensions along which adolescent jobs could be compared (opportunities for learning, opportunities for exercising initiative or autonomy, and opportunities for social interaction). These dimensions are encapsulated within Sauter, Murphy, and Hurrell's (1990) framework. In general, although the first factor mentioned above (career security) may not be critical to many young workers, the other five factors appear to be relevant to workers of all ages, and some are emerging as especially important to young workers in particular (O'Brien & Feather, 1990; Stern, Stone, Hopkins, & McMillion, 1990). We now consider what we know from the adult literature about each of these in turn, and relate this information to findings in the area concerning young workers.

Because of the unique nature of some youth employment, issues of career security may not be as important to younger workers as they would be to adults. Greenberger and Steinberg (1986) found that because most students do not plan to continue in the same type of jobs once they have completed their education, "future-oriented" aspects of a job such as fringe benefits and promotion are not very important. However, it should be noted that these findings may not apply equally well to all young workers. For example, this may be true for part-time workers who are in high school, but may be less so for those who are no longer in school. More research is necessary before career security factors should be considered as unimportant to youth. Interestingly, recent increases in part-time employment (whether voluntary or not) among young people may actually serve to protect them from unemployment. Because part-time jobs typically cost employers less (e.g., lower payroll taxes and fringe benefits), the average part-time job may now be as secure, if not more secure, than the average full-time job.

Perhaps the most influential theory concerning the issue of job autonomy is the job strain model (Karasek & Theorell, 1990), whereby the influence of work demands on health are moderated by the degree of control individuals have over their workload and work pace. Sauter et al. (1990) state that personal control (decision latitude) is the determining factor in generating any health consequences of work demands (p. 1150). Lack of input into decision making concerning one's job has been found to result in emotional distress, lowered self-esteem, job dissatisfaction, increased tension, anxiety, depression, irritation, somatic complaints, and alienation (Nord, 1977; Sauter et al., 1990; Wall et al., 1990). This lack of input has even been associated with increased mortality among workers (Astrand, Hanson, & Isacson, 1989; Theorell, Perski, Orth-Gomer, Hamsten, & de Faire, 1991).

In contrast, increasing workers' control over their jobs has been found to improve work motivation, performance, job satisfaction, and mental health, as well as serving to reduce employee turnover (Wall & Clegg, 1981; Wall et al., 1990), and acting as a buffer between the negative effects of job insecurity and ill health (Barling & Kelloway, 1996). Questioning the relationship between the degree of autonomy in young people's jobs and personal and work-related outcomes may be a promising future area of research in the area of youth employment quality. However, the beneficial effects of increased worker control may be limited by the fact that many of the jobs typically occupied by young workers are also of low demand (e.g., in terms of skill use).

Role stress theory suggests that there are several possible types of role stressors on the job, and role conflict, role ambiguity, and role overload have been identified as three key factors in job stress (Kahn, Wolfe, Quinn, Snoek, & Rosenthal, 1964; Kahn, 1980). Some consequences of these role stressors include increased job-related tension, decreased job satisfaction, less organizational confidence, decreased satisfaction with work relationships, decreased self-esteem, and increased anxiety and depression (Kahn, 1980). Role ambiguity and role conflict are also negatively related to commitment and involvement among workers (Fisher & Gitelson, 1983). Loughlin and Barling (1998) found role stressors to be related to part-time workers' career maturity, work-related motivation, and cynicism.

Interpersonal relationships in the workplace are a necessary component of most jobs. Individuals typically interact with peers, supervisors, or subordinates, and the social context in which work takes place provides meaning to work. Having poor relationships at work has been related to depression and job dissatisfaction (e.g., Karasek, Schwartz, & Theorell, 1982). Indeed, Jackson (1988) has shown that the loss of the social contacts and support available at work is one of the main factors associated with the negative effects of unemployment. Sauter et al. (1990) state that work relationships can either buffer or exacerbate the adverse effects of exposure to job risk factors, depending on the quality of the work relationships. For young workers, Greenberger et al. (1980) found that the workplace is not necessarily a source

25

of close personal relationships for teenagers. Because they do not nec- essarily have high-quality jobs, teenagers often work alone, under time pressure, or on irregular shifts and these conditions are likely to inter- fere with the development and maintenance of close personal relation- ships in the workplace. In fact, Greenberger et al. (1980) state that "if the workplace is to enable adolescents to establish meaningful relation- ships with others, especially adults, work settings quite different from those now available in the private sector will have to be generated" (p. 201). This is even more true today. Jobs offering students "positive experiences" (i.e., those using job skills and eliciting high job involve- ment) seem to lead to the development of closer relationships with work associates.

Previous research has found that three critical psychological states must be fulfilled by a person's job content to provide motivation and satisfaction:

1. A feeling of personal responsibility for one's work
2. Experiencing one's work as meaningful, and
3. Having knowledge of the results of one's performance. (Hackman & Oldham, 1980)

In general, "narrow, fragmented, invariant, and short-cycle tasks that provide little stimulation, allow little use of skills or expression of creativity, and have little intrinsic meaning for workers" lead to job dissatisfaction and poor mental health (Sauter et al., 1990, p. 1151). Stern et al. (1990) found that employment quality (e.g., opportunities to learn on the job) was significantly correlated with young people's cynicism toward work. Skill usage also appears to be critical to young workers, and psychological benefits are most pronounced when the job provides skills that will be useful in the future (Mortimer, Finch, Ryu, & Shanahan, 1991; Mortimer et al., 1992; O'Brien & Feather, 1990).

In addition to the work quality factors mentioned above, Warr (1987) includes several extrinsic work factors that affect work outcomes among adults, for example, pay level and pay equity. Other authors have also commented on the importance of extrinsic job factors (e.g., Jahoda, 1982). Little research has been conducted on young workers in this regard. Some recent research suggests that gender inequality in wage expectations is present in youth employment (see chap. 4, this volume). However, much research remains to be done on the effects of extrinsic factors on the employment experiences of young workers.

RELATIONSHIPS BETWEEN EMPLOYMENT QUALITY AND YOUNG PEOPLE'S WORK-RELATED ATTITUDES AND BEHAVIOR

Perhaps the most interesting questions concerning the quality of young people's employment stem from the relationship between this quality and young people's current and future work-related attitudes and behavior. Instead of knowledge and skills, which are often lacking in jobs for youth (Garson, 1988), what young people often seem to learn from employment is work-related attitudes and appropriate (or inappropriate) work behaviors (Stern et al., 1990). If work-related attitudes are most impressionable during the younger years and then relatively stable thereafter (Gottfredson, 1981; Krosnick & Alwin, 1989; Staw & Ross, 1985), paid jobs may affect subsequent work-related attitudes and behaviors. Given that teenagers are more influenced by their work environments than adults (Lorence & Mortimer, 1985), any positive or negative influences are likely to be exaggerated. High-quality employment may leave young people feeling more positive about work in general, and have a beneficial effect on their occupational development. In contrast, low-quality teenage employment may leave them negatively disposed to their work, which would be manifested in negative work-related attitudes (e.g., higher cynicism).

Preliminary work in this area has shown that employment quality (e.g., opportunities to learn on the job, or role stressors) is positively correlated with teenagers' motivation to do good work and negatively correlated with their cynicism (Loughlin & Barling, 1998; Stern et al., 1990). O'Brien and Feather (1990) also found that young workers in "poor-quality" full-time employment (i.e., with little opportunity to use their skills and education) had more negative work values than workers in "good-quality" employment. Indeed, there were no differences in psychological well-being between those in poor-quality employment and an unemployed contrast group. Krahn and Lowe (1988) found that young workers are less satisfied with their jobs in general than are older workers. Because employment quality may have long-lasting effects on young people's work-related attitudes and behavior, understanding the nature and experiences of their employment is now an important challenge confronting researchers, managers, and policy makers.

UNDEREMPLOYMENT: A PARTICULAR PROBLEM FOR YOUNG WORKERS?

As the preceding discussion implies, young workers are disproportionately likely to experience underemployment. According to Sheets, Nord, and Phelps (1987), underemployment includes the following: the unemployed (i.e., those actively seeking a job but unable to find work); discouraged workers (i.e., those who have given up seeking full-time employment owing to an inability to find a job); involuntary part-time workers (i.e., those working fewer than 35 hr per week but wanting full-time work); and low-income workers (full-time low-wage workers and intermittent employees who are employed part- or full-time during the year but are unable to secure stable full-time employment). When these forms of labor force participation are taken into account, typical underemployment rates are at least double if not more the official labor force unemployment rates reported.

Not all workers are equally affected by underemployment. Youth (as well as less educated workers, women, and minorities) are over-represented in all categories of the underemployed (Soltero, 1996). In fact, the situation for young workers has actually deteriorated somewhat over the past decade (Betcherman & Morissette, 1994). Since the early 1980s there has been a steady decline in the relative hourly wages of young workers in Canada, the United States, and the United Kingdom (even after controlling for education, industry, and occupation; Betcherman & Morissette, 1994). In the past, many repetitive low-quality jobs (e.g., assembly line jobs) attracted higher compensation, often as a result of union demands (i.e., discontentment pay). However, many young workers are now being saddled with both poor-quality jobs and poor wages (particularly among the least educated).

Young workers are more likely to be underemployed for several reasons. First, age is a proxy for experience, and is highly correlated with seniority. Similarly, age is a proxy for education. In addition to perceived lack of experience, young workers may also be disadvantaged if employers perceive them as more likely to quit; shirk responsibility; and be less productive, less dependable, and less cooperative. Finally, union membership is a buffer against underemployment because it increases worker power, provides its members with access to internal labor markets, and acts as a collective voice and alternate institutional change mechanism (Barling, Fullagar, & Kelloway, 1992). However, young workers are much less likely to be union members than are their older counterparts (see chap. 9, this volume, for a more complete discussion of young workers and unions).

EDUCATION AND TRAINING: A ROUTE TO HIGH-QUALITY EMPLOYMENT FOR YOUNG WORKERS?

As labor market opportunities have diminished over the past decade, school enrollment rates have risen: For example, whereas 32.1% of the 15- to 24-year-old population in Canada were enrolled full-time in 1981, 53.5% were enrolled in 1992. Between 1982 and 1991 the number of 18- to 21-year-olds enrolled in undergraduate universities had jumped over 10%, to 30.1% in 1991 (Betcherman & Morissette, 1994). In general, the educational attainment of the youth labor force has continued to rise. As this has occurred, the job prospects for young people with relatively low levels of schooling have deteriorated. In addition to the established negative relationship between years of schooling and unemployment rates, poorly educated young workers are at a growing disadvantage: Between 1981 and 1989, the relative unemployment rate decreased for those with a postsecondary diploma, certificate, or degree, while the relative unemployment rate increased for those with only secondary schooling or less. For those young workers who do not complete high school, there is a high probability that they will be under- or unemployed, potentially becoming a "chronic underclass" with no real entrance into the world of decent work (Lewington, 1997). Students may now be recognizing that without a high school diploma as well as some additional postsecondary education, their job prospects are very bleak. In fact, in Canada, four out of five high school students who had graduated by 1995 went on to take more training through a certificate, diploma, or degree program (Lewington, 1997).

Although higher levels of education can certainly buffer young people from some of the challenges facing young workers in general, it should be noted that higher credentials do not necessarily lead to higher opportunities. Furthermore, requiring individuals to gain additional skills, education, or both prior to entering the labor force is an ideal way for business to pass the cost of education onto the public, while gaining the advantages of a well-educated workforce. According to Hurn (1985), "modern societies have failed to provide skilled or challenging work for all but a minority of the population, and for a very large number of individuals the training they receive in schools is largely unnecessary or irrelevant" (p. 312). As we have seen in European as well as North American countries, whenever there is high unemployment, youth training is typically championed as necessary to solve the "youth employment problem" (e.g., Britain; Finn, 1987). In this regard, it is wise to bear in mind that unemployment is typically due more to a lack of jobs than a lack of skilled workers. Thus, one must be somewhat cautious about advocating education or training as the panacea for the current "youth employment problem" (e.g., the predominance of service sector jobs). Like the adult employment situation, massive economic and global changes have likely contributed as much to the creation of this problem as have a lack of education or training on the part of young workers.

CONCLUSION: THE NATURE OF
YOUTH EMPLOYMENT

We have considered numerous issues related to the quantity and quality of youth employment. Before concluding, two issues that will affect future research are worthy of elaboration. First, the very definition of *youth employment*, which includes workers between the ages of 15 and 24 years, is perhaps too broad for conceptual reasons. This definition captures two very different groups of workers, full-time students working part-time, and individuals who have either completed high school or dropped out of high school without obtaining any postsecondary education. These two groups seek employment for different reasons, work for different amounts of time each week, may well obtain different quality jobs, and probably spend the money they earn differently (see chap. 4, this volume). Given these differences, the question remains whether the findings from one group will generalize to the other.

Second, this chapter has highlighted the importance of the quality of employment for young people. At the same time, concern has been expressed because the literature to date indicates that young people are unlikely to find high-quality employment. However, this research has been limited to young workers employed in the formal sector. Future research should also consider young people employed in the informal sector (e.g., baby-sitting); such jobs may be high in responsibility and yield different findings from the research currently available.

In terms of practical suggestions, there are some possibilities for immediate action to improve the quality of young people's work experiences. First, the importance of high-quality work for young workers needs to be acknowledged explicitly and immediately. Second, we need to highlight those aspects of employment that might be most salient to youth, and most amenable to change (e.g., occupational health and safety, social contacts on the job or mentorship relationships).

In conclusion, it is clear that the quality of young people's employment is at least as important to them as the number of hours they work. The quality of young people's employment may have serious implications not only for young workers, but also for society. We should be concerned about what young people are learning about the world of work, and about the effects of this learning on subsequent occupational and personal development (see chap. 3, this volume). For example, young workers are overrepresented among discouraged workers. Recently, some authors have expressed concern that young discouraged workers who are denied access to legitimate means of earning a living and deriving self-fulfillment, may resort to illegal means to do so (Soltero, 1996). It behooves researchers, policy makers, and organizational decision makers to begin focusing on the quality of young people's employment experiences.

REFERENCES

Astrand, N. E., Hanson, B. S., & Isacson, S. O. (1989). Job demands, job decision latitude, job support and social network factors as predictors of mortality in a Swedish pulp and paper company. *British Journal of Industrial Medicine, 46,* 334–340.

Barling, J. (1990). *Employment, stress and family functioning.* Chichester, England: Wiley.

Barling, J., Fullagar, C., & Kelloway, E. K. (1992). *The union and its members: A psychological approach.* New York: Oxford University Press.

Barling, J., & Kelloway, E. K. (1996). Job insecurity and health: The moderating role of workplace control. *Stress Medicine, 12,* 253–259.

Barling, J., Rogers, K. A., & Kelloway, E. K. (1995). Some effects of teenager's part-time employment: The quantity and quality of work makes the difference. *Journal of Organizational Behavior, 16,* 143–154.

Betcherman, G., & Morissette, R. (1994). *Recent youth labour market experiences in Canada.* Business and Labour Market Analysis, 63. Ottawa, Ontario: Statistics Canada.

Carr, R. V., Wright, J. D., & Brody, C. J. (1996). Effects of high school work experience a decade later: Evidence from the national longitudinal survey. *Sociology of Education, 69,* 66–81.

Cheng, M. (1995). *Issues related to student part-time work: What did research find in the Toronto situation and other context?* (Research Report, No. 215). Toronto, Ontario, Canada: Toronto Board of Education, Research Services.

D'Amico, R. (1984). Does employment during high school impair academic progress? *Sociology of Education, 57,* 152–164.

Economic Council of Canada. (1990). *Good jobs: Employment in the service economy.* Ottawa, Ontario, Canada: Minister of Supply and Services Canada.

Finn, D. (1987). *Training without jobs: New deals and broken promises: From raising the school leaving age to the youth training scheme.* London: MacMillan Education.

Fisher, C. D., & Gitelson, R. (1983). A meta-analysis of the correlates of role conflict and ambiguity. *Journal of Applied Psychology, 68,* 320–333.

Garson, B. (1988). *The electronic sweatshop: How computers are transforming the office of the future into the factory of the past.* New York: Penguin Books.

Gottfredson, D. C. (1985). Youth employment, crime and schooling: A longitudinal study of a national sample. *Developmental Psychology, 21,* 419–432.

Gottfredson, L. S. (1981). Circumscription and compromise: A developmental theory of occupational aspirations. *Journal of Counseling Psychology, 28,* 545–579.

Greenberger, E., & Steinberg, L. D. (1986). *When teenagers work: The psychological and social costs of adolescent employment.* New York: Basic Books.

Greenberger, E., Steinberg, L. D., & Ruggiero, M. (1982). A job is a job is a job . . . or is it? *Work and Occupations, 9,* 79–96.

Greenberger, E., Steinberg, L. D., Vaux, A., & McAuliffe, S. (1980). Adolescents who work: Effects of part-time employment on family and peer relations. *Journal of Youth and Adolescence, 9,* 189–202.

Hackman, J. R., & Oldham, G. R. (1980). *Work redesign.* Reading, MA: Addison-Wesley.

Hurn, C. J. (1985). *The limits and possibilities of schooling: An introduction to the sociology of education.* Boston: Allyn & Bacon.

Jackson, P. R. (1988). Personal networks, social mobilization and unemployment. *Psychological Medicine, 18,* 397–404.

Jahoda, M. (1982). *Employment and unemployment: A social psychological perspective.* Cambridge, England: Cambridge University Press.

Kahn, R. L. (1980). Conflict, ambiguity and overload: Three elements in job stress. In D. Katz, R. L. Kahn, & J. S. Adams (Eds.), *The study of organizations: Findings from field and laboratory* (pp. 418–428). San Francisco: Jossey-Bass.

Kahn, R. L., Wolfe, D. M., Quinn, R. P., Snoek, D., & Rosenthal, R. A. (1964). *Role stress: Studies in role conflict and ambiguity.* New York: Wiley.

Karasek, R. A., Schwartz, J., & Theorell, T. (1982). *Job characteristics, occupation, and coronary heart disease* (Final report on Grant No. R-01-OH00906). Cincinnati, OH: National Institute for Occupational Safety & Health.

Karasek, R. A., & Theorell, T. (1990). *Healthy work: Stress, productivity and the reconstruction of working life.* New York: Basic Books.

Krahn, H. (1991). Youth employment. In R. Barnhorst & L. C. Johnson (Eds.), *The state of the child in Ontario* (pp. 139–159). Toronto, Ontario, Canada: Oxford University Press.

Krahn, H., & Lowe, G. S. (1988). *Work, industry and Canadian society.* Toronto, Ontario, Canada: Nelson Canada.

Krosnick, J. A., & Alwin, D. F. (1989). Aging and susceptibility to attitude change. *Journal of Personality and Social Psychology, 57,* 416–425.

Lantos, T. (1992). The silence of the kids: Children at risk in the workplace. *Labor Law Journal, 43,* 67–70.

Lewington, J. (1997, January 28). Real dropout rate only 15%: Returners tallied in new study. *The Globe and Mail,* A6.

Lorence, J., & Mortimer, J. T. (1985). Job involvement through the life course: A panel study of three age groups. *American Sociological Review, 50,* 618–638.

Loughlin, C. A., & Barling, J. (1997). *Young workers study: Occupational health and safety in Brockville.* Unpublished manuscript, Queen's University, Kingston, Ontario, Canada.

Loughlin, C. A., & Barling, J. (1998). Teenagers' part-time employment and their work-related attitudes and aspirations. *Journal of Organizational Behavior, 19,* 197–207.

Mortimer, J. T., Finch, M. D., Ryu, S., & Shanahan, M. J. (1991, April). Evidence from a prospective longitudinal study of work experience and adolescent development. In J. T. Mortimer (Chair), *New evidence on the benefits and costs of employment, work intensity, and work quality for adolescent development.* Symposium conducted at the 1991 biennial meeting of the Society for Research on Child Development, Seattle, WA.

Mortimer, J. T., Finch, M. D., Shanahan, M. J., & Ryu, S. (1992). Work experience, mental health, and behavioral adjustment in adolescence. *Journal of Research on Adolescence, 2,* 25–58.

Mortimer, J. T., Lorence, J., & Kumka, D. S. (1986). *Work, family and personality: Transition to adulthood.* Norwood, NJ: Ablex.

Mortimer, J. T., & Shanahan, M. J. (1991, June). *Adolescent work experience and relations with peers.* Paper presented at the 1991 American Sociological Association Meeting, Cincinnati, OH.

Nord, W. R. (1977). Job satisfaction reconsidered. *American Psychologist, 32,* 1026–1035.

O'Brien, G. E., & Feather, N. T. (1990). The relative effects of unemployment and quality of employment on the affect, work values and personal control of adolescents. *Journal of Occupational Psychology, 63,* 151–165.

Sauter, S. L., Murphy, L. R., & Hurrell, J. J. (1990). Prevention of work-related psychological disorders: A national strategy proposed by the National Institute for Occupational Safety and Health (NIOSH). *American Psychologist, 45,* 1146–1158.

Sheets, R. G., Nord, S., & Phelps, J. J. (1987). *The impact of service industries on underemployment in metropolitan economies.* Toronto, Ontario, Canada: Lexington Books.

Soltero, J. M. (1996). *Inequality in the workplace: Underemployment among Mexicans, African Americans, and Whites.* New York: Garland Publishing.

Staw, B. M., & Ross, J. (1985). Stability in the midst of change: A dispositional approach to job attitudes. *Journal of Applied Psychology, 70,* 469–480.

Steinberg, L. D., & Dornbusch, S. M. (1991). Negative correlates of part-time employment during adolescence: Replication and elaboration. *Developmental Psychology, 27,* 304–313.

Steinberg, L. D., Fegley, S., & Dornbusch, S. M. (1993). Negative impact of part-time work on adolescent adjustment: Evidence from a longitudinal study. *Developmental Psychology, 29,* 171–180.

Stern, D., Stone, J. R., III, Hopkins, C., & McMillion, M. (1990). Quality of students' work experience and orientation toward work. *Youth and Society, 22,* 263–282.

Sunter, D. (1992). Juggling school and work. *Perspectives on labour and income, 4,* 15–21.

Tetrick, L. E., & Barling, J. (1995). *Changing employment relations: Behavioral*

35

and social perspectives. Washington, DC: American Psychological Association.

Theorell, T., Perski, A., Orth-Gomer, K., Hamsten, A., & de Faire, U. (1991). The effects of the strain of returning to work on the risk of cardiac death after a first myocardial infarction before the age of 45. *International Journal of Cardiology, 30*, 61–67.

Wall, T. D., & Clegg, C. W. (1981). A longitudinal field study of a group work redesign. *Journal of Occupational Behavior, 2*, 31–49.

Wall, T. D., Corbett, J. M., Martin, R., Clegg, C. W., & Jackson, P. R. (1990). Advanced manufacturing technology, work design, and performance: A change study. *Journal of Applied Psychology, 75*, 691–697.

Warr, P. (1987). *Work, unemployment and mental health.* Oxford, England: Oxford University Press.

Winefield, A. H., Winefield, H. R., Tiggemann, M., & Goldney, R. D. (1991). A longitudinal study of the psychological effects of unemployment and unsatisfactory employment on young adults. *Journal of Applied Psychology, 76*, 424–431.

Yamoor, C. M., & Mortimer, J. T. (1990). Age and gender differences in the effects of employment on adolescent achievement and well-being. *Youth and Society, 22*, 225–240.

3

Learning to Work: The Development of Work Beliefs

E. Kevin Kelloway and Steve Harvey

Although developmental psychologists have long since abandoned the model of the child as a *tabula rasa*, in many respects organizational psychologists continue to act as if employees enter the workplace as a blank slate. That is, organizational psychologists continue to theorize and conduct research that focuses on the organizational setting as *the* causal factor, while simultaneously excluding the possible impact of individual factors on organizational behavior. This "disappearance of the individual" from organizational psychology is well documented (Nord & Fox, 1996), and is by no means a recent trend. Almost 20 years ago, Salancik and Pfeffer (1977) commented that

> The field has very nearly eliminated individual-level variables from the study of job attitudes. The field is no longer interested in what the individual brings to the work setting in terms of behavioral tendencies, traits, and personality. (p. 440)

Preparation of this chapter was supported by a Social Sciences and Humanities Research Council of Canada Research Grant (No. 410-95-0155) to the first author. Correspondence regarding the manuscript may be sent to E. Kevin Kelloway at the Psychology Department, University of Guelph, Guelph, Ontario, Canada, N1G 2W1 or kkellowa@uoguelph.ca.

Our primary purpose in this chapter is to suggest that there is substantial evidence to support the notion that young people enter the workplace with well-developed sets of work-related attitudes, beliefs, and values. Moreover, these individual factors likely continue to influence the development and expression of organizational attitudes and behaviors long after the individual has acquired work experience.

There is certainly evidence that ignoring the role of the individual has led to the construction of a truncated body of knowledge concerning organizational behavior. For example, until relatively recently, almost all the contemporary understanding of job satisfaction attributes satisfaction to workplace factors (Spector, 1997). In direct contrast to this perspective, Staw and Ross (1985) reported a longitudinal study of the job satisfaction of 1,500 accountants over a 10-year period. They found that job satisfaction remained remarkably stable over time even when the individuals had changed jobs or careers. Based on their data, Staw and Ross (1985) suggest that there is evidence for a dispositional influence on job satisfaction (see Staw, Bell, & Clausen, 1986). Others (e.g., Arvey, Bouchard, Segal, & Abraham, 1989; Levin & Stokes, 1989) have since reached similar conclusions regarding the importance of individual factors as determinants of job attitudes.

In a similar vein, there is evidence that employee commitment to the organization is influenced by "commitment propensity" (Meyer & Allen, 1997). Defined as (a) personal characteristics, (b) pre-entry expectations, and (c) the volition and irrevocability of organizational choice (Mowday, Porter, & Steers, 1982), *commitment propensity* measured prior to entry into the workforce has been found to predict subsequent employee commitment (Lee, Ashford, Walsh, & Mowday, 1992; Pierce & Dunham, 1987) even over a 4-year time span (Lee et al., 1992). However, once again, the research on individual differences to such predispositions is limited and in need of further attention (Meyer & Allen, 1997).

These findings, which are familiar to organizational psychologists, offer some support for the suggestion that young people enter the workforce with a set of tendencies, temperaments, or predispositions that shape their subsequent work and organizational experiences. They also illustrate that by excluding the individual from organizational theorizing (Nord & Fox, 1996), we run the risk of constraining the explanatory power of our theories and research. Although some pre-entry, individual difference research focuses on genetic determinants of work-related constructs (e.g., Arvey et al., 1989), our focus in this chapter is on what young people learn about work prior to entry in the workforce, and how this might have an impact on organizational behavior. Therefore, we focus on individuals' acquired knowledge, beliefs, attitudes, and values in relation to work and working. Excluded from our discussion are the development of individual difference variables such as personality. Although personality is subject, in part, to early learning and is known to influence organizational behavior, its development is well documented elsewhere.

In considering what individuals learn about work prior to formal entry into the workforce, at least three questions of considerable interest to organizational psychologists emerge:

1. What do young people learn about work prior to their entry into the workplace?
2. How do they acquire this information?
3. How is pre-employment learning manifested in the workplace?

We organize our discussion by considering each of these questions in turn. The review is by no means exhaustive but rather illustrative of the fact that much learning with respect to work occurs from an early age.

WHAT DO YOUNG PEOPLE LEARN PRIOR TO THEIR ENTRY INTO THE WORKPLACE?

We review the three aforementioned questions by drawing upon two lines of research. First, developmental psychologists have devoted some attention to the development of economic constructs (such as work and employment) in children (e.g., Berti & Bombi, 1988; Bowes & Goodnow, 1996; Dickinson & Emler, 1992). Such research has sought to explain what children and adolescents understand about the nature of work and its social context. Findings suggest that children form a surprisingly sophisticated mental framework of work early on, and that they are therefore well prepared to assimilate a great deal of value-laden information about work as they enter their teen years.

Second, organizational psychologists have examined the development of work beliefs (such as the Protestant work ethic; Furnham, 1990), attitudes (Barling, Kelloway, & Bremermann, 1991; Kelloway & Newton, 1996; Kelloway & Watts, 1994), and motivations (e.g., Mc-Clelland, 1961). This research is driven primarily by the notion that many work-related values, attitudes, and beliefs are largely acquired through the process of social learning prior to one's entry into the workforce, and that parents are a primary source of such learning.

Development of Economic Constructs

The acquisition of economic constructs, such as work and employment, has been examined in the context of the development of cognitive abilities and, typically within a Piagetian framework (e.g., Berti & Bombi, 1988). In general, the research evidence indicates an increasing depth of understanding of the workplace with increasing age. Between the ages of 4 and 11 years, children's understanding of employment increases rapidly (Berti & Bombi, 1988; Furth, 1980; Jahoda, 1979).

The youngest children (i.e., approximately 4 years of age) typically define work as "a place to go" (Dickinson & Emler, 1992) with no connection between wages and employment. By the age of 6–7 years, however, children make a clear connection between working and wages (Bowes & Goodnow, 1996; Dickinson & Emler, 1992). Indeed, some data suggest that the connection between working and wages is established as early as 3 years old and is generalized to most but not all occupations. At these early ages, children's notions of waged employment may coexist with beliefs that one can obtain money from other sources (i.e., from the bank, from a shopkeeper; Berti & Bombi, 1988). These alternate explanations dissipate with increasing understanding of the nature of work and economic exchange.

Based on interviews with 60 middle-class children between the ages of 6 and 14, Berti and Bombi (1988) identify four overlapping stages in the child's developing conception of work. At stage one (ages 6–7 years) children recognize that one works to earn money although (a) children identify a narrow range of activities that constitute "work," and (b) they do not recognize how, or why, money is exchanged for labor. In the second stage (ages 7–9 years), the perceived range of work activities widens and the concept of hierarchical relations (i.e., the existence of a "boss") emerges. However, children remain unclear about how the boss obtains money to pay the workers. At stage three (ages 8–11 years), the concepts of hierarchical relations are solidified and generalized (i.e., children recognize both economic and legislative hierarchies). Finally, at stage four (ages 10–14 years) children recognize the circulation of money. Children at this stage clearly recognize that companies obtain money by selling goods or services, and that this revenue provides a wage for employees.

Berti and Bombi (1988) suggest that this developmental sequence is characterized by three parameters. First, children recognize an increasing number of economic actors. Second, children increasingly recognize the type of relationships in which these actors are engaged. Finally, children can construct complex economic systems that recognize the relationships between the consumer, the employer, and the employee.

As children acquire knowledge about economic relationships, they also acquire knowledge about the socioeconomic context of employment. For example, there are data suggesting that children progressively acquire understanding about wage relations. Several studies (e.g., Connell, 1977; Emler & Dickinson, 1985; Siegal, 1981) report that children become progressively willing to accept wage differentials as they acquire understanding about the nature of work. Similarly, by adolescence, children's rankings of occupational prestige reflect the socioeconomic position of occupations (Dickinson, 1990). Moreover, adolescents' differentiation between the wage or prestige level of occupations parallel that of adults (e.g., through appeals to distributive justice where rewards are obtained through education, effort, hours worked, social importance of the job; Dickinson, 1990).

It is important to note here, as do Dickinson and Emler (1992), that although children come to a common understanding of the rank order of various occupations, their estimates of the wage difference between occupations are frequently inaccurate. In particular, children *underestimate* both the absolute wage of, and the wage inequality between, occupations (Emler & Dickinson, 1985; Siegal, 1991); moreover, these inaccuracies may vary by social class (Emler & Dickinson, 1985). As Dickinson and Emler (1992) note, one implication of these class differences is that middle- and working-class children aged 10–12 years have vastly different assumptions about the attainable economic rewards from different occupations. These findings are consistent with many studies on occupational choice wherein socioeconomic status shows a strong, positive relationship to occupational status aspirations, expectations, and its attainment (Schulenberg, Vondracek, & Crouter, 1984).

As implied by the aforementioned studies, knowledge of occupational prestige has direct implications for the development of career choice and occupational preference. Several theories have been postulated regarding career choice (e.g., Ginzberg, 1988; Gottfredson, 1981; Holland, 1985). However, we only briefly outline one such theory that, like the others, suggests children's thinking and understanding of work has matured to such a point in early adolescence that they are already considering careers, even though they remain somewhat vague on details (see Bowes & Goodnow, 1996).

Gottfredson (1981) has identified four stages in the development of occupational preference. In the initial stage (ages 3–5 years) children's knowledge of occupations is limited to adult roles. In the second stage (ages 6–8 years) occupational preferences start to become sex-typed as children acquire their own sense of gender identity and gender stereotypes about occupations. In the third stage (ages 9–13 years), the influence of social class appears, and children begin to orient toward occupations that are consistent with their own socioeconomic status. Finally, within the boundaries laid down by gender and social class, the child's own interests, values, and competencies further refine the choice of occupation.

Due to numerous mitigating factors, one must guard against rigid interpretations of the stated boundaries and the age-related nature of these stages and those of other theories. With respect to boundaries, for example, contrary to some theories, a study of 11th graders conducted by Erez, Borochov, and Mannheim (1989) found that adolescents' reported sex-role stereotypes were more predictive of the work features desired in employment than were the students' biological sex. As for the age-related nature of stages, one must recognize that they are average estimates with the potential for greater deviations. Indeed, Bowes and Goodnow (1996, p. 315) point out that the development of children's knowledge of work will be helped or constrained by three factors: (a) the state of the information available, (b) the individual's interest in understanding, and (c) the extent to which the understanding required is within the individual's capacity to understand.

Children also acquire perceptions of social relationships in the workplace prior to their entry into the workforce. For example, data reported by Dickinson and Emler (1992) suggest that adolescents develop an increasingly sophisticated view of industrial conflict and industrial relations in the workplace. At the ages of 10–12 years, only 26% of children were able to describe the role of labor unions. By the ages of 14–16 years, 85% of the adolescents could give reasonably accurate accounts of the role of trade unions (Dickinson & Emler, 1992).

Thus, the available data uniformly suggest that concepts of work and employment relations are well developed in childhood. As Dickinson and Emler (1992) conclude:

> By the time young people enter the labour market they are equipped with the argumentative terms of employment relations. They are already discussing the cash value of jobs in terms of skill, responsibility, effort, and qualifications, and therefore prepared for a particular framework for debating and negotiating a definition of a fair day's pay. (p. 28)

Development of Work Beliefs and Attitudes

Although there is clear evidence that children acquire some understanding of the workplace prior to their entry into the workforce, less attention has been paid to the development of work beliefs, values, and attitudes. Nonetheless, there is some evidence that children have well-developed beliefs and attitudes about work. For the most part, researchers have drawn on Bandura's (1977) social learning theory to suggest that beliefs, attitudes, and values about work are acquired through a socialization process. Consequently, much of this research has focused on the role of parents as socializing agents of a child's work attitudes, values, and beliefs.

Witjing, Arnold, and Conrad (1978), for example, found children and parents held similar work values among a sample of children in the sixth, ninth, tenth, and twelfth grades. Furnham (1987) reported similarity between parents' and children's Protestant work ethic, economic beliefs, external locus of control, and need for achievement. Similar findings demonstrating congruency in work values between parents and children have been reported by Thomas and Wiegert (1971) and by Perrone (1973). On the other hand, note that not all studies support the parental value linkage. In a study of college students and their parents, Vodanovich and Kramer (1989) failed to find support for the similarity of work values between parents and their children.

Several more recent studies have suggested that in addition to values and beliefs there is some evidence for the intergenerational transmission of work-related attitudes. Based on the observations that parental influence is the most important factor in whether young people join a trade union and that union leaders often come from union families, Barling et al. (1991) proposed that children acquire union attitudes through a process of family socialization and suggested that children develop attitudes toward unions that are similar to their parents. Subsequent research has supported this suggestion, reporting that union attitudes among first-year college students are similar to those of their parents (e.g., Kelloway & Newton, 1996; Kelloway & Watts, 1994).

These results are consistent with the observation that children routinely observe their parents' reactions to work (Barling, Dupre, & Hepburn, 1998). Even from an early age (e.g., 7–8 years) children can accurately report on parents' job satisfaction (Abramovitch & Johnson, 1992; Piotrkowski & Stark, 1987). Moreover, children's perceptions of parental work attitudes and experiences shape the development of children's own work beliefs and attitudes (Barling et al., 1991; Barling et al., 1998; Kelloway & Newton, 1996; Kelloway & Watts, 1994).

How Do Children Learn About the Workplace?

Almost uniformly, researchers have examined the development of knowledge and beliefs about work in the context of a model of economic socialization (e.g., Berti & Bombi, 1988; Dickinson & Emler, 1992). A prima facie case for economic socialization can be made based on the observation that children's acquisition and acceptance of economic concepts is influenced by their social environment. For example, children of small business owners may show an earlier understanding of economic exchange than do children who are more removed from the parents' workplace (Berti & Bombi, 1988; Jahoda, 1979). More generally, children's understanding of work and employment is influenced by their parents' employment and economic circumstances (Dickinson & Emler, 1992).

Dickinson & Emler (1992) identify at least five agents of economic socialization (i.e., language, family, mass media, peers, and school). However, most of the available research has focused on the role of parents as socialization agents. In particular, researchers have focused on the socialization of economic concepts through both vicarious learning and direct attempts at instruction. Our review of vicarious learning will focus on select studies examining the learning of attitudes and beliefs.

With regard to vicarious learning, Bandura (1977) suggested that "much social learning occurs on the basis of casual or directed observation of behavior as it is performed by others in everyday situations" (p. 39). The emphasis on social learning is clear throughout the literature. Furnham (1987, 1990), for example, suggested that parents communicate their values, beliefs, and attitudes in the way they discuss their jobs, perform activities at home, and discuss their achievements. Similarly, both Barling et al. (1991) and Piotrkowski and Stark (1987) suggested that children develop attitudes and beliefs as they observe their parents' work-related behaviors and listen to their parents talk about their work.

This emphasis on the process of vicarious learning has led to research focusing on the child's perception of parental experiences, beliefs, attitudes, and values as a predictor of the child's own beliefs, values, and attitudes. For example, Barling et al. (1991) proposed and supported a model in which the child's perception of a parent's union participation attitude would predict his or her own attitudes toward unions. Children's perceptions of their parent's union participation also predicted their own Marxist work beliefs which, in turn, also predicted children's union attitudes.

The Barling et al. (1991) study was based solely on children's self-reports, thereby precluding the question of whether children were accurate observers of their parents. However, Barling et al. (1991) suggested that accuracy of observation was a secondary question. It is the child's *perception* of parental attitudes and values, not the accuracy of the perception, that lends the greatest predictive power. Nonetheless, the question of accuracy has arisen in several studies with mixed results. For example, both Abramovitch and Johnson (1992) and Piotrkowski and Stark (1987) found that children were accurate perceivers of parental work experiences and work attitudes. In a related literature on social values and beliefs, however, both Acock and Bengston (1980) and Whitbeck and Gecas (1988) found contrary results; that is, children did not accurately perceive parental work values. With respect to these latter studies, note that children's perception of parental values or beliefs were related to their own, suggesting that children perceive themselves to be similar to their parents. Again, children's perception, not the accuracy of that perception, may be the most salient influence in shaping children's own attitudes.

In the wake of such discrepancies, four recent studies have elaborated on the socialization model proposed by Barling et al. (1991) and the accuracy of children's perceptions. First, Kelloway and Watts (1994) collected data from 87 students and their parents. They reported moderate to substantial correlations between parents' and children's reports of parental union participation ($r = .56$) and parental union attitudes ($r = .58$). Moreover, parental participation and parental union attitudes predicted children's perceptions which, in turn, predicted children's union attitudes.

Next, Kelloway and Newton (1996) extended the model by formally testing the hypothesis that children's perceptions of parental attitudes or experiences were the most salient predictors of children's attitudes. An important extension was the empirically supported hypothesis that a child's observation of parental dissatisfaction at work might better predict children's Marxist work beliefs (i.e., the belief that work is necessary but is organized so as to exploit workers; Buchholz, 1978, 1979) than their perceptions of parental union participation or Marxist work beliefs per se.

Based on data from 120 first-year undergraduate students and their parents, Kelloway and Newton (1996) found that children's perceptions of parental union participation and parental union attitudes mediated the relationship between parents' participation and attitudes and children's own attitudes. Moreover, children's union attitudes were predicted by their Marxist work beliefs, which were predicted by perceptions of parental job dissatisfaction. Once again, children were found to accurately report on parental union participation ($r = .70$), parental union attitudes ($r = .55$), and parental job satisfaction ($r = .63$), although children underestimated the level of parental job satisfaction.

Finally, Kelloway, Newsome, and Bullen (1997) extended the family socialization model by considering the influence of parents' job characteristics on the development of children's work beliefs. Based on data from 60 undergraduate students and their parents, Kelloway et al. (1997) found that students could accurately report on parents' work autonomy, skill variety, and job satisfaction. Most importantly, student perceptions of parental job autonomy predicted students' own Protestant work ethic beliefs (the measure of Protestant work ethic used in the study emphasized the value of independent action; see Furnham, 1990). Student perceptions of parental skill use at work predicted humanistic work beliefs (i.e., the belief that work can be source of fulfillment, see Buchholz, 1978, 1979). As in the previous study, student perceptions of parental job dissatisfaction predicted students' Marxist work beliefs, including the fact that they once again underestimated the level of parental job satisfaction.

Recently, Barling et al. (1998) examined the consequences of parental job insecurity on children's work beliefs and work attitudes. Based on a sample of 134 undergraduate students and their parents, the study indicated that parental experiences of layoffs and job insecurity significantly predicted children's perceptions of parental job insecurity. In turn, children's perceptions of parental job insecurity predicted children's own work beliefs and work attitudes.

Taken together, these results offer considerable support for the suggestion that children develop attitudes and beliefs about work as they listen to their parents talk about their jobs and engage in work-related activities. As mentioned earlier, these results are consistent with the view that a good deal of economic socialization occurs through a process of vicarious learning. Moreover, although there is a growing interest in the social learning of work attitudes and beliefs in particular, more research is needed examining the social learning of work values or preferences (i.e., the desired aspects of a job).

The learning discussed thus far is naturally occurring. However, parents also actively try to shape the attitudes, beliefs, and values of their children, and we now turn our attention to the effects of such efforts.

Perhaps the best known account of the influence of socialization on work beliefs and values is McClelland's (1961) explanation of the development of the need for achievement. McClelland explicitly linked need for achievement with parental socializing activities such as early mastery training. Moreover, McClelland focused on the role of stories containing achievement-oriented imagery as an important influence on the development of need for achievement. Thus, McClelland (1961) suggested that parents actively inculcate a need for achievement in their children by exposing them to achievement-oriented information and mastery training.

Perhaps a more direct means of economic socialization is through the use of allowances or pocket money (Furnham, 1990). Davis and Taylor (1979) suggest that the use of allowances teaches money handling skills such as saving, budgeting, and borrowing, and inculcates a sense of responsibility. Davis and Taylor (1979) argued further that children should receive explicit education in competition, profits, taxes, and investing, and suggest that there are many benefits to be obtained through a child holding a job. Specifically, they suggest that early experience with employment will foster time-management skills, a knowledge of competitive systems, an appreciation of the inevitability and consequences of failure, and an appreciation of the need to make choices.

These views seem to be shared by parents. Furnham and Thomas (1984) found that the vast majority of adults believed in giving children some form of allowance as a means of education in economic concepts. Similarly, Greenberger and Steinberg (1986) report that parents believe that holding a job as a teenager builds character; that is, a sense of responsibility, dependability, and the ability to delay gratification. As Furnham (1990) notes, "There appears to be sufficient evidence that parents with PWE [Protestant work ethic] beliefs stress the importance of postponement of gratification and saving; the planning of the use of money; and that money has to be earned" (p. 117).

Children may also share these beliefs. Greenberger and Steinberg (1981) report that students who held part-time jobs expressed pride in their dependability as employees. Despite these shared beliefs, the actual effect of early work experiences on children's economic socialization is more complex. For example, there is some concern that holding a part-time job might be associated with a decline in school performance (see chap. 4, this volume). Moreover, Greenberger and Steinberg (1986) summarize the results of their research by suggesting that although children may learn a sense of responsibility from holding a part-time job, it may be an egocentric form of responsibility that shows little concern for the needs of others. Research also points out the flaw in assuming that employment affects young people uniformly (e.g., see the discussion on the "quality" of employment, chap. 2, this volume).

Given that part-time employment is the modal pattern for North American high school students, the question arises as to what work values, attitudes, and beliefs are learned through such employment. In their study of Canadian high school students, Loughlin and Barling (1998) found no effects of job quality on the development of career motivation, job involvement, cynicism, and career maturity. Nor were any of these outcomes predicted by employment quantity (i.e., the number of hours worked). Even when students had acquired direct experience with the workplace, the effects of parental socialization remained the strongest influences on students' work beliefs. Loughlin and Barling (1998) suggested that part-time employment may be sufficiently uninvolving (i.e., undertaken primarily for financial gain and seen as temporary) that it has relatively little influence on the development of work beliefs.

How Does Pre-Employment Learning Affect Organizational Behavior?

If the effects of early economic socialization were largely undone, or disrupted by, entry into the workplace, then the question of what children learn about work would have little relevance to organizational psychologists. Although researchers recognize the paucity of the existing data, there is some evidence to suggest that the effects of pre-employment socialization continue well after the individual has entered the workplace.

Pre-employment learning can have an effect on the expression of organizational attitudes and behaviors in at least two ways. First, attitudes, values, and beliefs acquired in childhood or adolescence can find direct expression as predictors of organizational behavior. Second, consistent with the propositions of social learning theory (Bandura, 1977), the early development of attitudes and beliefs can influence how individuals interpret their own experiences. In the simplest case, individuals who develop positive union attitudes as children and adolescents might be more receptive to union membership and influence as they enter full-time employment. Similarly, the development of strong Marxist work beliefs prior to employment might act as a predisposition to the development of job dissatisfaction.

There is some empirical support for both of these notions. For example, several studies of union attitudes and behaviors support the notion that family-of-origin influences continue to play a powerful role in adulthood as direct predictors of other forms of behavior. First, in their study of a white-collar British trade union, Nicholson, Ursell, and Lubbock (1981) reported that parents' orientation to unions was significantly, albeit modestly, related to individuals' participation in the union. Second, Gallagher and Jeong (1989) provided a more direct test and reported that, although parental union status was not associated with union attitudes, parental union attitudes were significantly associated with individuals' union attitudes. Finally, Kelloway, Catano, and Carroll (1997) studied a sample of union shop stewards and found that perceptions of parental union attitudes predicted both stewards' union attitudes and stewards' militancy.

The findings of Lee et al. (1992) regarding propensity for commitment provide initial support for the second model of family-of-origin influences on organizational behavior. They found that individuals with a high propensity to commit to the organization were more likely to view the same set of events in a positive manner than were individuals with a low propensity to commit. That is, individual differences (i.e., beliefs, values, attitudes) may at least partially determine individual perceptions of the workplace, which in turn, result in the expression of organizational attitudes and behaviors. In a similar manner, Kelloway and Newton (1996; see also Kelloway et al., 1997) suggested that the development of Marxist work beliefs may act as a predisposition for job dissatisfaction. That is, if individuals enter the workplace with the belief that they are there to be exploited, they are likely to interpret events to fit this belief. Barling et al. (1998) reported that perceptions of parental job insecurity resulted in children developing attitudes such as alienation and cynicism. In turn, these attitudes would be expected to substantially color the children's perceptions of the working environment.

CONCLUSION

As the foregoing review attests, there are sufficient data supporting three central conclusions about how children learn to work. First, children acquire substantial information about work, working, and the nature of employment relationships long before they enter the workforce. Although the stereotype of young people as naive newcomers to the workplace is well established, the available evidence suggests that young people enter the workforce with a sophisticated understanding of work and employment. From very young ages children acquire an understanding of economic constructs, including the exchange of labor for money and power dynamics in employment relationships. Moreover, there is some evidence to suggest that this information is not received in a value-neutral fashion. That is, as children acquire general knowledge, they also develop beliefs, values, and attitudes about the workplace. In particular, the available evidence suggests that children develop values, beliefs, and attitudes similar to those held by their parents. This information plays a role in shaping occupational choice and, as we suggest later, in developing and shaping organizational behavior.

Second, this information is acquired through a process of economic socialization in which parents play a large, but not an exclusive, role. As a result, children's learning about work is not value-neutral, it is conditioned by socioeconomic factors as well as children's observations of their parents' employment experiences. Children learn about the workplace from a variety of sources including the media, their peers, and their own direct experience with part-time employment. By far the most research attention has been paid to the role of parents as economic socialization agents. In general, the research suggests that children have access to a great deal of information about their parents' jobs and feelings toward them. This information provides the basis for children to develop their own beliefs about the nature of work and what to expect in the workplace.

Finally, although this last conclusion remains more tentative than the preceding two, there is evidence that pre-employment learning about work continues to exert an effect on individual attitudes and behaviors long after individuals enter the workforce and acquire more direct experience with the nature of work and employment. These influences are both direct and indirect: direct in that attitudes developed through vicarious learning (e.g., family socialization) continue to manifest after the individual has acquired more direct experience with the workforce, indirect in that work beliefs and attitudes developed prior to entry into the workforce may act as predisposing factors for the development of work attitudes and behaviors.

These findings, in conjunction with the increasing recognition of the poverty of situation-based accounts of organizational behavior (e.g., Staw & Ross, 1985), provide a basis for speculating that the groundwork for organizational behavior is formed long before the individual enters the workforce. Certainly, the literature summarized herein suggests that individuals acquire a wealth of value-laden information about the workplace long before they themselves become employed. The emerging challenge for researchers is to examine how and to what degree these beliefs, values, attitudes, and other acquired knowledge are stable throughout employment, and how they might then play a role in shaping organizational behavior.

The point here is not so much the need to include pre-entry values, attitudes, and beliefs in our models, as this is clearly done in many studies in this and other areas. Rather, there is a need to specify and examine complete models of influence in organizations wherein the pre-entry socialization influences (e.g., parents) are included as relevant variables and measured along with the other traditional influences (e.g., organizational socialization). As Dawis (1991) put it in reviewing work values, interests, and preferences more generally, such questions are "empirically unexplored territory" (p. 859).

REFERENCES

Abramovitch, R., & Johnson, L. C. (1992). Children's perceptions of parental work. *Canadian Journal of Behavioral Science, 24,* 319–332.

Acock, A. C., & Bengston, V. L. (1980). Actual versus perceived similarity among parents and youth. *Journal of Marriage and the Family, 42,* 501–515.

Arvey, R. D., Bouchard, T. J., Jr., Segal, N. L., & Abraham, L. M. (1989). Job satisfaction: Environmental and genetic components. *Journal of Applied Psychology, 74,* 187–192.

Bandura, A. (1977). *Social learning theory.* Englewood Cliffs, NJ: Prentice Hall.

Barling, J., Dupre, K. E., & Hepburn, C. G. (1998). Effects of parents' job insecurity on children's work beliefs and attitudes. *Journal of Applied Psychology, 83,* 112–118.

Barling, J., Kelloway, E. K., & Bremermann, E. H. (1991). Pre-employment predictors of union attitudes: The role of family socialization and work beliefs. *Journal of Applied Psychology, 76*, 725–731.

Berti, A. E., & Bombi, A. S. (1988). *The child's construction of economics.* Cambridge, England: Cambridge University Press.

Bowes, J. M., & Goodnow, J. J. (1996). Work for home, school, or labor force: The nature and sources of changes in understanding. *Psychological Bulletin, 120*, 300–321.

Buchholz, R. A. (1978). The work ethic reconsidered. *Industrial and Labor Relations Review, 31*, 450–459.

Buchholz, R. A. (1979). An empirical study of contemporary beliefs about work in American society. *Journal of Applied Psychology, 63*, 219–227.

Connell, R. W. (1977). *Ruling class, ruling culture.* Cambridge, England: Cambridge University Press.

Davis, K., & Taylor, T. (1979). *Kids and cash: Solving a parent's dilemma.* La Jolla, CA: Oak Tree.

Dawis, R. V. (1991). Vocational interests, values and preferences. In M. D. Dunnette & L. M. Hough (Eds.), *Handbook of industrial and organizational psychology* (Vol. 2, 2nd ed., pp. 833–872). Palo Alto, CA: Consulting Psychologists Press.

Dickinson, J. (1990). Adolescent representations of socio-economic status. *British Journal of Developmental Psychology, 8*, 351–371.

Dickinson, J., & Emler, N. (1992). *Developing conceptions of work.* In J. F. Hartley & G. M. Stephenson (Eds.), *Employment relations: The psychology of influence and control at work* (pp. 19–44). Cambridge, MA: Blackwell.

Emler, N., & Dickinson, J. (1985). Children's representation of economic inequalities: The effects of social class. *British Journal of Developmental Psychology, 3*, 191–198.

Erez, M., Borochov, O., & Mannheim, B. (1989). Work values of youth: Effects of sex or sex role typing? *Journal of Vocational Behavior, 34*, 350–366.

Furnham, A. (1987). Predicting Protestant work ethic beliefs. *European Journal of Personality, 1*, 93–106.

Furnham, A. (1990). *The Protestant work ethic: The psychology of work-related beliefs and behaviors.* New York: Routledge.

Furnham, A., & Thomas, P. (1984). Adults' perceptions of the economic socialization of children. *Journal of Adolescence, 7*, 217–231.

Furth, H. G. (1980). *The world of grown-ups.* New York: Elsevier.

Gallagher, D. G., & Jeong, Y. A. (1989, October). *Methodological concerns with behavioral studies of union membership.* Paper presented at the 10th Annual Southern Regional Industrial Relations Academic Seminar, West Virginia University, Morgantown.

Ginzberg, E. (1988). Toward a theory of occupational choice. *The Career Development Quarterly, 36,* 358–363.

Gottfredson, L. S. (1981). Circumscription and compromise: A developmental theory of occupational aspirations. *Journal of Counseling Psychology, 28,* 545–579.

Greenberger, E., & Steinberg, L. D. (1981). The workplace as a context for the socialization of youth. *Journal of Youth and Adolescence, 10,* 185–210.

Greenberger, E., & Steinberg, L. D. (1986). *When teen-agers work: The psychological and social costs of adolescent employment.* New York: Basic Books.

Holland, J. L. (1985). *Making vocational choices: A theory of vocational personalities and work environments* (2nd ed.). Englewood Cliffs, NJ: Prentice Hall.

Jahoda, G. (1979). The construction of economic reality by some Glaswegian children. *European Journal of Social Psychology, 9,* 115–127.

Kelloway, E. K., Catano, V. M., & Carroll, A. E. (1997). *Predictors of shop steward militancy.* Manuscript submitted for publication.

Kelloway, E. K., Newsome, S., & Bullen, L. (1997). *Parental work experiences and children's work beliefs.* Manuscript submitted for publication.

Kelloway, E. K., & Newton, T. (1996). Pre-employment predictors of union attitudes: The roles of parental work and union attitudes. *Canadian Journal of Behavioral Science, 28,* 113–120.

Kelloway, E. K., & Watts, L. (1994). Pre-employment predictors of union attitudes: Replication and extension. *Journal of Applied Psychology, 79,* 631–634.

Lee, T. W., Ashford, S. J., Walsh, J. P., & Mowday, R. T. (1992). Commitment propensity, organizational commitment and voluntary turnover: A longitudinal study of organizational entry processes. *Journal of Management, 18,* 15–32.

Levin, I., & Stokes, J. P. (1989). Dispositional approach to job satisfaction: Role of negative affectivity. *Journal of Applied Psychology, 74,* 752–758.

Loughlin, C. A., & Barling, J. (1998). Teenagers' part-time employment and their work-related attitudes and aspirations. *Journal of Organizational Behavior, 19,* 197–207.

McClelland, D. (1961). *The achieving society.* New York: Free Press.

Meyer, J. P., & Allen, N. J. (1997). *Commitment in the workplace: Theory, research, and application.* Thousand Oaks, CA: Sage.

Mowday, R. T., Porter, L. W., & Steers, R. (1982). *Organizational linkages: The psychology of commitment, absenteeism, and turnover.* San Diego, CA: Academic Press.

Nicholson, N., Ursell, G., & Lubbock, J. (1981). Membership participation in a white-collar union. *Industrial Relations, 20,* 162–177.

Nord, W. R., & Fox, S. (1996). The individual in organizational studies: The great disappearing act? In S. R. Clegg, C. Hardy, & W. R. Nord (Eds.), *Handbook of Organizational Studies* (pp. 148–174). Thousand Oaks, CA: Sage.

Perrone, P. A. (1973). A longitudinal study of occupational values of adolescents. *Vocational Counseling, 22,* 116–223.

Pierce, J. L., & Dunham, R. B. (1987). Organizational commitment: Pre-employment propensity and initial work experiences. *Journal of Management, 13,* 163–178.

Piotrkowski, C. S., & Stark, E. (1987). Children and adolescents look at their parents' jobs. In J. H. Lewko (Ed.), *How children and adolescents view the world of work* (pp. 3–19). San Francisco: Jossey-Bass.

Salancik, G. R., & Pfeffer, J. (1977). An examination of need–satisfaction models of job attitudes. *Administrative Science Quarterly, 22,* 427–456.

Schulenberg, J. E., Vondracek, F. W., & Crouter, A. C. (1984). The influence of the family on vocational development. *Journal of Marriage and the Family, 10,* 129–143.

Siegal, M. (1981). Children's perceptions of adult economic needs. *Child Development, 52,* 379–382.

Spector, P. (1997). *Job satisfaction.* Thousand Oaks, CA: Sage.

Staw, B. M., Bell, N. E., & Clausen, J. A. (1986). The dispositional approach to job attitudes: A lifetime longitudinal test. *Administrative Science Quarterly, 31,* 56–77.

Staw, B. M., & Ross, J. (1985). Stability in the midst of change: A dispositional approach to job attitudes. *Journal of Applied Psychology, 70,* 469–480.

Thomas, H. B., & Wiegert, A. J. (1971). Socialization and adolescent conformity to significant others: A cross-national study. *American Sociological Review, 36*, 308–319.

Vodanovich, S. J., & Kramer, T. J. (1989). An examination of the work values of parents and their children. *The Career Development Quarterly, 37*, 365–374.

Whitbeck, L. B., & Gecas, V. (1988). Value attributions and value transmission between parents and children. *Journal of Marriage and the Family, 50*, 829–840.

Witjing, J., Arnold, C., & Conrad, K. (1978). Generational differences in work values between parents and children and between boys and girls across grade levels, 6, 9, 10, and 12. *Journal of Vocational Behavior, 12*, 245–260.

4

Gender Differences in Employment and Income Experiences Among Young People

Serge Desmarais and James Curtis

This chapter begins from a basic principle of social science: that in many aspects of people's lives, current and past experiences shape their future expectations. We then apply this idea to young people's experiences with income from employment, and views about entitlement to income. There has been little directly relevant research on these topics among youth. Certainly, though, exposure to paid work has been shown to begin early in the life cycle, often before the age of 12 in activities such as yard work, baby-sitting, and so forth (Mortimer, Finch, Owens, & Shanahan, 1990). Further, studies show that paid work has become an increasingly important component of teenage life in the past 20 years. Over 60% of American high school students ages 16–19 reported working part-time by the mid-1980s (U.S. Bureau of the Census, 1989, 1993; see also, Manning, 1990), and there have been similar reported rates of work participation among youth recently in many industrialized countries (McKechnie, Lindsay, Hobbs, & Lavalette, 1996;

We gratefully acknowledge that financial support for this chapter and related work was provided by a research grant from the Social Sciences and Humanities Research Council of Canada.

Organization for Economic Cooperation and Development, OECD, 1996). This increasing participation of young people in the workforce suggests that they are being exposed early on to the norms and expectations of the workplace, a workplace that we know is characterized by high rates of sex segregation (e.g., Jacobs & Lim, 1992; Reskin, 1993) and gender-based disparities in income in North America (e.g., Armstrong & Armstrong, 1994; Marini, 1989). Boys and girls may well become socialized, through this early experience with work, to have different expectations of employment, including about the pay they should receive for the work they perform. Further, these expectations are likely to be reinforced in many families, schools, and the media (Blau & Ferber, 1986; see also Ridgeway, 1997).

This chapter examines how young people's early experiences in the workforce, as part-time workers while still in school, reinforce gender-based orientations toward perceived income entitlement. The central premises are that there are gender differences in the early work experience of young people, and that these differentially affect the female and male perceptions of income entitlement. In this way, youth employment may contribute to the gendered patterns of entitlement to pay that have been well documented among college students and adult workers—wherein women compared with men describe themselves as deserving less and as being relatively more satisfied with the lower level of pay they receive (see Crosby, 1982 and Major, 1989, 1994, for reviews).

To address these issues, we first summarize research on the employment circumstances of young people in North America. We primarily examine the differences and similarities in the work experience of young women and men. We next review research that explores the connection between work and income experience and perceived income entitlement among college students and working adults. Then we present new data from a recent national study with which we test the relationship between the earnings experience and perceived income entitlement of young people ages 16–19 and 20–24. We conclude with a discussion of the practical implications of our findings and suggest directions for further research.

RESEARCH ON GENDER, WORK, AND PAY AMONG YOUTH

Work Participation, Job Segregation, and Income

As noted previously, a great majority of teenagers work a substantial number of hours. Although surveys in the United States vary considerably in their estimates, most recent national studies report that between 40% and 60% of high school students are engaged in the paid labor force, with as many as 90% working during at least part of the school year (e.g., Bachman & Schulenberg, 1993; Manning, 1990; Stevens, Puchtell, Ryu, & Mortimer, 1992; Sweet, Bumpass, & Call, 1988; U.S. Bureau of the Census, 1993). Moreover, the work is steady; for example, in one study over half of employed high school seniors reported working more than 20 hours per week for several weeks of the year (Steinberg & Dornbusch, 1991). In addition the work history of most young people begins early in life, with more than 50% of adolescents beginning their first jobs by the age of 12 (e.g., Mortimer et al., 1990; Stevens et al., 1992).

This pattern of early participation in the labor force seems to hold across the genders; that is, studies report no gender difference in the rate of work participation of boys and girls (Manning, 1990; Mortimer et al., 1990). Earlier research suggested that boys' involvement in the labor force was more extensive, that boys hold their first jobs at younger ages and work significantly more hours than girls (Greenberger & Steinberg, 1986; Lewin-Epstein, 1981; White & Brinkerhoff, 1981). However, recent studies have highlighted an increasing similarity in these aspects of boys' and girls' early work experiences (Manning, 1990; Yamoor & Mortimer, 1990). Indeed, some studies suggest that girls may now enter paid work at younger ages than boys (Mortimer et al., 1990; Mortimer, Finch, Shanahan, & Ryu, 1992).

Despite the apparent convergence in the early employment experience of male and female adolescents, there remains some persistent gender differences in youth employment. Like that of older adults, the work of young people has been shown to be highly segregated by gender. Girls are more likely to work in baby-sitting, and boys are more often employed in manual or skilled work and in formal work settings (Greenberger & Steinberg, 1983, 1986; Lewin-Epstein, 1981; Medrich, Roizen, Rubin, & Buckley, 1982; Mortimer et al., 1990; Stevens et al., 1992; U.S. Bureau of Labor Statistics, 1981; White & Brinkerhoff, 1981; Yamoor & Mortimer, 1990). As teens get older, sex segregation seems to become more pronounced, and adolescent girls are more likely than boys to be employed in so-called "benevolent" jobs, where family or neighbors are employers, while their male counterparts more frequently are employed in a wider range of jobs in the greater community. Further, the range of jobs increases more rapidly with age for males (Greenberger & Steinberg, 1986; Mortimer et al., 1990).

A pattern of gender difference in earnings has also been documented. Although—of late—adolescent girls report working about the same number of hours as adolescent boys per week, they continue to earn significantly lower hourly wages than their male peers (Greenberger & Steinberg, 1983, 1986; Lewin-Epstein, 1981; Mortimer et al., 1990; Mortimer, Finch, Dennehy, Lee, & Beebe, 1994). Hourly wages are also higher in job types that are dominated by young males (Greenberger & Steinberg, 1983; Medrich et al., 1982).

Academic Performance and Occupational Aspirations

Studies have also shown that work has a significant impact on the academic, occupational, and economic intentions of teenage boys and girls (see, e.g., Marini & Brinton, 1984; Sewell, Hauser, & Wolf, 1980). Early researchers advocated adolescent work as a means of facilitating transition to adulthood; the work was said to promote independence, social responsibility, and a positive orientation to occupational achievement (Elder, 1974; Hamilton & Crouter, 1980; for review, see also Safyer, Hawkins Leahy, & Colan, 1995). Yet this viewpoint did not stand up to further empirical evidence. Rather, youth employment has been shown to be associated with negative short-term consequences for school performance, educational attainment, and school completion (Greenberger & Steinberg, 1986; Mortimer & Finch, 1986; Mortimer et al., 1992; Steinberg & Dornbusch, 1991; cf. D'Amico, 1984), especially if the part-time job requires excessive hours of work per week (see, e.g., Bachman & Schulenberg, 1993; D'Amico, 1984; Mortimer & Finch, 1986; Steitz & Owen, 1982; Steinberg, Fegley, & Dornbusch, 1993). On the other hand, part-time employment during adolescence has also been linked to positive effects on later levels of career attainment and income (Carr, Wright, & Brody, 1996; D'Amico, 1984). Finally, some studies have found virtually no impact of part-time work on school behavior, grades, and investment in school among young people (Mortimer, Shanahan, & Ryu, 1993; see also chaps. 2, 3, 5, this volume).

As is the case for work participation and income, research shows some similarities and some differences between the educational experiences of boys and girls. Young women have greater educational achievement than in the past, and their levels of attainment are similar to young men's (Shapiro & Crowley, 1982; Tangri & Jenkins, 1986). Further, the majority of research now reports that boys' and girls' educational and occupational aspirations and expectations do not differ greatly as far as levels of attainment are concerned. Women and men continue to choose different types of professional training (e.g., there were fewer women in law, medicine, and engineering), but these differences, too, are slowly changing (see, e.g., Crowley & Shapiro, 1982; Danzinger, 1983; Farmer, 1983; Marini & Brinton, 1984; Rosen & Aneshensel, 1978; Stevens et al., 1992; Subich, Barrett, Doverspike, & Alexander, 1989). Most students (both sexes) aspire to postsecondary education (Danzinger, 1983; Rosen & Aneshensel, 1978), and many also aspire to complete college (Crowley & Shapiro, 1982). Some data suggest that girls not only meet, but also surpass boys in occupational aspirations (Farmer, 1983, 1985; Stevens et al., 1992).

Despite the fact that most high school and college men and women anticipate having employment, a few important gender differences persist (high school, see Bush, Simmons, Hutchinson, & Blyth, 1978; Crowley & Shapiro, 1982; Shapiro & Crowley, 1982; college, see Crowley & Shapiro, 1982; Shapiro & Crowley, 1982; Tangri & Jenkins, 1986). Girls more often plan to work part-time and intermittently rather than full-time, to accommodate competing demands of work and home (Machung, 1989; O'Connell, Betz, & Kurtz, 1989), although boys and girls alike aspire to a combination of work, marriage, and parenthood (Farmer, 1983; Shapiro & Crowley, 1982).

Early work involvement appears to have different ramifications for boys and girls. Work appears to reinforce the traditional experience of boys and promote their optimism about the future. Duration of work experience has been shown to enhance boys' educational plans, achievement orientation, and confidence that they will realize their career, family, and community goals. They expect larger families, longer duration of paid work, and more traditional family lives in which they alone provide financial support compared to boys who have not worked (Stevens et al., 1992). Among girls, formal work experience has been shown to be associated with a lower expectation of taking on traditional family roles, older estimates for marriage age, and reduced anticipation of marriage and parenthood (Stevens et al., 1992).

Psychological Well-Being

Youth employment can also affect the psychological well-being and social relationships of adolescents. Although many studies have shown that employment has a substantial impact on the well-being of adults (see, e.g., Kohn & Schooler, 1983), the developmental impact of adolescent employment is less well understood (Fine, Mortimer, & Roberts, 1990). It has been proposed that work experience could have different outcomes on the well-being of boys and girls because of the general cultural expectation that boys will work in adulthood and the conflict between work and family life for girls (Yamoor & Mortimer, 1990, p. 227). Findings here are mixed. Studies have reported some psychological benefits for both boys and girls who perceive their jobs as providing them with useful skills (Mortimer et al., 1992), whereas other research suggests that part-time employment is associated with increases in depression for both boys and girls (Shanahan, Finch, Mortimer, & Ryu, 1991). Some studies (Greenberger, 1988; Steinberg & Dornbusch, 1991) have identified gains in self-reliance for girls, but not for boys. This may result because girls entering the labor force at an early age represent a departure from traditional gender role expectations and this entry is viewed as an act of independence. Some findings, though, paint a more negative picture of the effects of part-time employment on girls' well-being; in one study, 15- and 16-year-old girls' life satisfaction was diminished by employment, whereas the opposite was true for boys (Yamoor & Mortimer, 1990).

Youth employment has also been shown to be associated with small but meaningful gains on self-report measures of dependability, persistence, motivation to perform work well, and greater satisfaction from completing tasks (Greenberger, 1983), with no indication of differences between boys and girls. Finally, there is research showing that work is associated with an increased sense of independence from parental control for girls and boys alike (Bachman, Johnston, & O'Malley, 1987; Greenberger, 1988).

Social Relationships

Some research has examined the impact of youth employment on personal and social relationships with family, peers, or other adults. Research by Greenberger and Steinberg (1981) suggests that there is little in the work experience of teenagers that would help them improve their relationships with adult coworkers. The workplace does not appear to be a source of meaningful relationships with adults for most young people, and contact with coworkers outside the workplace is rare. Also, the majority of job settings where teens work require little training (Greenberger, 1988) and tend to provide only short-term placements. As a result, adults in the workplace may tend to spend little time with teens and may show little interest in their lives.

One way in which youth employment impacts on relationships within the family is that it reduces significantly the amount of time adolescents spend with parents and siblings (Greenberger & Steinberg, 1986; Greenberger, Steinberg, Vaux, & McAulliffe, 1980; Ianni, 1989; Steinberg & Dornbusch, 1991). Despite this, it does not seem to be the case that teenagers who work are less close to their parents (Mortimer & Shanahan, 1994). Greenberger et al. (1980) emphasize that the relational patterns in the family are already well established by the time teenagers enter the part-time job market, which may explain the minimal effects on family relations.

There appear to be a few exceptions to this pattern. Part-time work, or the earnings associated with work, have been shown to lead to disagreement between adolescents and their parents regarding the use of the money (Williams & Prohofsky, 1986). Also, teenage girls who work may tend to be less close to their parents than teenage girls who do not (Greenberger et al., 1980; Mortimer and Shanahan, 1994), but this may simply reflect the fact that those who are less close to their family are those who are more likely to seek work in the first place (Greenberger et al., 1980). Another possibility suggested by Mortimer and Shanahan (1994) is that parents are less likely to perceive employment as an important socialization experience for girls compared with boys. Work may still be perceived by many parents as inconsistent with girls' future role expectations, and it may be seen as interfering with the performance of house chores. Finally, youth employment does not seem to interfere with the amount of time adolescents spend with peers, nor does it seem to impair the quality of peer relationships (for review see Safyer et al., 1995).

Use of Employment Income

An obvious consequence of youth employment is the increased income available to young people, and how that income is used has been the source of some research. One question asked in the literature is whether teenagers who work contribute to the economic well-being of the family. Research suggests that the majority of teenagers who work do not contribute much of their earnings to their families' coffers (Greenberger et al., 1980), with the exception of rural teens, whose contributions to the family are much higher—even four times as likely—as those teens who live in cities (Shanahan, Elder Jr., Burchinal, & Conger, 1996). An explanation offered for this general pattern of results is that adolescent work is more common among middle-class families than among lower-class families (Mortimer et al., 1992; Safyer et al., 1995). Also, teens from higher socioeconomic levels begin to work at an earlier age than do those from more economically disadvantaged backgrounds (Mortimer et al., 1992). However, it is likely the case that parents of working teens give less additional money to their young people, controlling for class of family.

A recent survey closely examined how teenagers spend their income (Manning, 1990). Eighty percent of working teens were required by their parents to use their earnings for special purchases. Substantial numbers of teens were also expected to use earnings for regular expenses (57%) and educational expenses (44%), and only 8% of working teenagers were expected to contribute to family expenditures. The proportion of teens who used their money for family-related expenses increased significantly with the number of hours worked. Of course, to the extent that the young worker spends money on regular and educational expenses, they are contributing indirectly to the family's discretionary expenses, and to its overall income.

Work-related earnings have also been shown to create some discord between parents and children, whereby teenagers who work part-time were significantly more likely to disagree about money with their parents than teens who did no work (Ianni, 1989; Williams & Prohofsky, 1986; see also Manning, 1990). Despite parental efforts to control how teens use their earnings, there is evidence that income allows teens to become more independent as a result of their increased freedom in spending decisions (Greenberger & Steinberg, 1986). Therefore, greater earnings apparently are correlated with increased attempts on the part of parents to control spending patterns. Generally, regarding issues associated with the use of employment income or its effect on relationships with parents, no gender differences are reported.

Working teens also pay for more of their own expenses than do nonworking teens. Recent U.S. data show that by the time they are in the 10th grade, more than 50% of adolescents report saving their earnings for long-range goals, primarily for their future education (Shanahan et al., 1996). However, earnings are seen primarily by teenagers as a means to achieve a higher standard of living for themselves (Bachman, 1983). This is consistent with other data wherein almost 70% of teens report that their involvement in work is motivated by a desire to buy things (Mortimer et al., 1990). Many teenagers spend their earnings on items that parents used to provide, such as clothing, but often teens save money for other items that parents may not be able to afford, such as a car (Greenberger & Steinberg, 1986).

Summary of Research on Youth Employment

Considerable research exists on ramifications of youth employment. Some of it deals with gender comparisons, and some with gender differences. However, none of the current research focuses on gender differences *in experiences with earnings* and possible consequences these have for teenagers' views of entitlement by gender.

Overall, teenage employment seems to have some positive outcomes, perhaps improving work habits, increasing occupational and educational aspirations, and fostering independence. There is also some negative impact such that part-time work, if excessively time-consuming, seems to be linked to lesser educational achievement and may increase familial disagreements, primarily over money. Each of these patterns likely holds across the genders.

On the matter of gender differences, it appears that the experiences of young people in the labor force do vary by gender on some dimensions but not on others. For girls, work may foster greater feelings of self-reliance and may encourage expectations of less traditional work and family arrangements. The opposite appears to be true with boys, for whom work reinforces traditional values and gender role orientation. Of course, what is traditional varies for females and males.

Possibly the strongest and most consistent gender difference in youth employment is in patterns of work segregation and lower payment of female youth that replicate the conditions found in adult employment, although the wage differential is less for youth workers than among adult workers (see Mortimer, Dennehy, Lee, & Finch, 1994). As Armstrong and Armstrong (1994) have recently argued, the wage differentials are unlikely to disappear until either the segregation or the inequitable wages that accompany women's work disappear (p. 45). Thus, youth employment reflects what is occurring among adult workers.

The recent similarity detected in the work participation and occupational expectations of boys and girls does not minimize the importance of two gender differences observed: the lower income payment of teenage girls and the sex-segregated job market of teens. A question for researchers is whether this gender-based experience with work and income leads boys and girls to have different expectations about the pay they deserve to earn, and whether similar pay experience, when it occurs, leads females and males to think similarly about the pay to which they are entitled. Recent research with college-student and adult workers has highlighted the significant impact of recent pay experience on income these workers perceive entitlement to, however thus far, no study has examined directly how adolescents' work experiences impact their income expectations. What follows is a description of the relevant research on college students and adults, showing that comparison processes, including comparing one's own work and pay experience among jobs, affect people's perceived entitlement about income. Then, we examine additional new data on the issue from samples of young people ages 16–19 and 20–24.

PREVIOUS RESEARCH ON GENDER AND PERCEIVED ENTITLEMENT AMONG COLLEGE STUDENTS AND ADULTS

The concept of entitlement is central to research that examines the long-term impact of gender-based inequality in work circumstances and income. To have a sense of entitlement toward a specific outcome, people must feel that they have a right to receive that outcome (Major, 1994); it is the judgment that someone or some group of people are entitled to a particular set of outcomes by virtue of who they are or what they have done (Lerner, 1987).

The fact that there are gender differences in perceived income entitlement has already been well established in the social psychological literature, primarily through experimental studies in the laboratory with college student participants (Callahan-Levy & Messé, 1979; Major, McFarlin, & Gagnon, 1984; Moore, 1990; for reviews of the literature see Kahn, O'Leary, Krulewitz, & Lamm, 1980; Major, 1987, 1989, 1994; Major & Deaux, 1982; see also Crosby, 1982). These researchers have found that women pay themselves less than men do when allocating rewards to themselves and others.

The explanations offered in the literature for female participants' perceptions of lower entitlement, compared with male counterparts, are of two types. The first set of explanations are rooted in differential gender socialization. Women are taught more often, for instance, to value interpersonal aspects of work, whereas men are more likely taught to concern themselves with productivity or monetary rewards (see, e.g., Adams, 1965; Boldizar, Perry, & Perry, 1988; Kahn et al., 1980; Stake, 1983, 1985). Women may also be socialized to value pay and promotion less than men (e.g., Crosby, 1982; Major & Konar, 1984; Nieva & Gutek, 1981). There may also be gender differences in people's evaluations of their work such that, in comparison to men, women are shown to evaluate their own performances more negatively (Major & Forcey, 1985) and to make external attributions for their success (Lenney, 1977). All these suggestions have in common the idea that the past socialization experiences of women and men, and their consequences, explain gender differences in perceived pay entitlement.

The second explanation emphasizes that gender differences in income entitlement may result in part because women are unlikely to encounter comparison standards that support the idea of equal rewards for women and men (Bylsma & Major, 1992, 1994; Bylsma, Major, & Cozzarelli, 1995; Major et al., 1984; Major, 1987, 1989). Although Major and her coworkers do not dispute the likelihood of effects from past socialization, they have emphasized that there are few instances in the current experiences of women compared with men that support the idea that they should receive high pay. In laboratory studies, women and men differed in their pay allocations to self when clear external comparison standards were unavailable to the participants, but not when particular types of external sources of comparison were made salient (Bylsma & Major, 1992, 1994; Bylsma et al., 1995; Major & Konar, 1984; Major et al., 1984; Major & Testa, 1989). When participants of each gender were informed by experimental manipulation that similar others received a specific rate of pay, they drew on this information in making decisions about their pay entitlement; in this situation, women and men pay themselves similarly. Also, when available comparison standards indicated that women have lower rates of pay than men, the usual patterns of gender differences in perceived pay entitlement were revealed; that is, women took less pay for themselves than did men (see Bylsma & Major, 1992, 1994, and Bylsma et al., 1995). Together, these studies point to the fact that contemporaneous comparison standards, where present, are central to women's and men's perceived sense of personal entitlement.

The two explanations offered for the reported gender differences in income entitlement effectively amount to a vicious cycle for women. On the one hand, the socialization history often informs women that they should approach the world of work differently from men by being oriented more toward the social aspects of work and less toward promotions and monetary rewards. Women also apparently learn to downplay their work effort or contributions, compared with men. Further, an important consequence of the well-documented sex segregation of the workplace is that when women try to compare their income to other similarly qualified people or others in a similar position, they usually compare themselves with other women who are similarly underpaid. Hence, these processes, together act to reduce women's expectations of income.

We might expect that the pattern just described also applies to the early work experiences of teens. Young women come to the work world with the different socialization about the meaning of work; then, most likely, the structural factors of gender inequality at work reinforce the assumption that young women's approach to work is different from that of men of the same age. Young women are paid less than men and the gender segregation of work reinforces this notion by means of social comparison. Just like adult women, girls who try to determine whether they are paid a fair wage have available only the comparison standard of other underpaid girls, and their own comparatively low pay rates from previous jobs.

Because the world of work presents female and male workers with another standard against which to judge their entitlement—their *own* pay experiences—this, too, should reinforce gender differences in perceptions of entitlement to pay. Our research (Desmarais, 1993; Desmarais & Curtis, 1997a, 1997c) has given particular attention to the comparison standard of a participant's *recent actual pay for work*. Our findings to date have shown the importance of income experience in explaining perceived income entitlement of women and men. In one study, with data from secondary analyses of a national sample of workers (Lambert, Brown, Curtis, Kay, & Wilson, 1986) we showed that recent income experience acts as a strongly influential standard of comparison from which people estimate their entitlement from their jobs. This was particularly evident among women, for whom recent income was the only statistically significant predictor when considered along with six other social background (e.g., age and education) and job characteristic predictors (e.g., type of occupation, number of years in the same occupation, number of subordinates, whether he or she was self-employed). Because income was comparatively low for women, it contributed to their lower sense of personal entitlement with respect to pay. Before controls—and even after controls for the social background factors and other characteristics of work—women gave responses of lower personal entitlement than men. However, after taking into account the effects of levels of earned income, women and men reported similar levels of deserved income. These results were also replicated in a survey study of first-year university students (Desmarais & Curtis, 1997c). Here, women reported deserving less than did men for the jobs they held the previous summer. Further, the women had worked fewer hours for less pay, in the previous summer, compared with the men. Just like for adult workers, however, youth workers' gender differences in pay entitlement were shown to disappear once we controlled for the initial gender difference in earnings.

In other laboratory studies, we were able to examine some of the factors that increase the relationship between pay history and pay entitlement. For instance, we were able to show that cueing female students concerning their recent income experience (which was similar to that of male counterparts in the study) greatly increased their perceived pay entitlement; for males, there was little effect on perceived entitlement from cueing about recent income (Desmarais & Curtis, 1997b).

Our most recent work (Desmarais & Curtis, 1997a), based on data from a national adult sample (see General Social Survey; Statistics Canada, 1994), has expanded further this line of analysis. The analyses continue to show the persistent pattern of gender difference in income expectation for the present job before and after controls for various social background and work circumstance factors; that is, women report that they deserve less than do men. Surprisingly, unlike the results of our previous studies based on the earlier set of national data and the student sample, we found a persistent significant difference in perceived income entitlement *even when controls are included* for respondents' recent wage levels.

The research just described leads us to expect that there will be similar patterns among working young people. To date, no one has examined whether the patterns of gender difference in pay among teens influences their expectations about pay. In the next section, we report the results of relevant analyses from representative national subsamples of people ages 16–19 and 20–24.

NEW DATA ON GENDER AND PERCEIVED INCOME ENTITLEMENT AMONG YOUTH

Data Source

We examined the connection between income and perceived income entitlement among youth by performing analyses on recent data from a national Canadian survey of work and income (see General Social Survey; Statistics Canada, 1994). This data source is appropriate for our present purposes because it includes a nationally representative cross-section of Canadian respondents ages 16–65 who were asked about their actual incomes in Canadian dollars for the part-time or full-time work they did the previous year. In addition, respondents were asked about their perceived income entitlement as follows: What in your opinion was the wage or salary you deserved for this work, all things considered? Other relevant questions were asked concerning the weekly number of hours of work performed by each respondent and the total number of weeks worked during the previous year.

The findings reported below are derived from subsamples of participants that include all respondents ages 16–19 years (a total of 347 men and 398 women) and respondents ages 20–24 years (321 men and 328 women). For comparison purposes, we also report findings on the group of respondents ages 25–65 years (3,148 men and 2,820 women) (see Table 1). For the groups of younger respondents, we performed two separate sets of analyses. First, using all respondents in each subsample without concern for their status as students or nonstudents, we examined the percentage of women and men who reported being employed during the previous year. We then computed the average income and perceived income entitlement of the young women and men who had worked. Further, we compared the sexes on the number of hours of work they performed per week on average and the number of weeks they reported working in the previous year. We also examined the relationship between earnings and perceived entitlement across genders. In a second set of gender comparisons, we replicated the analyses just listed, this time with only those respondents who identified themselves as full-time students (for the 16- to 19-year-olds: 284 men and 313 women; for the 20- to 24-year-olds: 202 men and 247 women).

Results

Considering first the data for the full subsample of respondents ages 16–19, results showed much similarity in the work experience of the young women and men. Fully 63.2% of men and 58.3% of women reported being employed, either full-time or part-time, in the year prior to the survey ($z = 0.1$, ns). Gender differences were not obtained for comparisons of the reported average number of hours worked per week, (for men: $M = 23.42$; for women: $M = 21.19$), $t(257) = 1.30$, ns, or for the mean number of weeks of work in the year prior to the survey (for men: $M = 28.86$; for women: $M = 31.00$), $t(393) = 1.11$, ns. However, as expected, the data show a significantly different income experience for women and men (see Table 1). The mean income level for male respondents was \$6,300.68, significantly higher than that reported by

Table 1

Earned Income, Perceived Income Entitlement, and the Discrepancy Between the Two by Gender for Various Age-Defined Subsamples

Subsample	Actual income[a] ($)	Income entitlement[a] ($)	Discrepancy ($)
16–19 years old (students only)			
Male	4,624.62	5,254.35	256.92
Female	3,325.64	3,640.68	259.76
16–19 years old (all)			
Male	6,300.68	6,973.03	279.16
Female	4,838.67	5,272.22	415.51
20–24 years old (students only)			
Male	12,033.08	12,225.80	674.59
Female	9,145.41	10,763.23	1,676.43
20–24 years old (all)			
Male	18,137.62	20,608.56	2,121.44
Female	13,972.62	15,645.62	1,487.79
25–64 years old			
Male	37,581.17	42,515.19	4,478.31
Female	25,138.20	29,431.54	3,727.01

Note. All the gender differences in the first two columns are statistically significant; only the gender differences for all subgroups ages 25–64 are statistically significant in the third column.
[a]All income and income entitlement estimates are in Canadian dollars.

women, ($4,838.67), $t(272) = 8.37$, $p < .01$. The female to male earnings ratio was .78, which is just slightly higher than the 70–75% gender wage gap reported for all full-year workers in Canada and the United States (Christofides & Swidinsky, 1994; Godley, Hafer, Riggar, & Maki,

1983; Marini, 1989; Statistics Canada, 1995). The perceived income entitlement of the male and female respondents also differed significantly. Men reported an average deserved annual income of $6,973.03; whereas women's estimates were much lower at $5,272.22, $t(254) = 9.66$, $p < .01$.

Thus, despite a great similarity in the work participation of young women and men, there remains a substantial gender difference in income and, as a result, in perceived income entitlement. We next tested for the impact of income history on the perceived income entitlement of young workers calculating a discrepancy index for each respondent, by subtracting the actual income reported from the deserved income. This discrepancy index indicates the increase in pay desired by each person above his or her current level of income. In other words, the index takes into account in its calculation each person's current income level, thereby controlling for initial differences in actual income which have been shown to vary systematically by gender. The results of this analysis suggest that the initial differences in perceived income entitlement are a result of the actual gender difference in actual income. Men report deserving an average of $279.16 above their current income level, which does not differ significantly from the $415.51 reported by women, $t(252) = 0.60$, ns.

Our second set of analyses examined the data of young people who described themselves as full-time students. Of these respondents, 58.4% of men and 52.9% of women indicated that they had worked part-time during the previous year ($z = .02$, ns). This level of participation in part-time work by students is comparable to that of recent surveys, primarily conducted in the United States (Bachman & Schulenberg, 1993; Sweet, Bumpass, & Call, 1988; U.S. Bureau of the Census, 1993; see also OECD, 1996). As in the first set of analyses, we found no gender difference in the work exposure of our respondents. Men worked an average of 28.19 weeks in the previous year, which is comparable to the 28.94 weeks of work reported by women, $t(285) = .32$, ns. We also found no difference in the average number of hours worked per week among our male and female students (for men: $M = 18.02$; for women: $M = 17.46$), $t(105) = .90$, ns.

However, these analyses do show a significant gender difference in income experience and perceived income entitlement. Male students reported a mean annual income of $4,624.62, which is significantly higher than the $3,325.64 average salary reported by female students, $t(191) = 8.27, p < .01$. Similarly, men reported a higher average perceived income entitlement ($5,254.35) than women ($3,640.68), $t(177) = 10.70, p < .001$. Once again, we examined the impact of income on perceived income entitlement by calculating for each student a discrepancy index between reported income earned and perceived income entitlement (entitlement minus income). As in our first set of analyses, the data show that despite the already reported gender difference in income earned and deserved, there is no significant difference in discrepancy scores. Women reported a discrepancy of $259.76 between what they earned and felt they deserved to earn for the previous year of work; whereas men reported this discrepancy to be equal to $256.92 ($t(175) = .02, ns$).

The pattern reported for the 16- to 19-year-olds was replicated for respondents ages 20–24. First, considering all respondents in that age group, we found that a significantly higher proportion of men (85.60%) than women (73.78%) worked either full-time or part-time in the year prior to the survey ($z = 3.70, p < .001$). A similar sex difference was also obtained for the average number of hours of work done per week (for men: 39.03 hr; for women: 32.28 hr), $t(463) = 5.67, p < .001$, though we found the reverse effect when we compared the total number of weeks worked in the year prior to the survey. In this case, women worked a significantly higher number of weeks (41.26 weeks) than did men (38.32 weeks), $t(647) = 2.27, p < .05$.

As expected, the sex differences for respondents' actual income and their reported income entitlement were significant and in the predicted direction. Women reported an average income of $13,972.62, which is significantly lower than the men's average income of $18,137.62, $t(506) = 3.98, p < .001$. Similarly, the average income entitlement of men ($20,608.56) was significantly higher than that reported by women ($15,645.62), $t(468) = 4.12, p < .001$. However, as in the previous set of analyses for the 16- to 19-year-olds, we found no difference when

77

comparing the discrepancy of men's and women's income and income entitlement. Here, men reported an average discrepancy score of $2,121.44, which did not differ statistically from women's reported average of $1,487.79, $t(466) = 1.65$, ns.

We performed the analyses again with the subsample of respondents ages 20–24 who described themselves as full-time students working on a part-time basis. Although we are dealing with few respondents, the data are very much consistent with the pattern described previously. Male and female students' rate of work participation was very similar, with 74.42% of men and 74.36% of women employed part-time in the year prior to the survey ($z = .01$, ns). Despite the great similarity in work participation rates for the sexes, women reported working significantly more weeks in the year prior to the survey (for women: 36.88 weeks; for men: 31.83 weeks), $t(209) = 2.06$, $p < .05$, although they worked fewer hours per week on average (for women: 26.16; for men: 29.02), $t(120) = 1.10$, $p < .05$, and earned significantly less than did comparable men (for women: $9,145.46; for men: $12,033.08), $t(144) = 1.99$, $p < .05$. Similarly, female students reported a lower estimate of their income entitlement ($10,763.23) than did males ($12,258.04), $t(130) = 2.06$, $p < .05$. Unlike in the previous sets of analyses, however, we did find a significant difference in the discrepancy score between earned income and income entitlement, whereby more women felt they deserved money above and beyond their income ($1,676.43) than did men ($647.59), $t(130) = 2.03$, $p < .05$.

CONCLUSION

Research has demonstrated that there has come to be increased similarity in the extent of part-time and full-time work by young females and males. Also, the occupational aspirations of young girls and boys are quite similar, as are their educational aspirations and educational attainment levels. Further, part-time work seems to have more or less the same set of consequences among young men and young women for work and educational aspirations, and for self-images and social relationships. Marked differences still obtain between young women and men, though, in the type of work and level of income experienced. These particular differences, we hypothesized, probably help lead to lower estimates of pay entitlement among young working women compared with their male counterparts. We provided a test of this hypothesis after presenting theoretical explanations for why this might occur, and after showing that effects of income earned on perceived entitlement occur among older workers; that is, among adult full-time workers and among college-age workers.

We found substantial gender differences in the income earned and perceived income entitlement of young women and men. Whether or not they were full-time students, young women were paid significantly less than were young men for the work they did in the previous year. Further, young women on average reported lower levels of income entitlement than did young men of the same age. The gender differences in entitlement perceptions were shown to be associated with differences in recent pay. When pay from the previous year was taken into account, young women and men reported similar levels of income entitlement, somewhat above their earned income. These patterns held whether we looked at participants age 16–19 or 20–24. The new data we presented also replicated certain findings from past research. Similar to recent U.S. data on the work experiences of teens (Manning, 1990; Yamoor & Mortimer, 1990), we found no gender differences among teenagers in the reported number of working hours per week or in the average number of weeks of work in the last year.

Coupled with our other survey results for college-age people and data from laboratory experiments (cf. Desmarais & Curtis, 1997a, 1997b, 1997c), these results suggest that when they are asked to appraise their income entitlement, both genders use their own income as an appropriate standard, that is as a reference point for the worth of their work. This is likely due to the fact that one's own income experience is a saliently available and useful comparison standard.

We should underscore, though, it is likely that some of the explanation goes to people's social comparisons with other workers' incomes. A person's own pay will often be quite similar to that of others in the same job. This means that the effects of the two factors will be closely related. When participants think of their past income, they may also be reminded of the income of similar others. Likewise, reminding people of the situations of their "comparison others" at work may also remind them of their own pay. Only by manipulating pay and information of comparison others in experimental situations can the two processes be made entirely separate. This should be one of the next steps in research. However, for the above-mentioned reasons, the contribution that each of the two processes makes *in the real world of work* will generally be difficult to determine. The two explanatory processes are likely inextricably involved in the world of work, and both are probably important predictors of perceived entitlements. What is clear from our results from young workers is that *recent* income earned and perceived income entitlement are closely correlated and that gender differences in perceived entitlement are essentially nonexistent if we control for income earned.

The idea that recent pay experience leads to perceptions of entitlement among young people also can be extended in ways that go beyond the data available to us thus far. We can ask whether other aspects of pay experience among young people contribute to their perceived entitlement. For instance, we wonder whether income entitlements are solely a function of recent pay, or whether they are the result of a person's total income, including the money received from earlier jobs. Whether earlier pay experience, in addition to recent pay experience, provides explanatory import for current perceived entitlement is unclear. Doubt is cast on this idea by our results showing that among young and older workers, the circumstances of people's recent pay largely account for gender differences in perceived current entitlement to pay. It may be that the comparison standard of one's own pay for a particular job is mostly influential only for estimates of entitlement to pay from roughly the same type of job. These questions must be answered in further studies.

Judging from our present results as well as those of our other studies, it appears that women's and men's perceptions of entitlement will be similar if women are paid the same as men. An exception to this may be some recent results we have obtained from laboratory studies with college students (Desmarais & Curtis, 1997b). These have shown that reminding women of their recent earnings leads them to exhibit pay behavior similar to comparison men, but that this does *not* occur when they are not so reminded. Otherwise, women report that they deserve less pay than do men—even when they have had the same recent pay experience as the men. This suggests, among other possibilities, that without prompting about their income experiences, women may draw largely on the gender norms in thinking about entitlements. Men in the same situation may draw on the gender norms and their work experiences in thinking about what they should be paid. When women are reminded of their work and pay, this seems to prompt them to think more highly of their entitlement. Men who are reminded, on the other hand, seem not to be affected in the same way. The results suggest that, if anything, they are led to temper what would be their estimates of entitlement from the sources of estimation they otherwise draw on. These interpretations, too, must be tested in further studies including among young people.

REFERENCES

Adams, J. S. (1965). Inequity in social exchange. In L. Berkowitz (Ed.), *Advances in experimental social psychology* (Vol. 2, pp. 267–299). New York: Academic Press.

Armstrong, P., & Armstrong, H. (1994). *The double ghetto* (3rd ed.). Toronto, Ontario, Canada: McClelland & Stewart.

Bachman, J. G. (1983, Summer). Premature affluence: Do high school students earn too much? *Economic Outlook USA,* 64–67.

Bachman, J. G., Johnston, L. D., & O'Malley, P. M. (1987). *Monitoring the future: Questionnaire responses from the nation's high school seniors, 1986.* Ann Arbor, MI: Institute of Social Research, Survey Research Center.

Bachman, J. G., & Schulenberg, J. (1993). How part time work intensity relates to drug use, problem behavior, time use, and satisfaction among high school seniors: Are there consequences or merely correlates? *Developmental Psychology, 29,* 220–235.

Blau, F. D., & Ferber, M. A. (1986). *The economics of women, men, and work.* Englewood Cliffs, NJ: Prentice Hall.

Boldizar, J. P., Perry, D. G., & Perry, L. C. (1988). Gender and reward distributions: A test of two hypotheses. *Sex Roles, 19*, 569–579.

Bush, D., Simmons, R. G., Hutchinson, B., & Blyth, D. A. (1978). Adolescent perception of sex-roles in 1968 and 1975. *Public Opinion Quarterly, 41*, 459–474.

Bylsma, W. H., & Major, B. (1992). Two routes to eliminating gender differences in personal entitlement: Social comparisons and performance evaluation. *Psychology of Women Quarterly, 16*, 193–200.

Bylsma, W. H., & Major, B. (1994). Social comparisons and contentment: Exploring the psychological costs of the gender wage gap. *Psychology of Women Quarterly, 18*, 241–249.

Bylsma, W. H., Major, B., & Cozzarelli, B. (1995). The influence of legitimacy appraisals on the determinants of entitlement beliefs. *Basic and Applied Social Psychology, 17* (1 & 2), 223–237.

Callahan-Levy, C. M., & Messé, L. A. (1979). Sex differences in the allocation of pay. *Journal of Personality and Social Psychology, 37*, 433–446.

Carr, R. V., Wright, J. D., & Brody, C. J. (1996). Effects of high school work experience a decade later: Evidence from the National Longitudinal Survey. *Sociology of Education, 69*, 66–81.

Christofides, L. N., & Swidinsky, R. (1994). Wage determination by gender and visible minority status: Evidence from the 1989 LMAS. *Canadian Public Policy, XX*(1), 34–51.

Crosby, F. J. (1982). *Relative deprivation and working women.* New York: Oxford University Press.

Crowley, J. E., & Shapiro, D. (1982). Aspirations and expectations of youth in the United States: Part 1, education and fertility. *Youth and Society, 13*, 391–422.

D'Amico, R. (1984). Does employment during high school impair academic progress? *Sociology of Education, 57*, 152–164.

Danzinger, N. (1983). Sex related differences in the aspirations of high school students. *Sex Roles, 9*(6), 683–695.

Desmarais, S. (1993). *Gender, income history, and perceived income entitlement.* Unpublished doctoral dissertation, University of Waterloo, Ontario, Canada.

Desmarais, S., & Curtis, J. E. (1997a). *Gender and perceived income entitlement:*

Analyses for a national sample of full-time workers. Paper presented at the VI International Conference on Social Justice Research, Potsdam, Germany.

Desmarais, S., & Curtis, J. E. (1997b). Gender and perceived pay entitlement: Testing for effects of experience with income. *Journal of Personality and Social Psychology, 72*(1), 141–150.

Desmarais, S., & Curtis, J. E. (1997c). Gender differences in pay histories and views on pay entitlement among university students. *Sex Roles, 37,* 623–642.

Elder, G. H., Jr. (1974). *Children of the Great Depression.* Chicago: University of Chicago Press.

Farmer, H. S. (1983). Career and homemaking plans for high school youth. *Journal of Counseling Psychology, 30*(1), 40–45.

Farmer, H. S. (1985). Model of career and achievement motivation for women and men. *Journal of Counseling Psychology, 32*(3), 363–390.

Fine, G. A., Mortimer, J. T., & Roberts, D. F. (1990). Leisure, work, and the mass media. In S. Feldman & G. Elliot (Eds.), *At the threshold: The developing adolescent* (pp. 225–252). Cambridge, MA: Harvard University Press.

Godley, S. H., Hafer, M., Riggar, T. F., & Maki, D. R. (1983, February). Gender and job function: Differences in salary, educational levels, and experience. *Journal of Rehabilitation Administration, 7,* 22–26.

Greenberger, E. (1983). A researcher in the policy arena: The case of child labor. *American Psychologist, 38,* 104–111.

Greenberger, E. (1988). Working in teenage America. In J. T. Mortimer & K. M. Borman (Eds.), *Work experience and psychological development through the life span* (pp. 21–50). Boulder, CO: Westview Press.

Greenberger, E., & Steinberg, L. D. (1981). The workplace as a context for the socialization of youth. *Journal of Youth and Adolescence, 10,* 185–210.

Greenberger, E., & Steinberg, L. D. (1983). Sex differences in early labor force experience: Harbinger of things to come. *Social Forces, 62,* 467–486.

Greenberger, E., & Steinberg, L. D. (1986). *When teenagers work: The psychological and social costs of adolescent employment.* New York: Basic Books.

Greenberger, E., Steinberg, L. D., Vaux, A., & McAulliffe, S. (1980). Adolescents who work: Effects of part-time employment on family and peer relationships. *Journal of Youth and Adolescence, 9,* 189–202.

Hamilton, S. F., & Crouter, A. C. (1980). Work and growth: A review of research on the impact of work experience on adolescent development. *Journal of Youth and Adolescence, 9,* 323–338.

Ianni, F. A. J. (1989). *The search for structure: A report on American youth today.* New York: Free Press.

Jacobs, J. A., & Lim, S. T. (1992). Trends in occupational and industrial sex segregation in 56 countries, 1960–1980. *Work and Occupation, 19,* 450–486.

Kahn, A., O'Leary, V. E., Krulewitz, J. E., & Lamm, H. (1980). Equity and equality: Male and female means to a just end. *Basic and Applied Social Psychology, 1,* 173–197.

Kohn, M. L., & Schooler, C. (1983). *Work and personality: An inquiry into the impact of social stratification.* Norwood, NJ: Ablex.

Lambert, R. D., Brown, S. D., Curtis, J. E., Kay, B. J., & Wilson, J. M. (1986). *The 1984 Canadian National Election Study: Description and Codebook.* Waterloo, Ontario, Canada: University of Waterloo.

Lenney, E. (1977). Women's self-confidence in achievement settings. *Psychological Bulletin, 84,* 1–13.

Lerner, M. J. (1987). Integrating societal and psychological rules of entitlement: The basic task of each social actor and fundamental problem for the social sciences. *Social Justice Research, 1,* 107–125.

Lewin-Epstein, N. (1981). *Youth employment during high school.* Washington, DC: National Center for Educational Statistics.

Machung, A. (1989). Talking career, thinking job: Gender differences in career and family expectation of Berkeley seniors. *Feminist Studies, 15,* 35–39.

Major, B. (1987). Gender, justice and the psychology of entitlement. In P. Shaver & C. Hendrick (Eds.), *Review of personality and social psychology: Sex and gender* (Vol. 7, pp. 124–148). Thousand Oaks, CA: Sage.

Major, B. (1989). Gender differences in comparisons and entitlement: Implications for comparable worth. *Journal of Social Issues, 45*(4), 99–115.

Major, B. (1994). From disadvantage to deserving: Comparisons, justifications and the psychology of entitlement. In M. Zanna (Ed.), *Advances in Experimental Social Psychology, 26,* 293–355.

Major, B., & Deaux, K. (1982). Individual differences in justice behavior. In J. L. Greenberg & R. L. Cohen (Eds.), *Equity and justice in social behavior.* New York: Academic Press.

Major, B., & Forcey, B. (1985). Social comparisons and pay evaluations: Preferences for same-sex and same-job wage comparisons. *Journal of Experimental Social Psychology, 21,* 393–405.

Major, B., & Konar, J. (1984). An investigation of sex differences in pay expectations and their possible causes. *Academy of Management Journal, 27,* 777–792.

Major, B., McFarlin, D., & Gagnon, D. (1984). Overworked and underpaid: On the nature of gender differences in personal entitlement. *Journal of Personality and Social Psychology, 47*(6), 1399–1412.

Major, B., & Testa, M. (1989). Social comparison processes and judgments of entitlement and satisfaction. *Journal of Experimental Social Psychology, 25,* 101–120.

Manning, W. D. (1990). Parenting employed teenagers. *Youth and Society, 22*(2), 184–200.

Marini, M. M. (1989). Sex differences in earnings. *Annual Review of Sociology, 15,* 343–380.

Marini, M. M., & Brinton, M. C. (1984). Sex stereotyping in occupational socialization. In B. Reskin (Ed.), *Sex segregation in the work place: Trends, explanations, and remedies.* Washington, DC: National Academy Press.

McKechnie, J., Lindsay, S., Hobbs, S., & Lavalette, M. (1996). Adolescents' perceptions of the role of part-time work. *Adolescence, 31,* 193–209.

Medrich, E. A., Roizen, J. A., Rubin, V., & Buckley, S. (1982). *The serious business of growing up.* Berkeley: University of California Press.

Moore, D. (1990). Discrimination and deprivation: The effects of social comparisons. *Social Justice Research, 4*(1), 49–64.

Mortimer, J. T., Dennehy, K., Lee, C., & Finch, M. D. (1994). Economic socialization in the American family: The prevalence, distribution, and consequences of allowance arrangements. *Family Relations, 43,* 23–29.

Mortimer, J. T., & Finch, M. D. (1986). The effects of part-time work on self-concept and achievement. In K. M. Borman & J. Reisman (Eds.), *Becoming a worker* (pp. 66–89). Norwood, NJ: Ablex.

Mortimer, J. T., Finch, M. D., Dennehy, K., Lee, C., & Beebe, T. (1994). Work experience in adolescence. *Journal of Vocational Education Research, 19,* 39–70.

Mortimer, J. T., Finch, M. D., Owens, T. J., & Shanahan, M. J. (1990). Gender and work in adolescence. *Youth and Society, 22*(2), 201–224.

Mortimer, J. T., Finch, M. D., Shanahan, M. J., & Ryu, S. (1992). Adolescent work history and behavioral adjustment. *Journal of Research on Adolescence, 2*(1), 59–80.

Mortimer, J. T., & Shanahan, M. J. (1994). Adolescent work experience and family relationships. *Work and Occupations, 21*(4), 369–384.

Mortimer, J. T., Shanahan, M., & Ryu, S. (1993). The effects of adolescent employment on school related orientation and behavior. In R. K. Silbereisen & E. Todt (Eds.), *Adolescence in context: The interplay of family, school, peers and work in adjustment* (pp. 304–326). New York: Springer-Verlag.

Nieva, V. F., & Gutek, B. A. (1981). *Women and work: A psychological perspective.* New York: Praeger.

O'Connell, L., Betz, M., & Kurtz, S. (1989). Plans for balancing work and family life: Do women pursuing nontraditional and traditional occupations differ? *Sex Roles, 20*(1–2), 35–45.

Organization for Economic Cooperation and Development. (1996). *Employment outlook, July.* Paris, France: Author.

Reskin, B. F. (1993). Sex segregation in the workplace. *Annual Review of Sociology, 19,* 241–270.

Ridgeway, C. L. (1997). Interaction and the conservation of gender inequality: Considering employment. *American Journal of Sociology, 62*(2), 218–235.

Rosen, B. C., & Aneshensel, C. S. (1978). Sex differences in the educational-occupational expectation process. *Social Forces, 67,* 164–186.

Safyer, A. W., Hawkins Leahy, B., & Colan, N. B. (1995). The impact of work on adolescent development. *Families in Society: The Journal of Contemporary Human Services, 1,* 38–45.

Sewell, W. H., Hauser, R. M., & Wolf, W. C. (1980). Sex, schooling, and occupational status. *American Journal of Sociology, 86,* 551–583.

Shanahan, M. J., Elder, G. H. Jr., Burchinal, M., & Conger, R. D. (1996). Adolescents' earnings and relationships with parents. In J. T. Mortimer & M. D. Finch (Eds.), *Adolescents, work, and family: An intergenerational developmental analysis* (pp. 97–128). Thousand Oaks, CA: Sage.

Shanahan, M. J., Finch, M. D., Mortimer, J. T., & Ryu, S. (1991). Adolescent work experience and depressive affect. *Social Psychology Quarterly, 54*(4), 299–317.

Shapiro, D., & Crowley, J. E. (1982). Aspirations and expectations of youth in the United States, Part 2: Employment activity. *Youth and Society, 14,* 33–58.

Stake, J. E. (1983). Factors in reward distribution: Allocator motive, gender, and protestant ethic endorsement. *Journal of Personality and Social Psychology, 44,* 410–418.

Stake, J. E. (1985). Exploring the basis of sex differences in third party allocations. *Journal of Personality and Social Psychology, 48,* 1621–1629.

Statistics Canada. (1994). *The 1994 General Social Survey C Cycle 9: Education, work and retirement.* Ottawa, Ontario, Canada: Author.

Statistics Canada. (1995). *Earnings of men and women, 1993.* Ottawa (Catalog No. 13-217). Ottawa, Ontario, Canada: Author.

Steinberg, L. D., & Dornbusch, S. M. (1991). Negative correlates of part-time employment during adolescence: Replication and elaboration. *Developmental Psychology, 27,* 304–313.

Steinberg, L. D., Fegley, S., & Dornbusch, S. (1993). Negative impact of part-time work on adolescent adjustment: Evidence from a longitudinal study. *Developmental Psychology, 29,* 171–180.

Steitz, J. A., & Owen, T. P. (1982). School activities and work: Effects on adolescent self-esteem. *Adolescence, 27,* 37–50.

Stevens, C. J., Puchtell, L. A., Ryu, S., & Mortimer, J. T. (1992). Adolescent work and boys' and girls' orientation to the future. *Sociological Quarterly, 33*(2), 153–169.

Subich, L. M., Barrett, G. V., Doverspike, D., & Alexander, R. A. (1989). The effects of sex-role-related factors on occupational choice and salary. In R. T. Michael, H. I. Hartmann, & B. O'Farrell (Eds.), *Pay equity: Empirical inquiries.* Washington, DC: National Academy Press.

Sweet, J. A., Bumpass, L. L., & Call, V. (1988). *The design and consent of the National Survey of Families and Households* (NSFH Working Paper No. 1). Madison, WI: University of Wisconsin, Center for Demography and Ecology.

Tangri, S. S., & Jenkins, S. R. (1986). Stability and change in role innovation and life plans. *Sex Roles, 14,* 647–662.

U.S. Bureau of Labor Statistics. (1981). *School and work among youth during the 1970's* (Bureau of Labor Statistics, Bulletin 2120). Washington, DC: U.S. Government Printing Office.

U.S. Bureau of the Census. (1989). *Statistical abstract of the United States, 1989.* Washington, DC: U.S. Government Printing Office.

U.S. Bureau of the Census. (1993). *Statistical abstract of the United States, 1993.* Washington, DC: U.S. Government Printing Office.

White, L. K., & Brinkerhoff, D. B. (1981). The sexual division of labor: Evidence from childhood. *Social Forces, 60,* 170–181.

Williams, F. L., & Prohofsky, S. S. (1986). Teenagers' perception of agreement over family expenditures, employment, and family life. *Journal of Youth and Adolescence, 15*(3), 243–257.

Yamoor, C. M., & Mortimer, J. T. (1990). An investigation of age and gender differences in the effects of employment on adolescent achievement and well-being. *Youth and Society, 22*(2), 225–240.

5

Developmental Consequences of Youth Employment

Michael R. Frone

Employment represents a major domain of adult life. As such, it receives considerable attention from researchers from diverse academic areas, such as psychology, sociology, economics, management, epidemiology, and public health. One issue examined in all of these disciplines is the consequences of employment. The potential consequences are as diverse as the disciplines studying them, and they can be grouped at various levels; for example, individual versus interpersonal versus organizational, attitudinal versus behavioral, or economic versus health-related. In contrast, less systematic research has been devoted to studying the outcomes of employment among adolescents. Most research on adolescent life and development has focused on the effects of family, peer group, and school contexts. This relative lack of attention to the employment context is at odds with both the developmental impetus of adolescence and with employment statistics in this age group.

Adolescence is a time of transition from childhood to adulthood (Adams, Montemayor, & Gullota, 1996; Feldman & Elliott, 1990; Steinberg,

---

Preparation of this chapter was supported by the National Institute on Alcohol Abuse and Alcoholism Scientist Development Award No. K21-AA00194.

1991). During middle (ages 16–18) to late (ages 19–21) adolescence, major developmental tasks include identity development, striving for autonomy, and striving for achievement (Adams et al., 1996; Feldman & Elliott, 1990; Steinberg, 1991; Vondracek, 1994). Seeking and obtaining part-time employment is one attempt by adolescents to fulfill these developmental tasks. Besides the developmental impetus of adolescence, employment statistics suggest that it is normative for adolescents in North America to be members of the part-time labor force while attending school (Mortimer & Shanahan, 1994). For example, Krahn (1991) reported that the labor force participation rate was 54% among full-time students between the ages of 15 and 19 in Ontario, Canada (see also Sunter, 1992). Using data from a national survey of U.S. families, Manning (1990) reported that 46.9% of students between the ages of 16 and 18 worked regularly during the school year. In addition, national surveys of U.S. high school seniors have revealed that 75% were employed during the school year, and of the employed seniors, 46% worked more than 20 hours per week (Bachman & Schulenberg, 1993).

During the 1970s, several social critics and blue-ribbon advisory panels suggested that adolescents should receive greater exposure to employment during high school (see Greenberger & Steinberg, 1981, 1986; Hamilton & Crouter, 1980; for reviews). The assumption was that employment would be beneficial by filling several developmental voids not addressed adequately by educational institutions. For example, it was argued that part-time work during adolescence might impart positive work values, reinforce the importance of academic skills for future career success, provide a better understanding of the workplace, increase adolescents' contact with adults, and build character. Despite this optimistic view of combining school and employment during adolescence, Hamilton and Crouter (1980) pointed out that very little credible data existed to support these early speculations.

In response to the dearth of empirical research on this issue, Greenberger and Steinberg (1986) undertook the first systematic study of adolescent employment. In summarizing their research, Greenberger and Steinberg (e.g., Greenberger, 1983; Greenberger & Steinberg, 1986; Steinberg, 1982, 1991) have articulated a position against part-time employment among adolescents who are full-time students (see chaps. 1, 2, this volume).

In contrast to the grim depiction of adolescent employment provided by Greenberger and Steinberg, recent descriptive research shows that a positive evaluation of part-time work experiences is reported by adolescents themselves (e.g., Green, 1990; Mortimer, Finch, Dennehy, Lee, & Beebe, 1994) and by the parents of employed adolescents (Phillips & Sandstrom, 1990). As noted by Mortimer, Shanahan, and Ryu (1994), jobs that seem routine and menial from the standpoint of an adult may be viewed quite differently by an adolescent just entering the paid workforce. In addition, longitudinal research by Mortimer, Finch, et al. (1994) reveals that with increasing age, adolescents move from less to more complex jobs and receive increasing amounts of training on the job.

Although not as extensive as the literature on adult employment, a body of research on adolescent employment has been developing during the past 10–15 years, with substantial growth in the 1990s. Early research simply examined work status and time commitment to work, whereas recent research has focused on time commitment and the quality or the nature of adolescent jobs. Moreover, even though cross-sectional research is still the norm, longitudinal studies have become more prevalent. Given the continuing debate about the costs and benefits of youth employment, the goal of this chapter is to provide a broad review of prior research on the developmental outcomes of adolescent employment.

REVIEW OF DEVELOPMENTAL OUTCOMES OF EMPLOYMENT AMONG ADOLESCENTS

In this section I review research that has examined the developmental outcomes of employment among adolescents who are still in school.[1] Regarding the construct domain of employment, prior research falls

---

[1]The present review was shaped by several restrictions. First, it covers studies from the late 1970s through early 1997. Second, the reviewed studies were restricted to those examining full-time students. The reason is that the primary concern has been with the costs and benefits of employment to adolescents who attend school full-time. Third, the review was restricted to studies of adolescents in North America. The reason is that until fairly recently, the issue of adolescent employment has not been a research concern in other industrialized countries. Finally, only studies of private-sector employment are reviewed because school- or government-sponsored job programs are likely to be different from those in the private sector in important ways, and the vast majority of employed adolescents hold jobs in the private sector.

into three general categories of work-related predictor variables: work status, work hours, and work quality. *Work status* refers to the simple comparison of adolescent workers and nonworkers. *Work hours* refer to the number of hours that adolescents work per week. *Work quality* represents various psychosocial dimensions of jobs (e.g., role ambiguity, work–school conflict). The distinction between these three general types of work-related predictors is important for two reasons. First, a gradual shift has occurred in the adolescent employment literature from examining the effects of work status to examining the effects of the number of work hours to examining the effects of the content and quality of adolescents' jobs. Second, after reviewing the general literature on part-time employment, Barling and Gallagher (1996) noted research should be "sensitive to potential difference among part-time jobs" (p. 248). Regarding the developmental outcomes, prior research has examined four broad categories of variables: academic, employment, family, and general. Each of these broad sets of outcomes is defined in more detail during the review.

Figure 1 depicts the basic conceptual model underlying prior research. Note that in addition to the two boxes representing the construct domains, Figure 1 shows two arrows connecting the boxes, which represent two hypotheses concerning cause and effect. The socialization hypothesis is the supposition that adolescent work status, work hours, or work quality have a causal effect on academic, employment, family, and general developmental outcomes. A thick arrow depicts this hypothesis, because it represents the primary causal direction that is im-

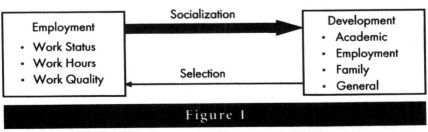

Figure 1

Conceptual model of adolescent employment and developmental outcomes guiding past research.

plicitly or explicitly expected in nearly all prior cross-sectional and lon-gitudinal studies on adolescent employment. Nonetheless, the causal direction between the employment and development variables may op-erate in the opposite direction. The selection hypothesis is based on the expectation that adolescents differentially select themselves into the workforce as a function of prior characteristics or developmental out-comes. For example, an adolescent who has a history of poor perfor-mance in school may be more likely than an adolescent who does well in school to join the formal workforce and to work more hours after turning 16 years old. A thin arrow depicts this hypothesis because few studies explicitly test this hypothesis. Note that the socialization and selection hypotheses are not mutually exclusive. For a given develop-mental variable, both hypotheses may be valid and would suggest that there is a reciprocal relation between adolescent employment and de-velopment.

This review is organized by the general categories of variables shown in Figure 1. Prior studies are grouped according to the four categories of developmental outcomes: academic, employment, family, and general. Further distinctions are made within the broad outcome categories where appropriate. Within each category of outcomes, find-ings are discussed based on the socialization hypothesis. Because most studies have been based on this hypothesis, the studies are grouped according to the three general categories of work-related antecedents: work status, work hours, and work quality. If research has tested the selection hypothesis for a given outcome category, this is reviewed last as one major category. Finally, although both cross-sectional and lon-gitudinal findings are reviewed, more weight will be given to prospective longitudinal results in generating conclusions.[2]

---

[2]Longitudinal analyses can be roughly classified as either prospective or contemporaneous. A pro-spective longitudinal analysis examines the effect of a predictor variable measured at time T on an outcome variable measured at time T + 1 while controlling for levels of the outcome variable assessed at time T. In contrast, a contemporaneous longitudinal analysis examines the relation of a predictor variable measured at time T + 1 to an outcome variable measured at time T + 1 while controlling for levels of the outcome variable at time T. By controlling for prior levels of the outcome variable, a contemporaneous longitudinal analysis is an improvement over a cross-sectional analysis because a significant predictor–outcome relation is less likely to be the result of unmeasured and stable common causes (e.g., Zapf, Dormann, & Frese, 1996). However, contem-

Academic Outcomes

To further structure this segment of the review, academic outcomes are classified into three subcategories: academic performance (grade point average, class rank, and standardized achievement scores), academic attachment (school-related intrinsic motivation, involvement in extracurricular activities, time spent on homework, school attendance, educational aspirations, and school misconduct), and educational attainment (high school completion, college attendance, and years of education completed).

Academic Performance

Work status. Ten cross-sectional studies examined the relation between work status and academic performance (grade point average, class rank, standardized achievement scores). Four studies found working adolescents had lower school performance scores than nonworking adolescents (Bachman & Schulenberg, 1993; High & Collins, 1992; Mortimer & Finch, 1986; Werner, 1989); four studies found no relation between work status and school performance (Gade & Peterson, 1980; Green & Jaquess, 1987; Mortimer, Shanahan, et al., 1994; Steinberg, Greenberger, Garduque, & McAuliffe, 1982); and two studies reported working adolescents showed higher levels of school performance than nonworking adolescents (Hammes & Haller, 1983; Schill, McCartin, & Meyer, 1985). These inconsistent cross-sectional results may be due to wide variability across studies regarding the control of potential confounding variables. Furthermore, the inconsistencies are not related to the type of school performance assessed. Grade point average was the most common measure reported and can be found in all three sets of studies. One longitudinal study by Steinberg, Greenberger, Garduque,

---

poraneous longitudinal analyses offer no advantage over cross-sectional analyses in terms of inferring cause and effect (e.g., Kessler, 1987). In contrast, prospective longitudinal analyses are generally superior to both cross-sectional and contemporaneous longitudinal analyses regarding inferences of causal direction. In the present review, all cross-sectional and contemporaneous longitudinal studies are labeled as cross-sectional. When longitudinal studies are considered, the discussion is limited to prospective longitudinal studies. Some articles provide both contemporaneous and prospective longitudinal analyses. In this case, both types of analyses are reviewed. However, the contemporaneous longitudinal analyses are grouped with the cross-sectional studies.

Ruggiero, and Vaux (1982) failed to support a relation between work status and grade point average.

Work hours. Twelve cross-sectional studies examined the relation between work hours and academic performance. Five studies failed to find a relation (Barling, Rogers, & Kelloway, 1995; D'Amico, 1984; Mortimer, Shanahan, et al., 1994; Warren & LePore, 1996; Yamoor & Mortimer, 1990), whereas seven studies reported some evidence of a negative relation between the number of weekly work hours and academic performance (Finch & Mortimer, 1985; Henke, Lyons, & Krachenberg, 1993; Lillydahl, 1990; K. A. Meyer, 1987; Mortimer, Finch, Ryu, Shanahan, & Call, 1996; Steinberg & Dornbusch, 1991; Steinberg, Greenberger, Garduque, & McAuliffe, 1982). Thus, the cross-sectional evidence is almost equally split between a negative relation and no relation between work hours and academic performance.

In contrast to the mixed cross-sectional findings, eight longitudinal studies provide a more consistent set of results. Although Marsh (1991) found that an increase in work hours from grade 10 to grade 11 was associated with lower academic performance in grade 12, statistical significance was mainly due to using a large sample (weighted $N = 4,000$). Because the absolute size of the standardized regression coefficients was small ($0 < \beta < .05$), little compelling evidence exists that work hours undermined academic performance in Marsh's (1991) sample. This conclusion is supported by the remaining seven longitudinal studies ($Ns = 176–5,656$; mean $N = 1,353$), all of which failed to support a causal effect of work hours on academic performance (Finch & Mortimer, 1985; Hotchkiss, 1986; Mortimer, Finch, et al., 1996; Mortimer & Johnson, 1997; Steinberg, Fegley, & Dornbusch, 1993; Steinberg, Greenberger, Garduque, Ruggiero, & Vaux, 1982; Warren & LePore, 1996).

Work quality. Both cross-sectional research (Barling et al., 1995; Call, 1996a; Mortimer, Shanahan, et al., 1994) and longitudinal research (Marsh, 1991) failed to find a relation between several dimensions of work quality and academic performance. In addition, although Barling et al. (1995) and Marsh (1991) explored work-quality by work-hours interactions, neither study found significant relations to academic performance.[3]

Selection. Seven longitudinal studies examined whether earlier measures of academic performance predict subsequent measures of either work status or work hours. Two studies support a selection effect (Mortimer & Johnson, 1997; Steinberg et al., 1993), whereas five studies failed to support a selection effect (Finch & Mortimer, 1985; Marsh, 1991; Mortimer & Finch, 1986; Mortimer, Finch, et al., 1996; Mortimer, Shanahan, et al., 1994). No studies have examined the relation of academic performance to subsequent measures of work quality.

Conclusions. A substantial set of studies examining the relations of work status and work hours to academic performance fails to support both the socialization hypothesis and the selection hypothesis. Although three studies examining work quality also support the general conclusion that employment and academic performance are unrelated, this conclusion may be premature. Too few studies have been conducted with too few dimensions of work quality to be able to draw any definitive conclusions. Additional research on work quality—which includes further examination of work-quality by work-hours interactions—and on academic performance is clearly warranted.

Academic Attachment

Work status. Nine cross-sectional studies examined the relation of work status to at least one of six general dimensions of academic attachment (school-related intrinsic motivation, involvement in extracurricular activities, time spent on homework, school attendance, educational aspirations, and school misconduct). Of the three studies that

[3]Several researchers have proposed that work hours and work quality may interact to predict developmental outcomes. This interactional hypothesis may be stated a bit differently depending on whether *work hours* or *work quality* is viewed as the moderator variable. In the former case, it is hypothesized that work quality will have a stronger effect on outcomes as the number of work hours (i.e., exposure) increases. In the latter case, it is hypothesized that work hours (i.e., exposure) will have a stronger negative impact on development as work quality decreases and a stronger positive impact on development as work quality increases. Finally, although Greenberger et al. (1981) attempted to explore interactions between work quality and work hours, we do not discuss their results because their analytic technique renders their interaction results uninterpretable (e.g., Aiken & West, 1991; Cohen, 1978).

examined the relation of work status to school-related intrinsic motivation, two studies found working students were less motivated than nonworking students (Mortimer & Finch, 1986; Steinberg, Greenberger, Garduque, & McAuliffe, 1982), and one study failed to support a relation (Mortimer, Shanahan, et al., 1994). Of the four studies that examined the relation between work status and involvement in extracurricular activities, three failed to find a significant relation (Gade & Peterson, 1980; Mortimer, Shanahan, et al., 1994; Steinberg, Greenberger, Garduque, & McAuliffe, 1982), and one study found working students were less involved than nonworking students (Green & Jaquess, 1987). One study found that employed students spend less time on homework than nonemployed students (Steinberg, Greenberger, Garduque, & McAuliffe, 1982), and one study failed to support this relation (Mortimer, Shanahan, et al., 1994). Drawing on the same sample of high school students, Steinberg, Greenberger, Garduque, and McAuliffe (1982) and Greenberger, Steinberg, and Vaux (1981) reported that working students exhibited poorer school attendance than nonworking students. Three studies found that employed youth had lower educational aspirations than nonemployed youth (Bachman & Schulenberg, 1993; Mortimer & Finch, 1986; Werner, 1989). Finally, two studies failed to find a relation between work status and school misconduct (Mortimer, Finch, Shanahan, & Ryu, 1992a; Mortimer, Shanahan, et al., 1994).

Two longitudinal studies examined the relation of work status to academic attachment. Steinberg, Greenberger, Garduque, Ruggiero, and Vaux (1982) found no relation of work status to school motivation, school attendance, and involvement in extracurricular activities. However, they found working students devoted less time to homework than did nonworking students. Gottfredson (1985) failed to find a longitudinal relation between work status and school-related intrinsic motivation, involvement in extracurricular activities, time spent on homework, school attendance, and educational aspirations.

Work hours. Twelve cross-sectional studies examined the relation of work hours to academic attachment. Of the three studies focusing on school-related intrinsic motivation, one study supported a negative relation (Steinberg & Dornbusch, 1991), and two failed to support a relation (Mortimer, Shanahan, et al., 1994; Warren & LePore, 1996). Three studies examined the relation of work hours to involvement in extracurricular activities; two found a significant negative relation (D'Amico, 1984; Steinberg & Dornbusch, 1991); and one failed to find a significant relation (Mortimer, Shanahan, et al., 1994). Of the five studies that assessed time spent on homework, two studies found a negative relation with work hours (D'Amico, 1984; Steinberg & Dornbusch, 1991), and three studies failed to find a significant relation (Barling et al., 1995; Mortimer, Finch, et al., 1996; Mortimer, Shanahan, et al., 1994). Three studies reported a negative relation between work hours and school attendance (Barling et al., 1995; Greenberger et al., 1981; Steinberg & Dornbusch, 1991). One study found a negative relation between work hours and academic aspirations (Bachman & Schulenberg, 1993), and two studies failed to support this relation (Stevens, Puchtell, Ryu, & Mortimer, 1992; Warren & LePore, 1996). Finally, prior cross-sectional research provides no compelling evidence of a relation between work hours and school misconduct (Mortimer, Finch, et al., 1996; Mortimer et al., 1992a, 1992b; Mortimer, Shanahan, et. al., 1994; Yamoor & Mortimer, 1990).

Eight longitudinal studies examined the relation of work hours to academic attachment. Of the four studies examining school-related intrinsic motivation, three studies supported a negative relation (Marsh, 1991; Steinberg, Greenberger, Garduque, Ruggiero, & Vaux, 1982; Steinberg et al., 1993), and one failed to support this relation (Warren & LePore, 1996). Two studies failed to find a significant effect of work hours on involvement in extracurricular activities (Hotchkiss, 1986; Steinberg, Greenberger, Garduque, Ruggiero, & Vaux, 1982). Of the four studies examining time spent on homework, two studies reported a negative effect of work hours (Steinberg, Greenberger, Garduque, Ruggiero, & Vaux, 1982; Steinberg et al., 1993), and two studies failed to find a significant relation (Marsh, 1991; Mortimer, Finch, et al., 1996). One study reported a negative effect of work hours on school attendance (Marsh, 1991), and two studies failed to support this relation (Hotchkiss, 1986; Steinberg, Greenberger, Garduque, Ruggiero, & Vaux, 1982). Three studies found a negative effect of work hours on academic aspirations (Finch & Mortimer, 1985; Marsh, 1991; Steinberg et al., 1993), and two studies failed to support this relation (Mortimer & Johnson, 1997; Warren & LePore, 1996). Finally, two studies found that work hours have a positive effect on school misconduct (Mortimer, Finch, et al., 1996; Steinberg et al., 1993), and one study failed to support this relation (Mortimer & Johnson, 1997).

Work quality. Four cross-sectional studies examined the relation of work quality to academic attachment. Greenberger et al. (1981) failed to find a relation between several dimensions of work quality and school attendance. Barling et al. (1995) examined the relation of work quality to school attendance and time spent on homework. Their results showed that role clarity was negatively related and work–school conflict was positively related to poor attendance. Moreover, as hypothesized, interaction analyses revealed that weekly work hours were more negatively related to school attendance and time spent on homework at lower levels of role clarity. Mortimer et al. (1992b) found that job complexity concerning things (e.g., materials, equipment, tools, or machines) was positively related to school misconduct among girls. Mortimer, Shanahan, et al. (1994) reported that opportunities for skill development were positively related to girls' intrinsic school motivation. Job complexity concerning data was negatively related to school misconduct among boys. Work stress and being held responsible for tasks beyond one's control were negatively related to time spent on homework among girls and were positively related to school misconduct among boys. No work quality variables were related to involvement in extracurricular activities.

A longitudinal study by Marsh (1991) explored the relation of work quality to school-related intrinsic motivation, time spent on homework, school attendance, and academic aspirations. The results showed that work satisfaction was negatively related to intrinsic school motivation and academic aspirations, whereas work importance was negatively related to all four measures of academic attachment. Additional analyses revealed that interactions between work quality and work hours did not predict any of the academic outcome variables.

Selection. Seven longitudinal studies explored whether earlier measures of academic attachment predict subsequent measures of either work status or work hours. Of the six studies that examined intrinsic school motivation, two found a negative relation to either work status (Steinberg et al., 1993) or work hours (Mortimer & Johnson, 1997), and four studies failed to support a selection effect (Gottfredson, 1985; Marsh, 1991; Mortimer, Shanahan, et al., 1994; Mortimer & Finch, 1986). One study found a positive effect of involvement in extracurricular activities on joining the workforce (Gottfredson, 1985), and one study failed to find a relation to work hours (Mortimer, Shanahan, et al., 1994). Four studies tested a selection effect for homework hours; one study found that time spent on homework was negatively associated with the likelihood of joining the workforce (Steinberg et al., 1993), and three studies found no evidence for selection (Marsh, 1991; Mortimer, Finch, et al., 1996; Mortimer, Shanahan, et al., 1994). One study failed to support a selection effect for school attendance on work hours (Marsh, 1991). Of the four studies assessing educational aspirations, two found a negative relation to either work status (Steinberg et al., 1993) or work hours (Marsh, 1991), and two studies found no relation (Gottfredson, 1985; Mortimer, Shanahan, et al., 1994). Finally, of the three studies examining school misconduct, one found evidence for selection (Mortimer, Shanahan, et al., 1994), and two did not (Mortimer, Finch, et al., 1996; Mortimer & Johnson, 1997). No studies have examined the relations of academic attachment to subsequent measures of work quality.

Conclusions. In contrast to the research on academic performance, research on academic attachment involves a broader variety of school-related variables and produces a less consistent pattern of results. The set of work status studies provides no compelling evidence to support a relation to academic attachment. The set of studies examining work hours supports a potential reciprocal relation between work hours and intrinsic school motivation and between work hours and educational aspirations. As for the socialization hypothesis, increasing work hours are associated with lower levels of school-related intrinsic motivation and educational aspirations. Regarding the selection hypothesis, lower levels of school-related intrinsic motivation and educational aspirations are related to increased hours devoted to work. Some evidence also exists for a negative socialization effect of work hours on time spent on homework, but no evidence for a selection effect. Little support exists for a relation between work hours and the remaining dimensions of academic attachment (i.e., involvement in extracurricular activities, school attendance, and school misconduct). Turning to work quality, no consistent evidence exists linking this aspect of employment to academic attachment. However, few studies have been conducted and few dimensions of work quality have been assessed. Thus, conclusions regarding this broad dimension of adolescent employment are premature without additional research.

Educational Attainment

Work status. Two longitudinal studies examined the relation of high school work status to at least one dimension of educational attainment (high school completion, college attendance, and years of education completed). Mortimer and Finch (1986) found that individuals employed during high school completed fewer years of education by the time they were 5 years out of high school than did individuals who did not work during high school. However, their analysis failed to control for potential sociodemographic differences between employed and nonemployed youth (e.g., gender, family socioeconomic status, type of high school program, academic ability). Steel (1991) addressed this limitation and found that high school employment status was not related to months enrolled in school 1–2 years after high school when controlling for a wide range of sociodemographic variables.

Work hours. Eight longitudinal studies considered the relation of the number of work hours in high school to future educational attainment. Of the four studies that examined the likelihood of completing high school, one study found a negative effect for high school work hours (Marsh, 1991), two studies failed to find a relation (Carr, Wright, & Brody, 1996; Warren & LePore, 1996), and one study (D'Amico, 1984) found that the percentage of weeks where respondents worked less than 20 hours was positively related to high school completion. Five studies explored the short-term relation of high school work hours to educational attainment from 1–5 years after completing high school. Although one of these five studies failed to find a significant relation (Finch & Mortimer, 1985), the four remaining studies supported a negative relation between the number of work hours during high school and either college attendance or the number of years of education completed (Marsh, 1991; R. H. Meyer & Wise, 1982; Mortimer & Johnson, 1997; Steel, 1991). Moreover, the negative relation between high school work hours and educational attainment 1–5 years after high school is primarily observed among males (R. H. Meyer & Wise, 1982; Mortimer & Johnson, 1997; Steel, 1991). One long-term study by Carr et al. (1996) found a negative relation between the number of hours worked during high school and educational attainment assessed 12 years later. As with the short-term studies, Carr et al. (1996) reported that this relation was observed only among males. (See chap. 4, this volume, for a discussion of gender effects on income.)

Work quality. Two longitudinal studies explored the relation of work quality to educational attainment. Steel (1991) found no relation between the quality of high school jobs and college attendance from 1 to 2 years after high school. Marsh (1991) reported that job-related training and ratings of work importance were negatively related to college attendance during the 2 years following high school.

Selection. By the nature of the educational attainment outcomes, differential selection is not a viable hypothesis. In other words, the variables reflecting educational attainment in adulthood cannot occur before or contemporaneous with the high school employment characteristics.

Conclusions. No evidence exists that work status is related to educational attainment. In addition, little evidence exists that the number of weekly work hours during high school is systematically related to high school completion. In contrast, evidence exists for both short-term and long-term negative effects of the number of work hours during high school on college attendance and years of education completed among males, but not among females. Because only one long-term study has been conducted, more research examining the long-term impact of high school work hours on future educational attainment is needed. Currently, it may be premature to conclude that the consistent short-term drop in educational attainment due to working longer hours in high school is never eliminated. Because only two narrow work quality studies have been conducted, it is unclear whether the quality of high school jobs is systematically related to educational attainment. However, more detailed research on work quality and educational attainment seems useful for understanding the processes underlying the negative relation between work hours and educational attainment.

Employment Outcomes

To further structure this segment of the review, employment outcomes are classified into three subcategories: career development (attitudes, values, aspiration, planning, and practical knowledge), work behaviors (accidents and deviance), and occupational attainment (earnings, employability, and occupational prestige).

Career Development

Work status. Three cross-sectional studies examined the relation of work status to at least one dimension of career development (work attitudes, work values, occupational aspirations, career planning or maturity, and practical knowledge). Regarding work attitudes, one study by Steinberg, Greenberger, Vaux, and Ruggiero (1981) found that adolescent workers reported more work-related cynicism than nonworkers, but no relation between work status and acceptance of unethical business practices was found. Of the two studies that assessed the importance of intrinsic and extrinsic work values, both failed to support a relation between work status and extrinsic work values, but found that workers reported higher intrinsic work values than nonworkers (Mortimer, Pimentel, Ryu, Nash, & Lee, 1996; Steinberg et al., 1981). One study failed to find a relation between work status and occupational aspirations (Steinberg et al., 1981). Finally, one study found that employed youth had higher levels of practical knowledge about business, economics, and consumerism than nonemployed youth (Steinberg, Greenberger, Garduque, & McAuliffe, 1982).

One longitudinal study by Steinberg, Greenberger, Garduque, Ruggiero, and Vaux (1982) found that employed youth reported higher levels of work-related cynicism and were more accepting of unethical business practices than nonemployed youth. However, additional analyses revealed that the direction of these relations differed unpredictably across gender and race subgroups.

Work hours. Eight cross-sectional studies explored the relation of work hours to career development. As for work attitudes, one study revealed that work hours were positively related to work-related cynicism (Steinberg et al., 1981) and one study failed to find a relation (Loughlin & Barling, 1998). One study reported that work hours were positively related to acceptance of unethical business practices among boys but not girls (Steinberg et al., 1981). One study failed to find a relation of work hours to work involvement and intrinsic work motivation (Loughlin & Barling, 1998). Two studies failed to find a relation between work hours and job satisfaction (Bachman & Schulenberg, 1993; Markel & Frone, 1998). Turning to intrinsic and extrinsic work values, two studies found no relations with work hours (Mortimer, Pimentel, et al., 1996; Steinberg et al., 1981). Three studies failed to find a significant relation between work hours and occupational aspirations (Loughlin & Barling, 1998; Steinberg et al., 1981; Stevens et al., 1992). Of the two studies examining career planning or maturity, one study supported a positive relation to work hours (Hamilton & Powers, 1990) and one study failed to find a relation (Loughlin & Barling, 1998). One study failed to find a relation between work hours and practical knowledge about business, economics, and consumerism (Steinberg, Greenberger, Garduque, Ruggiero, & Vaux, 1982).

Two longitudinal studies explored the relation of work hours to career development. One study failed to find a relation between work hours and work-related cynicism. The relation between work hours and acceptance of unethical business practices was nonsignificant for adolescents from blue-collar families, positive for white-collar families, and negative for professional families (Steinberg, Greenberger, Garduque, Ruggiero, & Vaux, 1982). The second study failed to find a relation between work hours and occupational aspirations (Marsh, 1991).

Work quality. Three cross-sectional studies examined the relation between work quality and career development. As for work attitudes, Stern, Stone, Hopkins, and McMillion (1990) examined intrinsic work motivation and work-related cynicism and found that both opportunity to learn on the job and physical challenge were positively related to intrinsic motivation. In addition, work–school conflict was positively related and skill use was negatively related to work-related cynicism. Loughlin and Barling (1998) examined the relations of work quality to work-related cynicism, work involvement, and intrinsic work motivation. A positive relation between role comfort (i.e., low levels of role ambiguity, role conflict, and role overload) and intrinsic motivation was found. In addition, both role comfort and satisfaction with interpersonal relations were negatively related to work-related cynicism. Mortimer, Pimentel, et al. (1996) found that the opportunity to develop skills at work was positively related to the importance of both intrinsic and extrinsic work values. Loughlin and Barling (1998) examined the relation of work quality to occupational aspirations and career maturity and found a positive relation between role comfort and career maturity.

A longitudinal study by Marsh (1991) found that work quality was unrelated to occupational aspirations. In addition, interactions between work quality and work hours did not predict occupational aspirations.

Selection. The possibility that dimensions of general career development (work attitudes, work values, occupational aspirations, and career planning or maturity) affect whether adolescents work, the number of hours they work, or the quality of their jobs has not received much attention. However, Mortimer, Pimentel, et al. (1996) reported evidence that the importance of intrinsic work values was related to later reports that one's job provided opportunities to develop skills at work and to be helpful to others.

Conclusions. No compelling evidence exists that work status or work hours are related to career development outcomes. Although few studies have been conducted, it seems likely that work quality is related to career development outcomes, especially work attitudes. However, more research is needed before specific conclusions can be drawn. Longitudinal research also is required to test the relative validity of the socialization and selection hypotheses.

Work Behaviors

Although work-related behaviors (e.g., injuries, performance, employee citizenship, and organizational deviance) represent an important set of employment outcomes, the adolescent employment literature has paid little attention to them. Because work behaviors can be observed only among employed adolescents, work status is not a viable predictor variable. Although the relation of work hours to work-related behaviors is possible to examine, only one study has examined this relation. Frone (1998) failed to find a relation between the number of work hours and work injuries. Four cross-sectional studies have examined the relation between work quality and work behaviors. Two of these four studies have focused on work-related injuries. Parker, Carl, French, and Martin (1994) explored the relation between work activities and work injuries. They found that the amount of weight adolescents lifted at work was positively related to sustaining a back injury; working with cooking equipment and oils was positively associated with burn injuries; and bagging and working as a stock clerk was associated with sustaining bruises and contusions. Frone (1998) found that workload, job boredom, exposure to environmental hazards, and on-the-job substance use (e.g., alcohol or drugs) were positively related and supervisors' performance monitoring was negatively related to work injuries (see also chap. 7, this volume).

Two studies examined the relation of work quality to work-related deviance. Ruggiero, Greenberger, and Steinberg (1982) found that poor environmental conditions and an opportunity for theft were positively related, and a poor social environment was negatively related to employee theft and nontheft deviance. Frone (1997) reported that off-the-job drinking with coworkers and exposure to on-the-job drinking by coworkers were positively related to on-the-job drinking by adolescents.

Because no longitudinal studies of adolescent employment and work-related behaviors have been conducted, there has been no attempt to provide separate tests of the socialization and selection hypotheses.

Conclusion. Although little research has been conducted on the work behaviors of adolescents, the studies described above suggest that additional research on the relation between work quality and work behaviors is warranted. Research in this area is important because the development of functional and dysfunctional work behaviors is relevant to adolescent health and well-being and future occupational and personal success.

Occupational Attainment

Work status. Three longitudinal studies examined the relation of high school work status to at least one dimension of occupational attainment (earnings, employability, and occupational prestige). Two of these studies focused on later earnings. Mortimer and Finch (1986) found that high school employment was positively related to earnings assessed 5 years after high school. However, their analysis failed to control for basic sociodemographic characteristics. Foster (1995) conducted a study that used data from brothers, where one worked at the age of 16 and one did not, to provide tight controls for potentially confounding background factors. Although the unadjusted analysis showed that high school employment was positively related to earnings reported from 6 to 19 years later, this relation was eliminated in the adjusted analysis. Regarding employability, one study found that high school work status was not related to the number of weeks employed 1–2 years after high school (Steel, 1991).

Work hours. Nine longitudinal studies examined the relation of work hours to occupational attainment. Of the four short-term studies assessing earnings from 1 to 5 years after high school, one study failed to find an effect for high school work hours (Finch & Mortimer, 1985), and three studies found support for a positive effect (R. H. Meyer & Wise, 1982; Mortimer & Johnson, 1997; Stern & Nakata, 1989). All three long-term studies assessing earnings or wages from 6 to 19 years after high school found a positive effect of high school work hours on earning or wages (Carr et al., 1996; Foster, 1995; Ruhm, 1995).

Five short-term studies examined the outcome of employability. Hamilton and Powers (1990) failed to find a relation between work hours and the likelihood of being employed 6 months after high school in a sample of working-class girls. In contrast, the remaining four studies supported a positive relation between high school work hours and employability (i.e., weeks worked) from 2 to 4 years after high school (R. H. Meyer & Wise, 1982; Mortimer & Johnson, 1997; Steel, 1991; Stern & Nakata, 1989). One long-term study by Carr et al. (1996) reported that high school work hours were positively related to being in the labor force and being employed 12 years after high school.

Two studies examined the relation of high school work hours to occupational prestige. One short-term study by Finch and Mortimer (1985) failed to find a significant relation between work hours and the occupational prestige of the job held 5 years after high school. In contrast, a long-term study by Ruhm (1995) found that the number of work hours during high school was positively related to the occupational prestige of jobs held 6 to 9 years after high school.

Work quality. Three short-term longitudinal studies examined the relation of work quality to occupational attainment. Stern and Nakata (1989) explored the relation of work quality to earnings and employability during the period from 1 to 2 years after high school. Their results showed that skill use and development were positively related to earnings and weeks worked, and that rights and compensation (i.e., having good extrinsic rewards) were positively related to weeks worked. Hamilton and Powers (1990) reported that an overall rating of the quality of high school jobs (i.e., skill use and development, interaction with adults, task variety, decision-making authority, level of responsibility, and level of fit between one's job and one's vocational preferences or plans) was positively related to the likelihood of being employed 6 months after high school. Steel (1991) found that high school job prestige, as measured by the Duncan Socioeconomic Index, was positively related to weeks of employment from 1 to 2 years after high school.

Selection. By the nature of the occupational attainment outcomes, differential selection is not a viable hypothesis. Variables representing occupational attainment during adulthood can never occur before or contemporaneous with the high school employment characteristics.

Conclusions. Work status during high school does not affect later occupational attainment. In contrast, longitudinal evidence exists for both short-term and long-term positive effects of high school work hours on earnings, employability, and occupational prestige. Nonetheless, research on work hours provides little insight into the underlying processes linking adolescent employment and later occupational attainment. Prior research on high school work quality begins to address this issue. The research reviewed above provides preliminary evidence that certain characteristics of adolescents' jobs (e.g., skill use and development) may be related to higher levels of employability. However, the few studies conducted have been limited by crude measures of work quality and a limited range of occupational attainment outcomes. Future research in this area should devote more attention to the quality of adolescent jobs. Little justification exists to conduct additional research on work status, and further research on work hours should be embedded in studies of work quality.

Family Outcomes

Work status. Four cross-sectional studies examined the relation of work status to at least one of three dimensions of family development (adolescent autonomy, family interpersonal relations, and family economics). As for adolescent autonomy, two studies suggest that employed youth may spend less time with their families and receive less parental monitoring than nonemployed youth (Greenberger, Steinberg, Vaux, & McAuliffe, 1980; Manning, 1990). Three studies provide little evidence that work status and family interpersonal relations are related (Greenberger et al., 1980; Manning, 1990; Mortimer & Shanahan, 1994). Turning to the family economy, two studies reported that employed adolescents were less likely to receive an allowance and more likely to have financial responsibility for a variety of purchases than nonemployed adolescents (Greenberger et al., 1980; Miller & Yung, 1990; see chap. 4, this volume).

Two longitudinal studies examined the relation between work status and family outcomes. Collectively, both studies failed to find a relation of work status to both adolescent autonomy and family interpersonal relations (Gottfredson, 1985; Steinberg, Greenberger, Garduque, Ruggiero, & Vaux, 1982).

Work hours. Five cross-sectional studies examined the relation of work hours to family development. Four studies support a positive relation between the number of work hours and adolescent autonomy (Greenberger et al., 1980; Manning, 1990; Mortimer & Shanahan, 1994; Steinberg & Dornbusch, 1991). Two studies found no support for a relation between work hours and overall family interpersonal relations (Greenberger et al., 1980; Manning, 1990), and two studies found that increasing work hours were positively related to poor interpersonal relations (Bachman & Schulenberg, 1993; Mortimer & Shanahan, 1994). No cross-sectional studies tested the relation between work hours and family economics.

Five longitudinal studies examined the relation of work hours to family development. Collectively, three studies failed to provide evidence of a relation between work hours and adolescent autonomy (Steinberg, Greenberger, Garduque, Ruggiero, & Vaux, 1982; Shanahan, Elder, Burchinal, & Conger, 1996b; Steinberg et al., 1993). Similarly, four studies failed to show a relation between work hours and family interpersonal relations (Mortimer & Shanahan, 1994; Shanahan, Elder, Burchinal, & Conger, 1996a, 1996b; Steinberg, Greenberger, Garduque, Ruggiero, & Vaux, 1982). No longitudinal studies tested the relation between work hours and family economics.

Work quality. A cross-sectional study by Call (1996a) failed to find a relation between several dimensions of work quality and family interpersonal relations. Similarly, a longitudinal study by Mortimer and Shanahan (1994) failed to support a relation between skill development and family interpersonal relations. No studies have examined the relation of work quality to adolescent autonomy or family economics.

Selection. Two longitudinal studies explored whether earlier family development variables predicted subsequent measures of adolescent employment. Mortimer and Shanahan (1994) found marginal support for an effect of family interpersonal relations on later work hours among boys but not among girls. However, family interpersonal relations were not related to later work quality (opportunities for skill development). Steinberg et al. (1993) reported that adolescent autonomy was positively related to the likelihood of entering the workforce.

Conclusions. In terms of absolute numbers, there have been relatively few studies exploring the relations between adolescent employment and family developmental outcomes. Unlike research looking at other types of developmental outcome variables, most of the cross-sectional studies testing the socialization hypothesis failed to control for two basic demographic variables (i.e., gender and age). For example, as noted earlier, cross-sectional research supports a positive relation between work hours and adolescent autonomy. However, the number of hours adolescents work per week and the degree of autonomy that parents afford their children are both positively related to the age of the adolescent. It is, therefore, highly likely that controlling for age would eliminate the observed relation between work hours and autonomy. This problem exists for the other family outcomes as well. Collectively, the longitudinal studies, which have better statistical controls, provide little evidence for either the socialization or the selection hypotheses with regard to family development. Because so few studies have been conducted in this area, it is prudent to suggest that no firm conclusions can be drawn at this time. Based on research investigating other types of developmental outcomes, it would be reasonable to forego studies of work status. Future research should devote primary attention to work quality, and any research on work hours should be embedded in a study of work quality.

General Developmental Outcomes

To further structure this segment of the review, general developmental outcomes are classified into three subcategories: psychological or somatic health (depression, somatic symptoms, and life satisfaction), personality (self-esteem, mastery, personal responsibility, social responsibility, and materialism), and behavioral outcomes (substance use, sexual behavior, general delinquency, and time use).

Psychological or Somatic Health

Work status. Four cross-sectional studies tested the relation between work status and at least one dimension of psychological or somatic health (depression, somatic symptoms, life satisfaction). One study found that working youth reported more psychological and somatic symptoms than nonemployed youth (Koeske & Koeske, 1989). One study found no relation between work status and psychological distress, but found that employed youth reported fewer somatic symptoms than nonemployed youth (Greenberger et al., 1981). The remaining two studies do not support a relation between work status and both psychological and somatic health (Mortimer et al., 1992a; Shanahan, Finch, Mortimer, & Ryu, 1991). No longitudinal studies have examined work status and adolescent health.

Work hours. Eight cross-sectional studies tested the relation of work hours to psychological and somatic health. Greenberger et al. (1981) reported that work hours were negatively related to both psychological and somatic symptoms. Steinberg and Dornbusch (1991) reported that work hours were positively related to both psychological and somatic symptoms (Steinberg & Dornbusch, 1991). The remaining six studies failed to support any relation of work hours to psychological and somatic symptoms (Bachman & Schulenberg, 1993; Mortimer, Finch, et al., 1996; Mortimer et al., 1992a, 1992b; Shanahan et al., 1991; Yamoor & Mortimer, 1990). Three longitudinal studies also reported that work hours were unrelated to psychological and somatic symptoms (Mortimer, Finch, et al., 1996; Mortimer & Johnson, 1997; Steinberg et al., 1993).

Work quality. Six cross-sectional studies examined the relation of work quality to psychological or somatic health. Two studies failed to support a relation between work quality and either psychological or somatic health (Greenberger et al., 1981; Mortimer et al., 1992b). In contrast, Frone and Windle (1995) found that job dissatisfaction was positively related to depression. Mortimer et al. (1992a) found that negative work–school spillover and job stress were positively related to depression, and positive work–school spillover and job complexity concerning things was negatively related to depression. In addition, negative work–school spillover was negatively related to psychological well-being, and positive work–school spillover, job security, job skill development, and job complexity concerning things was positively related to psychological well-being. Shanahan et al. (1991) reported that work stress, work–school conflict, and self-direction were positively related and job skill development was negatively related to depression among boys. Being held responsible for tasks outside one's control was positively related to depression among girls. Call (1996a) found that work satisfaction was positively related and work stress was negatively related to psychological well-being. Moreover, supervisor support and work satisfaction were negatively related, and work stress and job boredom were positively related to depression. No longitudinal studies have examined the socialization hypothesis regarding work quality and adolescent health.

Selection. Three longitudinal studies explored whether earlier measures of psychological or somatic health predict subsequent measures of work status (Gottfredson, 1985), work hours (Mortimer, Finch, et al., 1996), or work quality (Shanahan et al., 1991). All three studies failed to find evidence of selection.

Conclusions. Research on psychological and somatic health reveals no evidence for either socialization or selection effects with regard to work status and work hours. In contrast, research does support a relation between work quality and adolescent health. However, because only a few cross-sectional studies have been conducted, it is unclear whether the relation between work quality and health reflects socialization or selection effects. In addition, little can be concluded regarding the specific job characteristics that may be most likely to influence health. Additional research should explore the relation of work quality to adolescent health.

Personality

Work status. Four cross-sectional studies tested the relation between work status and at least one dimension of personality (self-esteem, mastery, personal responsibility, social responsibility, and materialism). All four studies failed to support a relation of work status to self-esteem, mastery, personal responsibility, and materialism (Finch, Shanahan, Mortimer, & Ryu, 1991; Gade & Peterson, 1980; Mortimer et al., 1992a; Steinberg et al., 1981). Consistent with the cross-sectional results, a longitudinal study by Steinberg, Greenberger, Garduque, Ruggiero, and Vaux (1982) failed to find a relation of work status to both personal and social responsibility, but found higher levels of materialism among employed males than among nonemployed males.

Work hours. Ten cross-sectional studies tested the relation between work hours and adolescent personality, none of which supported a relation of work hours to self-esteem, mastery, personal responsibility, social responsibility, and materialism (Bachman & Schulenberg, 1993; Barling et al., 1995; D'Amico, 1984; Finch et al., 1991; Mortimer, Finch, et al., 1996; Mortimer et al., 1992a, 1992b; Steinberg et al., 1981; Steinberg & Dornbusch, 1991; Steitz & Owen, 1992).

Five longitudinal studies tested the relation between work hours and adolescent personality, all of which failed to support a relation of work hours to self-esteem, mastery, personal responsibility, social responsibility, materialism, and locus of control (Marsh, 1991; Mortimer, Finch, et al., 1996; Mortimer & Johnson, 1997; Steinberg et al., 1993; Steinberg, Greenberger, Garduque, Ruggiero, & Vaux, 1982). Only one study found a positive relation between work hours and sociability (Marsh, 1991).

Work quality. Six cross-sectional studies examined the relation of work quality characteristics to adolescent personality. Mortimer et al. (1992b) found that job complexity was unrelated to self-esteem and mastery. Mortimer et al. (1992a) found that work stress was negatively related and job skill development positively related to self-esteem and mastery. In addition, negative work–school spillover was negatively related and positive work–school spillover and predictability were positively related to self-esteem among girls only. Barling et al. (1995) found that autonomy and role clarity were positively related to self-esteem. In addition, their results showed that skill variety, autonomy, and role clarity interacted with work hours to predict self-esteem. As hypothesized, work hours were negatively related to self-esteem when work quality was low, and work hours were positively related to self-esteem when work quality was high. Finch et al. (1991) reported that pay evaluation and advancement potential were positively related, and work–school conflict and being held responsible for things beyond one's control were negatively related to mastery. Call (1996a) examined the relation of work quality to self-esteem and mastery. This study revealed that work satisfaction was positively related and work stress was negatively related to self-esteem, and that supervisor support was positively related to mastery. Call (1996b) reported that the ability to be helpful to others at work was not related to levels of mastery.

A longitudinal study by Marsh (1991) examined the relation of work quality to self-esteem and social self-concept. The results showed that a job that encourages good work habits is positively related to both self-esteem and social self-concept. Additional analyses revealed that interactions between work quality and work hours did not predict either outcome variable.

Selection. Four longitudinal studies explored whether earlier measures of adolescent personality predicted subsequent measures of work hours or work quality. Three studies revealed no evidence that adolescent personality predicts the extent of work force involvement (Marsh, 1991; Mortimer, Finch, et al., 1996; Shanahan et al., 1991). The remaining study reported that mastery was negatively related to subsequent measures of work–school conflict, work stress, and being held responsible for things beyond one's control (Finch et al., 1991).

Conclusions. Research on adolescent personality provides no support for either socialization or selection effects with regard to work status and work hours. In contrast, research does support a relation between work quality and personality. However, because only a few cross-sectional studies have been conducted, it is unclear whether the relation between work quality and personality reflects socialization or selection effects. Furthermore, little can be concluded regarding which dimensions of work quality and personality are most likely to be related. Additional research should explore the relation of work quality to adolescent personality.

Behavioral Outcomes

Work status. Five cross-sectional studies examined the relation between work status and at least one behavioral outcome (substance use, sexual behavior, general delinquency, time use). Three studies failed to find a relation with cigarette and alcohol use (Greenberger et al., 1981; Jenkins, 1996; Mortimer et al., 1992a). However, Greenberger et al. (1981) reported that employed youth had higher levels of illicit drug use than nonemployed youth. One study of adolescent males revealed that work status was not related to several dimensions of sexual behavior (number of sexual partners, frequency of intercourse, impregnating a female, and fathering a child; Ku, Sonenstein, & Pleck, 1993). The remaining study found that employed youth exhibited lower levels of criminality than nonemployed youth (Good, Pirog-Good, & Sickles, 1986). Two longitudinal studies found no relation between work status and any form of substance use or delinquency (Gottfredson, 1985; Steinberg, Greenberger, Garduque, Ruggiero, & Vaux, 1982).

Work hours. Seven cross-sectional studies examined the relation between work hours and behavioral outcomes. Five studies supported a positive relation of work hours to cigarette, alcohol, or illicit drug use (Bachman & Schulenberg, 1993; Greenberger et al., 1981; Mortimer et al., 1992b; Mortimer, Finch, et al., 1996; Steinberg & Dornbusch, 1991). One study of adolescent males found that work hours were positively related to several dimensions of sexual behavior (number of sexual partners, frequency of intercourse, impregnating a female, and fathering a child; Ku et al., 1993). Two studies found a positive relation of work hours to delinquent behavior (Bachman & Schulenberg, 1993; Steinberg & Dornbusch, 1991). One study failed to find a relation between work hours and the extent to which adolescents plan each day (Barling et al., 1995). In contrast, Bachman and Schulenberg (1993) reported that work hours were negatively related to engaging in health-promotive behaviors, such as getting enough sleep, eating breakfast, and vigorous exercise.

Six longitudinal studies have examined the relation of work hours to behavioral outcomes. Of the six studies examining work hours and substance use, four studies found a positive relation (Brook & Newcomb, 1995; Mortimer & Johnson, 1997; Steinberg, Greenberger, Garduque, Ruggiero, & Vaux, 1982; Steinberg et al., 1993) and two studies failed to find a relation (Frone & Barnes, 1995; Mortimer, Finch, et al., 1996). In addition, Mortimer and Johnson (1997) reported that although work hours during high school were related to alcohol and cigarette use in the senior year, this effect did not extend to substance use assessed 4 years after high school. Finally, Steinberg et al. (1993) found that work hours were positively related to delinquent behavior.

Work quality. Five cross-sectional studies examined the relation of work quality characteristics to behavioral outcomes. Frone and Windle (1997) reported that job dissatisfaction was positively related to cigarette and alcohol use but was unrelated to illicit drug use. In contrast, three studies failed to find any relation between work quality and substance use (Greenberger et al., 1981; Mortimer et al., 1992a, 1992b). With regard to time management, Barling et al. (1995) reported that skill variety, autonomy, and role clarity were positively related to the extent to which adolescents plan each day. Moreover, as hypothesized, work-quality by work-hours interaction analyses showed that work hours were more negatively related to time management at low levels of role clarity.

Selection. Six longitudinal studies explored whether earlier measures of adolescent behavior predicted subsequent measures of work status or work hours. Three studies revealed no evidence that delinquent behavior predicts entry into the workforce or number of work hours (Good et al., 1986; Gottfredson, 1985; Steinberg et al., 1993). Of the five studies examining substance use, one study failed to find a selection effect (Steinberg et al., 1993), and four studies supported a positive relation of substance use to subsequent work status (Gottfredson, 1985) and work hours (Brook & Newcomb, 1995; Frone & Barnes, 1995; Mortimer, Finch, et al., 1996).

Conclusions. In general there is little evidence to support either socialization or selection effects between work status and behavioral outcomes. In contrast, there is consistent evidence that substance use and work hours may be reciprocally related, thereby supporting both the socialization and selection hypotheses. Moreover, there is some support for a relation between work hours and general delinquency and, among males, a relation between work hours and sexual promiscuity. However, more research needs to be conducted before any definitive conclusions can be drawn regarding delinquency and sexual promiscuity. Based on the few studies of work quality, there is not much evidence to suggest that work quality is related to behavioral outcomes. Nonetheless, based on the results involving the other outcomes reviewed earlier, this is a potentially fruitful area for future research.

GENERAL CONCLUSIONS

The goal of this review was to determine what conclusions are warranted regarding the relation between adolescent employment and development. Three categories of employment predictors (work status, work hours, and work quality) were examined in relation to four major dimensions of adolescent development: academic (academic performance, academic attachment, and educational attainment), employment (career development, work behaviors, and occupational attainment), family (adolescent autonomy, interpersonal relations, and family economy), and general development (psychological or somatic health, personality, and behaviors).

The results of this review overwhelmingly support the fact that simply being employed during adolescence has no appreciable relation to development. The relation of work hours to adolescent development is more complex and depends on the dimension of development under consideration. There is consistent evidence that the number of work hours is inconsequential for most of the development outcomes examined in this review (i.e., academic performance, career development, adolescent autonomy, family interpersonal relations, family economy, psychological or somatic health, and personality). Nonetheless, work hours may be associated with several adverse effects. Supporting the socialization hypothesis, working many hours per week during high school may undermine certain dimensions of educational attachment (intrinsic motivation and educational aspirations), lower levels of post-high school educational attainment among males only, and increase the likelihood of substance use and delinquent behavior. There also is evidence for the selection hypothesis in that youth who show early signs of academic detachment and higher levels of involvement with substance use are more likely to devote more hours to employment. Finally, there also is consistent evidence for a positive socialization effect in that working more hours in high school is related to higher levels of post-high school occupational attainment (earnings, employability, occupational prestige) among men and women.

Relative to work status and work hours, much less systematic research has been devoted to work quality. At this time, no reasonable conclusions can be offered regarding academic and family outcomes. However, there is growing evidence that various psychosocial dimensions of adolescent employment may be related to career development, work behaviors, occupational attainment, psychological or somatic health, and personality. The general pattern of results is such that high-quality work experiences are associated with developmentally beneficial outcomes, whereas poor-quality work experiences are associated with developmentally detrimental outcomes. Because few longitudinal studies have been conducted, it is not clear whether the relations between work quality and adolescent development represent socialization effects, selection effects, or both.

Based on this review, it is evident that adolescent employment (i.e., work hours and work quality) may have both positive and negative effects. However, prior research is rather limited in its ability to explain the underlying processes that link employment and development. The primary reason for this is that too much attention has been devoted to the study of work hours and too little has been devoted to work quality (see chap. 2, this volume). The number of weekly work hours provides a very limited and unidimensional representation of adolescents' work experience. In addition, when the number of work hours is related to a given outcome, it is often viewed as a surrogate for a richer and more proximal dimension of employment. For example, number of work hours may be positively related to alcohol use because adolescents who work long hours are more likely to associate with older coworkers, make more money, or be exposed to more job stress.

As noted throughout this chapter, the most promising avenue for future research on the relation between adolescent employment and development is the exploration of work quality. However, as also indicated in chap. 2 (this volume), little attention has been paid to the large employment literature developed by industrial/organizational (I/O) psychologists and management researchers. This rich literature on adult employment offers two important assets to the study of adolescent employment. The first involves measurement. Even though well-developed measures of various job characteristics exist in the I/O psychology and management literatures, prior adolescent employment studies have relied on ad hoc, study-specific scales. In many cases, complex constructs have been assessed with single items or with multi-item scales that do not even possess reasonable face validity. The second asset offered by the adult employment literature is a rich source of conceptual models that may help to clarify the processes linking employment and development. For example, Warr (1987) outlined a vitamin model of the work environment and mental health. As part of this model, nine principal work characteristics that define a "good" job are described. These nine work characteristics are likely to be salient predictors of adolescent developmental outcomes. Also, Markel and Frone (1998) developed and found empirical support for an integrative model of the relations among job characteristics (e.g., work load, job dissatisfaction, and job hours), work–school conflict, and several school outcomes (readiness or preparation, performance, and dissatisfaction). Their model was based, in part, on prior conceptual models of work–family conflict among adults (Frone, Barnes, & Farrell, 1994; Frone, Russell, & Cooper, 1992; Frone, Yardley, & Markel, 1997).

In conclusion, this review reveals that part-time employment may represent an important force in adolescent development. Although employment status per se is not related to developmental outcomes, the number of hours worked per week and work quality are related to developmentally beneficial and detrimental outcomes. Nonetheless, in comparison to other domains of adolescent life (i.e., school, peer group, and family), we know relatively little about the impact of employment on adolescent development. It is hoped that this review will motivate additional research in this important arena. However, if we are to develop an integrative understanding of the role of employment in adolescent development, more comprehensive models need to be developed that portray the interrelations among the employment, family, peer-group, and school contexts.

REFERENCES

Adams, G. R., Montemayor, R., & Gullota, T. P. (1996). *Psychosocial develop-ment during adolescence: Progress in developmental contextualism.* Thousand Oaks, CA: Sage.

Aiken, L. S., & West, S. G. (1991). *Multiple regression: Testing and interpreting interactions.* Thousand Oaks, CA: Sage.

Bachman, J. G., & Schulenberg, J. (1993). How part-time work intensity relates to drug use, problem behavior, time use, and satisfaction among high school seniors: Are these consequences or merely correlates? *Developmental Psychology, 29,* 220–235.

Barling, J., & Gallagher, D. G. (1996). Part-time employment. In C. L. Cooper & I. T. Robertson (Eds.), *International review of industrial and organizational psychology* (Vol. 11, pp. 243–277). New York: Wiley.

Barling, J., Rogers, K. A., & Kelloway, E. K. (1995). Some effects of teenagers' part-time employment: The quantity and quality of work make the difference. *Journal of Organizational Behavior, 16,* 143–154.

Brook, J. S., & Newcomb, M. D. (1995). Childhood aggression and unconventionality: Impact on later academic achievement, drug use, and workforce involvement. *Journal of Genetic Psychology, 156,* 393–410.

Call, K. T. (1996a). Adolescent work as an "arena of comfort" under conditions of family discomfort. In J. T. Mortimer & M. D. Finch (Eds.), *Adolescents, work, and family: An intergenerational developmental perspective* (pp. 129–166). Thousand Oaks, CA: Sage.

Call, K. T. (1996b). The implications of helpfulness for possible selves. In J. T. Mortimer & M. D. Finch (Eds.), *Adolescents, work, and family: An intergenerational developmental perspective* (pp. 63–96). Thousand Oaks, CA: Sage.

Carr, R. V., Wright, J. D., & Brody, C. J. (1996). Effects of high school work experience a decade later: Evidence from the national longitudinal survey. *Sociology of Education, 69,* 66–81.

Cohen, J. (1978). Partialed products are interactions; partialed vectors are curve components. *Psychological Bulletin, 85,* 858–866.

D'Amico, R. (1984). Does employment during high school impair academic progress? *Sociology of Education, 57,* 152–164.

Feldman, S. S., & Elliott, G. R. (1990). Capturing the adolescent experience.

In S. S. Feldman & G. R. Elliott (Eds.), *At the threshold: The developing adolescent* (pp. 1–13). Cambridge, MA: Harvard University Press.

Finch, M. D., & Mortimer, J. T. (1985). Adolescent work hours and the process of achievement. *Research in Sociology of Education and Socialization, 5,* 171–196.

Finch, M. D., Shanahan, M. J., Mortimer, J. T., & Ryu, S. (1991). Work experience and control orientation in adolescence. *American Sociological Review, 56,* 597–611.

Foster, E. M. (1995). Why teens do not benefit from work experience programs: Evidence from brother comparisons. *Journal of Policy Analysis and Management, 14,* 393–414.

Frone, M. R. (1997, July). *Alcohol exposure and drinking on the job among employed adolescents.* Poster session presented at the annual scientific meeting of the Research Society on Alcoholism, San Francisco, CA.

Frone, M. R. (1998). Predictors of work injuries among employed adolescents. *Journal of Applied Psychology, 83,* 565–576.

Frone, M. R., & Barnes, G. M. (1995, August). *Work intensity and substance use among adolescents: A longitudinal study.* Poster presented at the American Psychological Association convention, New York, NY.

Frone, M. R., Barnes, G. M., & Farrell, M. P. (1994). Relationship of work-family conflict to substance use among employed mothers: Examining the mediating role of negative affect. *Journal of Marriage and the Family, 56,* 1019–1030.

Frone, M. R., Russell, M., & Cooper, M. L. (1992). Antecedents and outcomes of work-family conflict: Testing a model of the work-family interface. *Journal of Applied Psychology, 77,* 65–78.

Frone, M. R., & Windle, M. (1995, September). *Job dissatisfaction, coping styles, and health outcomes among adolescents.* Poster session presented at the Work, Stress, and Health '95: Creating Healthier Workplaces Conference, sponsored by the American Psychological Association and the National Institute on Occupational Safety and Health, Washington, DC.

Frone, M. R., & Windle, M. (1997). Job dissatisfaction and substance use among employed high school students: The moderating influence of active and avoidant coping styles. *Substance Use and Misuse, 32,* 571–585.

Frone, M. R., Yardley, J. K., & Markel, K. S. (1997). Developing and testing an integrative model of the work-family interface [Special issue on work-family balance]. *Journal of Vocational Behavior, 50,* 145–167.

Gade, E., & Peterson, L. (1980). A comparison of working and nonworking high school students on school performance, socioeconomic status, and self-esteem. *Vocational Guidance Quarterly, 29,* 65–69.

Good, D. H., Pirog-Good, M. A., & Sickles, R. C. (1986). An analysis of youth crime and employment patterns. *Journal of Quantitative Criminology, 2,* 219–236.

Gottfredson, D. C. (1985). Youth employment, crime, and schooling: A longitudinal study of a national sample. *Developmental Psychology, 21,* 419–432.

Green, D. L. (1990). High school student employment in social context: Adolescents' perceptions of the role of part-time employment. *Adolescence, 25,* 425–434.

Green, G., & Jaquess, S. N. (1987). The effect of part-time employment on academic achievement. *Journal of Educational Research, 80,* 325–329.

Greenberger, E. (1983). A researcher in the policy arena: The case of child labor. *American Psychologist, 38,* 104–111.

Greenberger, E., & Steinberg, L. D. (1981). The workplace as a context for the socialization of youth. *Journal of Youth and Adolescence, 10,* 185–210.

Greenberger, E., & Steinberg, L. D. (1986). *When teenagers work: The psychological and social costs of adolescent employment.* New York: Basic Books.

Greenberger, E., Steinberg, L. D., & Vaux, A. (1981). Adolescents who work: Health and behavioral consequences of job stress. *Developmental Psychology, 17,* 691–703.

Greenberger, E., Steinberg, L. D., & Vaux, A., & McAuliffe, S. (1980). Adolescents who work: Effects of part-time employment on family and peer relations. *Journal of Youth and Adolescence, 9,* 189–202.

Hamilton, S. F., & Crouter, A. C. (1980). Work and growth: A review of research on the impact of work experience on adolescent development. *Journal of Youth and Adolescence, 9,* 323–338.

Hamilton, S. F., & Powers, J. L. (1990). Failed expectations: Working-class girls' transition from school to work. *Youth and Society, 22,* 241–262.

Hammes, J. F., & Haller, E. J. (1983). Making ends meet: Some of the consequences of part-time work for college students. *Journal of College Student Personnel, 24,* 529–534.

Henke, J. W., Jr., Lyons, T. F., & Krachenberg, A. R. (1993). Knowing your market: How working students balance work, grades, and course load. *Journal of Marketing for Higher Education, 4,* 191–203.

High, R., & Collins, J. W. (1992). High school employment at what cost? *The High School Journal, 75,* 90–93.

Hotchkiss, L. (1986). Work and schools—Complements or competitors? In K. M. Borman & R. Reisman (Eds.), *Becoming a worker* (pp. 90–115). Norwood, NJ: Ablex.

Jenkins, J. E. (1996). The influence of peer affiliation and student activities on adolescent drug involvement. *Adolescence, 31,* 297–306.

Kessler, R. C. (1987). The interplay of research design strategies and data analysis procedures in evaluating the effects of stress on health. In S. V. Kasl & C. L. Cooper (Eds.), *Stress and health: Issues in research methodology* (pp. 113–140). New York: Wiley.

Koeske, R. D., & Koeske, G. F. (1989). Working and nonworking students: Roles, support, and well-being. *Journal of Social Work Education, 25,* 244–256.

Krahn, H. (1991). Youth employment. In R. Barnhorst & L. C. Johnson (Eds.), *The state of the child in Ontario* (pp. 139–159). Toronto, Ontario, Canada: Oxford University Press.

Ku, L., Sonenstein, F. L., & Pleck, J. H. (1993). Neighborhood, family, and work: Influences on the premarital behaviors of adolescent males. *Social Forces, 72,* 479–503.

Lillydahl, J. H. (1990). Academic achievement and part-time employment of high school students. *Journal of Economic Education, 2,* 307–316.

Loughlin, C. A., & Barling, J. (1998). Teenagers' part-time employment and their work-related attitudes and aspirations. *Journal of Organizational Behavior, 19,* 197–207.

Manning, W. D. (1990). Parenting employed teenagers. *Youth and Society, 22,* 184–200.

Markel, K. S., & Frone, M. R. (1998). Job characteristics, work-school conflict, and academic outcomes: Testing a structural model. *Journal of Applied Psychology, 83,* 277–287.

Marsh, H. W. (1991). Employment during high school: Character building or a subversion of academic goal? *Sociology of Education, 64,* 172–189.

Meyer, K. A. (1987). The work commitment of adolescents: Progressive attachment to the work force. *Career Development Quarterly, 36,* 140–147.

Meyer, R. H., & Wise, D. A. (1982). High school preparation and early labor force experience. In R. B. Freeman & D. A. Wise (Eds.), *The youth labor market problem: Its nature, causes, and consequences* (pp. 277–347). Chicago: University of Chicago Press.

Miller, J., & Yung, S. (1990). The role of allowances in adolescent socialization. *Youth and Society, 22,* 137–159.

Mortimer, J. T., & Finch, M. D. (1986). The effects of part-time work on adolescent self-concept and achievement. In K. M. Borman & J. Reisman (Eds.), *Becoming a worker* (pp. 66–89). Norwood, NJ: Ablex.

Mortimer, J. T., Finch, M. D., Dennehy, K., Lee, C., & Beebe, T. (1994). Work experience in adolescence. *Journal of Vocational Education Research, 19,* 39–70.

Mortimer, J. T., Finch, M. D., Ryu, S., Shanahan, M. J., & Call, K. T. (1996). The effects of work intensity on adolescent mental health, achievement, and behavioral adjustment: New evidence from a prospective study. *Child Development, 67,* 1243–1261.

Mortimer, J. T., Finch, M. D., Shanahan, M., & Ryu, S. (1992a). Work experience, mental health, and behavioral adjustment in adolescence. *Journal of Research on Adolescence, 2,* 25–57.

Mortimer, J. T., Finch, M. D., Shanahan, M., & Ryu, S. (1992b). Adolescent work history and behavioral adjustment. *Journal of Research on Adolescence, 2,* 59–80.

Mortimer, J. T., & Johnson, M. K. (1997, August). *Adolescent work and the transition to adulthood.* Paper presented at the annual meeting of the American Sociological Association, Toronto, Ontario, Canada.

Mortimer, J. T., Pimentel, E. E., Ryu, S., Nash, K., & Lee, C. (1996). Part-time work and occupational value formation in adolescence. *Social Forces, 74,* 1405–1418.

Mortimer, J. T., & Shanahan, M. J. (1994). Adolescent work experience and family relationships. *Work and Occupations, 21,* 369–384.

Mortimer, J. T., Shanahan, M. J., & Ryu, S. (1994). The effects of adolescent employment on school-related orientation and behavior. In R. K. Silbereisen & E. Todt (Eds.), *Adolescence in context: The interplay of family, school, peers, and work in adjustment* (pp. 304–326). New York: Springer-Verlag.

Parker, D. L., Carl, W. R., French, L. R., & Martin, F. B. (1994). Characteristics of adolescent work injuries reported to the Minnesota department of labor and industry. *American Journal of Public Health, 84,* 606–611.

Phillips, S., & Sandstrom, K. L. (1990). Parental attitudes toward youth work. *Youth and Society, 22,* 160–183.

Ruggiero, M., Greenberger, E., & Steinberg, L. D. (1982). Occupational deviance among adolescent workers. *Youth and Society, 13,* 423–448.

Ruhm, C. J. (1995). The extent and consequences of high school employment. *Journal of Labor Research, 16,* 293–303.

Schill, W. J., McCartin, R., & Meyer, K. A. (1985). Youth employment: Its relationship to academic and family variables. *Journal of Vocational Behavior, 26,* 155–163.

Shanahan, M. J., Elder, G. H., Jr., Burchinal, M., & Conger, R. D. (1996a). Adolescent earnings and relationships with parents: The work-family nexus in urban and rural ecologies. In J. T. Mortimer & M. D. Finch (Eds.), *Adolescents, work, and family: An intergenerational development analysis* (pp. 97–128). Thousand Oaks, CA: Sage.

Shanahan, M. J., Elder, G. H., Jr., Burchinal, M., & Conger, R. D. (1996b). Adolescent paid labor and relationships with parents: Early work-family linkages. *Child Development, 67,* 2183–2200.

Shanahan, M. J., Finch, M., Mortimer, J. T., & Ryu, S. (1991). Adolescent work experience and depressive affect. *Social Psychology Quarterly, 54,* 299–317.

Steel, L. (1991). Early work experience among white and non-white youths: Implications for subsequent enrollment and employment. *Youth and Society, 22,* 419–447.

Steinberg, L. D. (1982). Jumping off the work experience bandwagon. *Journal of Youth and Adolescence, 11,* 183–205.

Steinberg, L. D. (1991). Adolescent transitions and alcohol and other drug use prevention. In E. N. Goplerud (Ed.), *Preventing adolescent drug use: From theory to practice* (pp. 13–51). Rockville, MD: Office for Substance Abuse Prevention.

Steinberg, L. D., & Dornbusch, S. M. (1991). Negative correlates of part-time employment during adolescence: Replication and elaboration. *Developmental Psychology, 27,* 304–313.

Steinberg, L. D., Fegley, S., & Dornbusch, S. M. (1993). Negative impact of part-time work on adolescent adjustment. *Developmental Psychology, 29,* 171–180.

Steinberg, L. D., Greenberger, E., Garduque, L., & McAuliffe, S. (1982). High school students in the labor force: Some costs and benefits to schooling and learning. *Educational Evaluation and Policy Analysis, 4,* 363–372.

Steinberg, L. D., Greenberger, E., Garduque, L., Ruggiero, M., & Vaux, A. (1982). Effects of working on adolescent development. *Developmental Psychology, 18,* 385–395.

Steinberg, L. D., Greenberger, E., Vaux, A., & Ruggiero, M. (1981). Early work experience: Effects on adolescent occupational socialization. *Youth and Society, 12,* 403–422.

Steitz, J. A., & Owen, T. P. (1992). School activities and work: Effects on adolescent self-esteem. *Adolescence, 27,* 37–50.

Stern, D., & Nakata, Y. (1989). Characteristics of high school students' paid jobs, and employment experience after graduation. In D. Stern & D. Eichorn (Eds.), *Adolescence and work: Influences of social structure, labor markets, and culture* (pp. 189–223). Hillsdale, NJ: Erlbaum.

Stern, D., Stone, J. R., III, Hopkins, C., & McMillion, M. (1990). Quality of students' work experience and orientation toward work. *Youth and Society, 22,* 263–282.

Stevens, C. J., Puchtell, L. A., Ryu, S., & Mortimer, J. T. (1992). Adolescent work and boys' and girls' orientations to the future. *Sociological Quarterly, 33,* 153–169.

Sunter, D. (1992). Juggling school and work. *Perspectives on Labour and Income, 4,* 15–21.

Vondracek, F. W. (1994). Vocational identity development in adolescence. In R. K. Silbereisen & E. Todt (Eds.), *Adolescence in context: The interplay of family, school, peers, and work in adjustment* (pp. 285–303). New York: Springer-Verlag.

Warr, P. (1987). *Work, unemployment, and mental health.* New York: Oxford University Press.

Warren, J. R., & LePore, P. C. (1996, August). *Employment during high school: Consequences for students' academic achievements, aspirations, and orientations.* Paper presented at the annual meeting of the American Sociological Association, New York, NY.

Werner, E. E. (1989). Adolescents and work: A longitudinal perspective on gender and cultural variability. In D. Stern & D. Eichorn (Eds.), *Adolescence and work: Influences of social structure, labor markets, and culture* (pp. 159–186). Hillsdale, NJ: Erlbaum.

Yamoor, C. M., & Mortimer, J. T. (1990). Age and gender differences in the effects of employment on adolescent achievement and well-being. *Youth and Society, 22,* 225–240.

Zapf, D., Dormann, C., & Frese, M. (1996). Longitudinal studies in organizational stress research: A review of the literature with reference to methodological issues. *Journal of Occupational Health Psychology, 1,* 145–169.

6

Child Labor and Exploitation

Chaya S. Piotrkowski and Joanne Carrubba

Child labor[1] refers to "economic activities carried out by persons less than 15 years of age" (International Labour Organization [ILO], 264th Session, 1995). *Economic activity* includes the production of goods and services, whether intended for the market, for exchange, or for consumption. The ILO now estimates that 250 million children worldwide,[2] ages 5–14 years old are working, half of them full-time ("U.N. sharply increases," 1996). Unlike adults who may be able to organize to protect themselves from harmful working conditions, children are easy to exploit and abuse not only because they are compliant and unlikely to complain about their working conditions, but also because they lack the power to change their working conditions or to negotiate the terms of their employment (Grootaert & Kanbur, 1995; UNICEF, 1997; U.S. Department of Labor, 1995). Consequently, many

---

[1] The term *child labor* sometimes is used to denote any economic activity by those under ages 16 or 18. Here we use the international standard adopted by the International Labour Organization (ILO) Convention 138 on the Minimum Age for Admission to Employment.

[2] Systematic information regarding the number of working children is not available. The great majority are found in the informal sector of the economy (ILO, 264th Session, 1995; Siddiqi & Patrinos, 1995), making the collection of prevalence data especially difficult.

work under illegal, deplorable, and dangerous conditions that seriously threaten their physical and mental health, their psychosocial development, and their education (Bequele & Myers, 1995; UNICEF, 1997). Child labor is harmful when it interferes with healthy development by imposing developmentally inappropriate physical, social, or psychological demands on children; when it directly exposes children to noxious conditions that harm them physically or psychologically; when it interferes with education; or when it is detrimental to children's full social and psychological development (UNICEF, 1997). Under these conditions, child labor violates Article 32 of the Convention on the Rights of the Child,[3] which recognizes that children have the right to protection from "economic exploitation and from performing any work that is likely to be hazardous or to interfere with the child's education, or to be harmful to the child's health or physical, mental, spiritual, moral or social development" (ILO, 1991, p. 209). Children are especially vulnerable to dangerous or stressful working conditions because they are emotionally, physically, and cognitively immature.

This chapter focuses on child labor that is directly harmful or adversely affects the psychosocial development or education of children under the age of 15. Although it also may be injurious, we omit a discussion of *light work*,[4] or work that children do for their families in households or on farms. We begin with a discussion of child labor abuses in developing countries and then focus on the problem of child labor in the United States. Our goals are to portray the face of the problem, not its extent, and to discuss the likely impact of child labor on children's physical and mental health, their psychosocial development, and their school performance.

By emphasizing child labor in the United States, we hope to demonstrate that abuses exist even in wealthy countries, where children are

---

[3] Entered into international law in 1990, as of this writing, only two countries (the United States and Somalia) have not ratified the Convention.

[4] *Light work* is broadly conceptualized as work that is not likely to harm children's health or development or to prejudice their attendance in school or in a training program or to interfere with their capacity to benefit from instruction received. It is allowed under certain conditions from the age of 12 or 13 (Sinclair & Trah, 1991). Currently, there are no accepted standards for what constitutes light work (World Health Organization [WHO], 1987).

considered to be "priceless" (Zelizer, 1985) and where child labor purportedly no longer exists. International attention has focused almost exclusively on child labor abuses in developing countries. It is a myth, however, to think that child labor has been entirely abolished in industrialized countries (UNICEF, 1997). In Turkey, which is the only industrialized country to conduct a recent survey of child labor, 8.3% of children ages 6–14 were economically active (ILO, 264th Session, 1995). It is estimated that between 15% and 26% of 11-year-olds are working in the United Kingdom (UNICEF, 1997). In wealthy nations, most child workers come from ethnic minority or immigrant groups. In Canada they may be Asian children; in the United States they may be from Latin America or Asia; in northern Europe, they are likely to be African or Turkish.

THE FACE OF EXPLOITIVE CHILD LABOR

Systematic research on child labor is almost nonexistent (Kruse, 1997; Richter & Jacobs, 1991). Therefore, we draw heavily on evidence from limited injury data, case reports, anecdotal journalistic accounts, qualitative studies, reports of advocacy groups, and government documents that, themselves, are limited. Typically, sampling is not systematic and data are incomplete, so that conclusions drawn from these sources must be considered tentative. Despite the limitations of the available information, it provides a starting point for developing an understanding of the consequences of abusive child labor practices for children under the age of 15. Sometimes data for 15-year-olds are reported when they are aggregated with younger children.

Child Labor in Developing Countries

Child labor is most common in the informal economies of developing countries, particularly those of Asia, Africa, and Latin America (Bequele, 1991; ILO, 264th Session, 1995; Leipziger & Sibharwal, 1995; UNICEF, 1997). It is estimated that more than 50% of child laborers are found in South Asia and Southeast Asia. Rates are highest in Africa, where one child in three is engaged in some sort of economic activity. In Latin

America, an estimated 15–20% of children work, and are paid only a fraction of what adults receive for comparable work (Grootaert & Kanbur, 1995; ILO, 264th Session, 1995; UNICEF, 1997; U.S. Department of Labor, 1995).

Child workers typically are found in agriculture, working long hours sometimes under inhumane and hazardous conditions for little or no pay, often as part of a family unit (U.S. Department of Labor, 1995). In some developing countries, children make up nearly one third of the agricultural workforce (UNICEF, 1997). Although specific prevalence data are not available, the evidence indicates that large numbers of children labor in the fields. For example, in Zimbabwe, some children work 60 hours per week picking cotton or coffee. In Indonesia, children work in the tobacco plantations. In Nepal, children work on tea estates, some for up to 14 hours per day. In Thailand, children work in the sugar and rubber plantations. Migration from rural to urban areas also is increasing the rate of child labor in urban areas of developing countries (Siddiqi & Patrinos, 1995), where it is found mainly in the trade and service industries, especially in domestic service, restaurants, and street vending, and to some extent in small-scale manufacturing of carpets, garments, and furniture (U.S. Department of Labor, 1994a). Rapid urbanization, population growth, and poverty also have resulted in a proliferation of so-called "street children" (UNICEF, 1997). For example, in the Philippines, early adolescents comb the streets as scavengers. Street workers also shine shoes, wash cars, carry luggage, sell trinkets, and so forth.

In its most extreme form, the exploitation of working children takes the form of slavery, or forced or bonded labor, still practiced in South Asia, Southeast Asia, and West Africa (U.S. Department of Labor, 1995). Children's work may be pledged by parents for payment of a debt, or for collateral, they may be kidnapped and imprisoned in brothels or sweatshops, or they may be given away or sold by their families (U.S. Department of Labor, 1995; UNICEF, 1997). Typically, their servitude never succeeds in eliminating the debt, they receive little or no pay, and they have little control over their lives. They are virtual prisoners.

The most widespread but invisible form of forced child labor is the use of domestic servants in the homes of affluent families throughout Asia, Africa, Latin America, and parts of southern Europe (U.S. Department of Labor, 1995; UNICEF, 1997). They are the world's "most forgotten children." Millions of children (usually girls from poor, rural families who may be as young as 6 or 10) are recruited, kidnapped, sold, or even adopted into domestic service. These children may sleep on floors, eat leftover scraps, and wear cast-off clothing. Few attend school, and they may be almost completely isolated. Forced child labor also is found in the agriculture, carpet and textile manufacture, quarrying and brick-making industries in Asia, Latin America, and Africa (ILO, 264th Session, 1995; U.S. Department of Labor, 1995). For example, according to the ILO and U.S. Department of Labor, in parts of India, children are kidnapped, lured away, or pledged by their parents for small sums of money to work in the carpet industry, where many are kept in captivity, working under deplorable conditions.

Child labor in the sex industry is a particularly egregious example of forced child labor (U.S. Department of Labor, 1995). Children are tricked, enticed, kidnapped, or sold by their parents into prostitution. Village loan sharks may act as procurers for city brothels, and children may be trafficked across borders. Sex tourist trades exist in Brazil, the Dominican Republic, Thailand, Africa, and elsewhere, but these children also serve local men. An estimated one million girls are lured or forced into sex work, and the numbers are increasing, with a growing demand for ever younger children, particularly in Asia (UNICEF, 1997; U.S. Department of Labor, 1995).

Although these distressing examples may shock our moral sensibilities, they underscore the extreme conditions under which many young children labor and the seriousness of the problems they face.

Child Labor in the United States

Like other industrialized countries, the United States has a long history of child labor, which was considered normal until recently (Zelizer, 1985). After several failed attempts to pass child labor legislation at the federal level, the Fair Labor Standards Act (FLSA) was passed in 1938. The FLSA restricts the ages, hours, and settings in which children under

18 years of age can be employed, particularly on school days.[5] All work on family farms is exempt from the FLSA. State laws generally are more restrictive than federal regulations.

Because of strong enforcement of the FLSA and generally favorable economic conditions, child labor outside of agriculture was not a widespread problem until the 1980s when violations increased (Committee on Environmental Health, 1995; General Accounting Office [GAO], 1990; Golodner, 1994). In the U.S. Department of Labor's 1- to 3-day "sweeps," Operation Child Watch identified more than 500 children under the age of 14 working under prohibited conditions (Baker, 1990). Based on data from 42 states, from 1983 to 1989, there was a 145% increase in the number of minors employed illegally, particularly in restaurants and grocery stores (GAO, 1990).

Data regarding the prevalence of child labor among children under 15 years of age are not systematically collected in the United States (NIOSH, 1997). There is evidence, however, that the employment of children has risen dramatically since 1940. It is estimated that about 30% of 14- and 15-year-olds worked in 1993, compared to 5% in 1940 (Halperin, 1993). In Washington state, 28% of eighth grade students surveyed reported having a part-time job during the school year (Miller, 1995). Extrapolating from the limited data, Kruse (1997) estimates that 683,000 children ages 12 and 13 are employed in an average week in nonagricultural jobs; many work in violation of child labor laws. Using multiple sources of data (1979–1997), Kruse also estimates that 73,000 14- and 15-year-olds and 33,700 children under age 14 are employed in violation of child labor laws in an average week, excluding prostitution, drug trafficking, and other such activities.

---

[5] In nonagricultural industries, hazardous work is not permitted for those under the age of 18. In these industries, the minimum working age is 16, although 14- and 15-year-old children may be employed in specified occupations, for limited hours. Fourteen-year-olds may deliver newspapers, ring up and bag groceries, wash cars, pump gas, and stock supermarket shelves (Belville, Pollack, Godbold, & Landrigan, 1993). Minors under 14 may not be employed in nonfarm occupations. Fourteen- and fifteen-year-olds may work a 40-hour week (up to 8 hr per day) when school is not in session, 3 hr a day after school, for a weekly maximum of 18 hr in a school week. They may work no later than 7 p.m. on school nights and no later than 9 p.m. during the summer (General Accounting Office, 1990). Work in agriculture is exempt from many of these provisions. For example, hazardous work in agriculture is prohibited only until age 16, and all work on family farms is totally excepted (Beyer, 1994).

Although child labor for children under age 15 generally has not been a focus of attention, the limited case reports and injury and fatality data suggest there is cause for concern. For example, in Maryland, the leg of a 13-year-old boy was torn off by a blowing machine while he was working in a car wash (Lantos, 1992). In 1980, 892 workers' compensation claims for work-related injuries were filed by 13- and 14-year-old children in only 24 states reporting these data (Halperin, 1993). In 1986, 7.4% of the workers' compensation awards made to children in New York state went to those under the age of 14 (Pollack, Landrigan, & Mallino, 1990). In the period from 1980 to 1987, 14-year-olds in New York state averaged 8.2 workers' compensation awards to minors per 10,000, with boys having higher average rates (10.6 per 10,000) than girls (4.2 per 10,000) (Belville, Pollack, Godbold, & Landrigan, 1993). Moreover, 14- and 15-year-olds were more likely than older adolescents to experience permanent disabilities. A review of workers' compensation claims in Washington state from 1988 to 1991, indicated that 12% of the work-related injuries or illnesses to minors occurred among 11- to 15-year-olds (Miller, 1995). These estimates are conservative because of underreporting. In addition, low-income youths are more likely than those in high-income families to work in hazardous occupations (GAO, 1991), suggesting that these youngsters may suffer a disproportionately high number of these injuries.

Children also are dying unnecessarily at work. From 1984 to 1987, the Occupational Safety and Health Administration investigated 14 work-related deaths of children under age 15, excluding most transportation accidents, work-related homicides, and industries regulated by other agencies (Suruda & Halperin, 1991). In 1984 and 1985, three work-related deaths of children ages 12–13 were recorded (Halperin, 1993). In 1988, an 11-year-old boy was killed when he became entangled in a box crusher while working in a supermarket (Pollack et al., 1990). In 1994, 25 work-related deaths of children under age 16 were identified through the Census of Fatal Occupational Injuries (Toscano, 1995). In 1995, a 14-year-old suffocated inside a storage bin when helping to package dried beans while working for a packing company in North Dakota ("Work safe," 1996). Estimates of work-related fatalities in children are likely to be conservative because data on those under 16 are not systematically collected (NIOSH, 1997).

Young children also work in the less visible sectors of the economy. For example, the children of immigrants, particularly those who are undocumented, are highly vulnerable to exploitation in sweatshops (Committee on Environmental Health, 1995). Child prostitutes represent another neglected group of child laborers (U.S. Department of Labor, 1995). In this chapter we focus on two other groups of children: migrant farmworker children in the formal economy and inner-city children working in the drug trade in the informal economy. The lack of systematic research and adequate prevalence data on these two populations permits only a skeletal outline of the problems they face.

Migrant Farmworker Children

Agriculture has surpassed mining as the most dangerous occupation (Committee on Environmental Health, 1995). Agriculture is also the least regulated sector of the U.S. economy and is one of the few industries where children may engage in work typically performed by adults. Although reliable data are unavailable (Kruse, 1997), it is likely that work by children under the age of 14 is common (DHHS, 1997).

There has been some research on the risk to children and youth working on farms (e.g., Cogbill, Busch, & Stiers, 1985; Swanson, Sachs, Dahlgren, & Tinguely, 1987), but data on migrant farmworker children are scant (Martin, 1994). Although there are no uniform definitions, in general, migrant farmworkers are those who travel to look for crop work. The vast majority are from Latin America (U.S. Department of Labor, 1994b). It is estimated that about 25,000 children of migrant farmers (aged 10 to 15 years) who are in the United States also work in the fields (R. Mines, personal communication, May 7, 1997). Even children as young as 6 years old work in the fields (Buirski, 1994).

Children who work on farms are afforded only limited protection under the FLSA. Federal law permits a child as young as 12 to work on a commercial farm if his or her parent also is employed there (Beyer, 1994), although state laws may be more restrictive. According to Mull (1993), migrant farmworker children may work on farms even if they are younger than 10 years old. Children 10 and 11 years old may work

136

without parental consent as hand-harvesters if the farm obtains a waiver from the Department of Labor, and those under 12 years old can be paid less than the minimum wage with written consent from a parent. They may work more than 40 hours per week, even during the school year, and work an unlimited number of hours before school. Those under 14 years old may even use knives and machetes and operate machinery (Mull, 1993).

Inner-City Children in the Drug Trade

An important part of the informal cash economy in many inner-city communities is *hustling*, a complex, money-making activity that includes a willingness to take advantage of whatever economic opportunities exist in a scarce economic environment, even if the wider society defines these activities as illegal (Whitehead, Peterson, & Kaljee, 1994). Involvement in the drug trade is one form of hustling to which children are introduced when they are quite young (Williams & Kornblum, 1985). Children 9 and 10 years old are employed to warn dealers when police are approaching, earning as much as $100 per day (Leviton, Schindler, & Orleans, 1994; Pogrebin, 1995; Williams & Kornblum, 1985). Slightly older children serve as runners to transport money or drugs, eventually becoming drug dealers. Inciardi and Pottieger (1991) found that many of the crime-involved youth they studied in Miami, Florida began working for crack dealers in their neighborhoods while they were in grade school. Williams and Kornblum (1985) described a "crew"[6] in Harlem which consisted of about 200 children 8 to 12 years old who collected guns and sold drugs.

Although the vast majority of inner-city children do not engage in drug trafficking, studies of urban neighborhoods in Washington, DC and Baltimore, Maryland indicate that from 5% of boys in the sixth and seventh grades to 13% of boys in the ninth and tenth grades are involved in drug trafficking (Stanton & Galbraith, 1994). Stanton and Galbraith conclude that approximately 1 in 10 African American pre- and early adolescent boys and 1 in 20 girls report having engaged in

---

[6] *Crews* are formally structured groups of poor youth who come together to fulfill a need for money, recognition, protection, and success (Williams & Kornblum, 1985).

drug trafficking. The percentages of children intending to traffick in drugs is even higher, especially among those already involved in trafficking (Li & Feigelman, 1994). Although White youth also engage in drug trafficking (e.g., Inciardi & Pottieger, 1991), the limited research has focused on African American boys, who are more visible to the juvenile justice system (Leviton et. al., 1994).

CONSEQUENCES OF CHILD LABOR

There is no systematic body of research on the effects of child labor on the health, psychosocial development, and the school performance of children under 15 years of age. Therefore, to develop a preliminary understanding of these consequences, we look to case reports and the clinical literature on child maltreatment. Because children's physical development is closely linked to their cognitive and psychosocial development, we first consider the effects of exploitive child labor on children's physical health and safety.

Children's Physical Health and Safety

Jobs that are safe for adults are not necessarily safe or appropriate for children, whose bodies are still growing and maturing (NIOSH, 1997; World Health Organization [WHO], 1987). Tools, equipment, and protective gear designed for adults may not protect children because they are physically smaller; because they lack the cognitive skills, experience, and safety training to understand the risks they face; and because they are powerless to protect themselves. For example, in the bangle industry of India, in which children under 14 years old are estimated to be one quarter of the workforce, children carry molten glass on rods that extend just a few feet from their bodies and draw molten glass from furnaces that their arms almost touch because they are so small (UNICEF, 1997). In agriculture, children cut cane with machetes, putting them at constant risk of mutilation (UNICEF, 1997). Children also are especially vulnerable to injuries from heavy machinery (Pollack et al., 1990). Another study by Pollack, Landrigan, and Mallino (as cited in Bequele & Myers, 1995) indicated that 20% of farmworker children surveyed in New York state, some as young as 12 years old, had driven tractors as part of their work. Additionally, two 14-year-old migrant farmworker children in Washington state died of tractor injuries. One fell asleep while working late hours and died when a tractor crushed his head; the other died of severe head injuries sustained in a tractor accident.

Many child laborers are exposed to toxic substances including known carcinogens and neurotoxins with as yet unknown short- and long-term consequences for their health (Landrigan & Carlson, 1995). Children may be more vulnerable to environmental toxins because they are developing rapidly, and developmental processes may easily be disrupted and compromised. They also have a longer time to develop chronic diseases resulting from early exposures to toxins, and they have greater exposures to toxins because of their size and patterns of food ingestion.

The particular toxins to which children are exposed vary by industry. For example, in the Sivakasi region of India, some 80,000 children—mostly girls, some as young as 5 years old—are employed in small factories making handmade matches, where they handle toxic chemicals and work up to 60 hours a week ("Little match girls," 1994; UNICEF, 1997). Children in the coal mines of Colombia breathe in coal dust; in porcelain and earthenware factories they breathe in silica dust; in the lock industry they inhale noxious fumes; in the brass factories they breathe dust used in polishing brass. In Tanzania, children experience nicotine poisoning from harvesting tobacco (UNICEF, 1997).

Children who work in agriculture are regularly exposed to pesticides, volatile organic compounds, such as fuel, airborne irritants, noise, vibration, and noxious gases. Of the farmworker children interviewed in New York state, Pollack et al. (as cited in Bequele & Myers, 1995) report that almost half had worked in fields still wet with pesticide, one third had been sprayed either directly or indirectly while working in the fields, and one third of the camps where the children lived had been sprayed directly or by drift. In Colombia's flower-export farms, children are exposed to pesticides banned in industrial countries (UNICEF, 1997). Little is known about the neurophysiological, behavioral, and cognitive effects of pesticides on children's development, because pesticide safety standards are predicated on the bodily size of adults (Beyer, 1994). Illnesses from such exposures are likely, and include lung cancer, mesothelioma, leukemia, neurological impairments, asthma, and behavioral disorders (Committee on Environmental Health, 1995; Landrigan & Belville, 1993). For example, skin, eye, respiratory, and neurological problems can develop in children exposed to agrochemicals in processing crops such as sisal (UNICEF, 1997).

Child laborers are also exposed to unsanitary conditions. Only one third of migrant farmworkers are guaranteed the right to drinking water, to hand-washing water, and access to toilet facilities in the field (U.S. Department of Labor, 1994b). Increased rates of parasitic infections, constant danger from infectious diseases such as hepatitis, measles, conjunctivitis, and impetigo, and lowered life expectancies are the norm for the migrant farmworker population in the United States (Mull, 1993; Winters-Smith & Larner, 1992). In developing countries, children who scavenge may be especially susceptible to developing ulcers; they also cut themselves and become susceptible to tetanus (UNICEF, 1997).

Children also may suffer musculoskeletal problems from carrying excessively heavy loads and working in difficult positions. In Colombia, small coal mines employ young boys to reach deposits that full-size adults cannot reach ("Child miners," 1994). These boys are often up by 4 a.m., working 8 hours or more below ground, hauling sacks of coal up narrow tunnels. Children working in the carpet industry in India may work at looms located in small earthen shacks, where they also live and sleep (U.S. Department of Labor, 1994a). These children have been known to lose part of their eyesight and to have deformed backs due to sitting for long periods in cramped quarters. In some factories, children crouch on their toes from morning until dusk, severely stunting their growth (UNICEF, 1997).

The health consequences of drug trafficking also are extremely serious (Moore, 1995). Drug trafficking appears to be associated with an increased likelihood of subsequent drug use and therefore risk of HIV infection (Dembo, Hughes, Jackson, & Mieczkowski, 1993; Li, Stanton,

Feigelman, & Black, 1994). Drug trafficking also is associated with greater risk of violent death. Young African American male children involved in drug trafficking are more likely to carry weapons such as bats, guns, and knives than those with no drug involvement (Black & Ricardo, 1994). Homicide is the second most common cause of death for African American youths ages 10–14, and drug trafficking is a cause of death among adolescents and young adults (Stanton & Galbraith, 1994). Adolescent drug dealers acknowledge that death is a high risk in their line of work (Dembo et al., 1993), but children's sense of invulnerability may make them minimize the risks to themselves. Street workers in developing countries also may be led into the world of drug trafficking, burglary, and prostitution, subcultures known for violence (UNICEF, 1997). Similarly, child prostitutes face unwanted pregnancies, drug addiction, sexually transmitted diseases, HIV and AIDS (U.S. Department of Labor, 1995; UNICEF, 1997).

Maltreatment and Children's Mental Health

Child maltreatment has been linked to child labor, particularly bonded labor. Abusive child labor practices are a form of extrafamilial child maltreatment (Doek, 1991) that may include physical, sexual, and emotional abuse. Sexual abuse is a fact of everyday life for child prostitutes. It has also been documented in other contexts, such as the carpet factories of Nepal (UNICEF, 1997) and among child laborers in Pakistan (Ahmed, 1991). Physical abuse is also not uncommon. In Bangkok, 31 children were rescued from a sweatshop producing paper cups. Many had been so badly beaten and malnourished that they had to be carried out of the small room in which they worked (Golodner, 1994). Children working in the carpet industry in India have been beaten to death for making mistakes, have been branded to show ownership, have been beaten with iron rods, hung upside down, and poked with scissors for infractions such as going to the toilet without permission (Bequele & Myers, 1995; U.S. Department of Labor, 1994a). Child domestic servants who are deprived of the support and nurturance of their families and isolated in households are particularly vulnerable to emotional, sexual, and physical abuse (UNICEF, 1997). In Dhaka, for example, child do-

141

mestic servants see their parents once every 9 months or less. They are exposed to emotional and sexual abuse, work extremely long hours, and experience humiliation from the children of their employers. Child domestics may even be starved and tortured (U.S. Department of Labor, 1995).

Unfortunately, no systematic research exists on the mental health consequences of the maltreatment of working children. Existing research on the psychological effects of child maltreatment focuses almost entirely on intrafamilial physical abuse or neglect and, in the case of sexual abuse, the distinction between extra- and intrafamilial abuse is not clear.

Finkelhor and Browne's (1986) conceptualization of the underlying dynamics that cause psychological symptoms and damage from sexual abuse is especially useful in helping to identify the potential mental health effects of the extrafamilial maltreatment of working children. The first two dynamics they describe—sexual traumatization and stigmatization—are particular to sexual abuse. Traumatic sexualization is the process whereby a child's sexuality, both feelings and attitudes, are shaped in developmentally inappropriate ways. We would anticipate such traumatization to occur among child prostitutes and other child workers subject to sexual abuse. Symptoms would probably include sexual preoccupations, compulsive sexual behavior, confusion about sexual identity and norms, and negative attitudes toward sex. In the trauma of stigmatization, the shame or guilt children feel may become incorporated into their self-image. In addition, children may be stigmatized by others, because of powerful religious or cultural taboos. Consistent with this notion, child prostitutes who return home may find themselves treated as outcasts and may return to prostitution after being rejected by their families (UNICEF, 1997). Symptoms of stigmatization include guilt, shame, lowered self-esteem, isolation, drug or alcohol abuse, criminal involvement, self-mutilation, and suicide.

The traumas of betrayal and powerlessness are two additional dynamics relevant for understanding the effects of maltreatment on child laborers. According to Finkelhor and Browne (1986), children feel betrayed when they learn that those on whom they are vitally dependent have harmed them by treating them callously or by not protecting them. We would expect that the trauma of betrayal would be especially likely to occur among children who are maltreated as a result of being bonded by their parents in payment of a debt, who are sent away from home to work as domestic servants, or who are forced to work in situations where they are abused to help augment family income. Symptoms of betrayal can include grief and depression, mistrust, excessive dependency, anger and hostility, and isolation.

The trauma of powerlessness contributes to children's feeling utterly helpless to escape abuse. Powerlessness is reinforced when children recognize they cannot halt the abuse, and instead, are trapped. As Becker-Lausen, Sanders, and Chinsky noted, "Children who are presented repeatedly with harsh and painful experience may come to expect life to be difficult and may develop a sense of hopelessness" (p. 567, 1995). The trauma of powerlessness would be an especially significant factor where children are essentially enslaved or cannot escape their abusive work situations. Symptoms of powerlessness include fear, anxiety, diminished self-efficacy, nightmares, phobias, depression, vulnerability to victimization, aggressive behavior, delinquency, and—as adults—eating disorders and dissociation. Physically abused children are also especially likely to show aggression, noncompliance, and other externalizing behaviors (e.g., Malinosky-Rummell & Hansen, 1993).

Emotional abuse is a core component of physical and sexual abuse and may occur by itself. It includes acts that degrade, corrupt, isolate, exploit, or mis-socialize children (Hart & Brassard, 1987). These actions are committed by those who have power over a child. Thus, abusive child labor practices typically involve the emotional abuse of children, regardless of whether physical or sexual abuse is also present. Emotional abuse is likely to have a particularly damaging effect on the self-esteem of children, because during their school-age years children consolidate their sense of worthiness and incorporate it into their self-concept (Zigler & Finn-Stevenson, 1987).

Results of research on the mental health correlates and long-term consequences of intrafamilial child maltreatment are consistent with these consequences of abuse (e.g., Becker-Lausen, Sanders, & Chinsky,

1995; Lamphear, 1985; Kendall-Tackett, Williams, & Finkelhor, 1993; Malinosky-Rummell & Hansen, 1993; Mullen, Martin, Anderson, Romans, & Herbison, 1996). Anecdotal evidence from observations of child laborers points to similar symptoms. Child domestic workers, who are especially at risk for sexual, physical, or emotional abuse because they are socially isolated, have been described as "cowed," "timid," and "listless" (UNICEF, 1997). Studies of child domestics in Kenya and Haiti indicate they suffer from feelings of inferiority. They also exhibit symptoms of depression, regressive behaviors, withdrawal, passivity, fear, anxiety, as well as sleep and eating disorders (UNICEF, 1997; WHO, 1987). Attempts at suicide also have been documented (Bequele & Myers, 1995). Rosario (as cited in Bequele & Myers, 1995) describes the psychological status of ragpickers in Thailand. These children are deeply insecure, hostile, and rebellious, and engage in self-destructive behavior.

Psychosocial Development

Even when child laborers do not experience overt maltreatment, the psychological consequences may nonetheless be serious. As children enter adolescence, they begin to consider their occupational futures, but this process may be compromised by child labor. In their study of employment among adolescents in the United States, Greenberger and Steinberg (1986) note that going to work every day in a monotonous job may deaden a young person's imagination, curiosity, and inner life, limiting motivation and mental exploration. Similarly, child laborers who work extremely long hours in monotonous work that requires attention because it is exacting or dangerous lack sufficient opportunities to exercise independent thought and to have an inner life of possibilities (WHO, 1987). Consistent with this notion, Ahmed (1991) found that the ambitions of the majority of child laborers studied were extremely limited: Most aspired to work in the same job they had. Similarly, migrant farmworker children have been observed to be listless and bored, introverted, and fatalistic, and to have feelings of worthlessness (WHO, 1987). In general, observers have noted that many working children display a sense of worthlessness, apathy, and coldness that may reflect stunted development (Bequele & Myers, 1995).

Children's employers may also become significant occupational role models. Direct personal experience is an important factor in shaping occupational knowledge and choices (e.g., DeFleur, 1963; Tittle, 1981). Drug dealers, with their visible signs of achievement, may serve as occupational role models for poor inner-city children and facilitate their transition into the drug trade. Children report frequent exposure to the drug trade, even among neighbors, family members, and friends (Feigelman, Stanton, & Ricardo, 1993; Li & Feigelman, 1994). Li and Feigelman (1994) found that both drug-trafficking and non-drug-trafficking children reported high rates of drug use and drug trafficking among neighbors, friends, and family members. They also found that young African American girls (median age of 11) who reported they expected to sell drugs, perceived drug dealing as "exciting" and drug dealers as "happy," suggesting they served as positive role models for these children. Dealers may also be viewed positively because they are perceived as "kind" and as giving money and gifts (Feigelman et al., 1993).

As children enter adolescence they make advances in moral behavior and social responsibility (Zigler & Finn-Stevenson, 1987). Child workers may be exposed to negative adult role models at a time when they are extremely impressionable, resulting in pseudomaturity and problem behaviors. For example, in the United States, drug trafficking is associated with the co-occurrence of other problem behaviors such as cigarette smoking, alcohol use, and illicit drug use (Inciardi & Pottieger, 1991; Li & Feigelman, 1994). Drug trafficking is also a significant contributor to juvenile arrests (Stanton & Galbraith, 1994). Moreover, boys who begin their criminal careers in late childhood or adolescence face the greatest risk of becoming chronic offenders (Patterson, DeBaryshe, & Ramsey, 1989). Similarly, behavior problems also have been noted among children working on the streets in developing countries, where they may become involved in drug use, criminal activities, and so forth (UNICEF, 1997, WHO, 1987).

Finally, the development of a positive identity and the sense of belonging are important tasks of adolescence (Erikson, 1968). Young African American boys learn that having status and respect as a man comes from their earning capacity and their ability to provide for their families. Insofar as drug trafficking promotes these goals, it also contributes to the development of a "gendered identity" (Leviton et al., 1994; Whitehead et al., 1994; Williams & Kornblum, 1985). The drug trade also may provide youngsters with a sense of "belonging" (Feigelman et al., 1993).

School Performance

Many of the world's child workers cannot attend school because school is not available or because it is too expensive. Where schooling is available, child labor may have serious adverse effects on school performance and on children's ability to develop essential cognitive and literacy skills. Child labor interferes with education in a number of ways. First, it absorbs a great deal of time, particularly when children's full-time labor is forced or necessary for the economic survival of their families, making school attendance difficult. Even when they do attend school, children's work can interfere with performance because they are physically exhausted (UNICEF, 1997). In a study of child laborers in Pakistan, Ahmed (1991) found that children under the age of nine averaged 8.5 hours per day at work, while 9- to 14-year-olds worked on average between 9 and 10 hours. In a study of 62 children employed in small workshops in the Sudan, all but one worked more than 8 hours per day; four worked more than 12 hours per day (WHO, 1987). Of the 400 young street hawkers observed in Nigeria, over 85% worked 6 or more days per week, and one third said they worked more than 6 hours per day. Many tried to combine street work with school.

In the United States, most of the child labor violations identified by the U.S. Department of Labor involved 14- and 15-year-old children working excessive hours, typically in restaurants and grocery stores (Baker, 1990). Anecdotal evidence suggests that many migrant farmworker children work 8 hours per day during the school week, and that many work as many as 4 hours before the school day starts (Mull, 1993). During peak seasons, children may miss school entirely (Martinez & Cranston-Gingras, 1996). Work was cited by more than one third of migrant farmworker students in a high school equivalency program in

Florida as the reason they dropped out of school (Martinez & Cranston-Gingras, 1996). As a result of their work schedules and the move from community to community, farmworker children have high rates of grade retention and age–grade discrepancies (Martinez & Cranston-Gingras, 1996). Their school dropout rate is conservatively estimated at 45%, which is almost twice the national average. In Florida, 85% of migrant farmworker children do not graduate from high school (Winters-Smith & Larner, 1992).

Second, Bequele and Myers (1995) observe that child labor may traumatize children, interfering with their concentration and causing behavioral problems at school. This observation is consistent with research in the United States on the effects of intrafamilial child maltreatment on children's school performance. Studies indicate that physical abuse and neglect represent significant risk factors for poor academic performance, grade repetition, and discipline problems in school (Eckenrode, Laird, & Doris, 1993; Wodarski, Kurtz, Gaudin, & Howing, 1990).

Third, child labor may also undermine the value placed on education. Among teenagers, a primary focus on income and material possessions and negative work socialization has been found to interfere with older students' willingness and ability to participate in the educational process (Greenberger & Steinberg, 1986). Similarly, drug trafficking and street work also are associated with school failure and truancy (Black & Ricardo, 1994; Li & Feigelman, 1994; UNICEF, 1997). By interfering with educational attainment, child labor thus perpetuates a vicious cycle of poverty.

DETERMINANTS OF CHILD LABOR

The specific determinants of child labor are complex and vary by country, but family poverty is widely recognized as a key factor. Some children may become bonded laborers to pay off debts; others work to augment family income and prevent abject poverty. For example, it is estimated that the incidence of poverty in Latin America would rise between 10% and 20% without the income of children (UNICEF, 1997).

Historically, children also have worked in order to manage economic risk (Grootaert & Kanbur, 1995; Zelizer, 1985). In poor households, any interruption of income may be life-threatening. Thus, child labor plays a "self-insurance" role in families' survival strategies.

In the United States, increased family poverty also has contributed to child labor abuses (GAO, 1990).[7] In New York City, The African American and Latino boys and girls under 18 years old who are involved in the sale and distribution of cocaine typically come from families whose income is below the poverty line (Williams, 1989). Among migrant farmworkers, low hourly wages and seasonal unemployment result in an average median income of $5,000 per year (U.S. Department of Labor, 1994b). Securing additional income is a top priority for all family members, so that farmworkers' children must work (Martinez & Cranston-Gingras, 1996; Winters-Smith & Larner, 1992). When adults are paid on the piece-rate system, children increase family wages by helping to pick crops and by carrying bushel baskets to and from the loading trucks (Mull, 1993).

In addition to limited economic and occupational opportunities, lack of access to adequate schooling may be a determinant of child labor (Siddiqi & Patrinos, 1995). For example, in parts of Africa, parents may view work as a preferred option for their children, where education is no longer a route to economic opportunities (Grootaert & Kanbur, 1995). In the United States, "hustling" in the drug trade may be viewed as a viable alternative career path for those who view future occupational alternatives as limited (Moore, 1995; Whitehead et al., 1994). It has been observed that some young drug traffickers may be particularly ambitious youth who are creating their own entrepreneurial opportunities (Leviton et al., 1994; Whitehead et al., 1994). For example, at the age of 14, Max had been involved in the cocaine trade for 3 years; he led a "crew" of youngsters who bought, cut, packaged, and sold cocaine

---

[7]Other factors that may have contributed to increases in child labor abuses in the United States include increased immigration resulting from unstable world conditions due to war and poverty and diminishing wages and employment opportunities for those with limited skills. The generally healthy economy may also have contributed to increases in child labor, for the shortage of adults and teenage workers in some areas may have led some employers to hire 14- and 15-year-olds (GAO, 1990).

on the street (Williams, 1989). Because it is relatively cheap to make and sell per unit, crack offers new entrepreneurial opportunities for poor youth at the same time that decent jobs in manufacturing have declined (Whitehead et al., 1994).

Poverty also may interact with normative developmental changes to encourage children's drug trafficking. In poor communities, there are fewer opportunities for children to take on "light work" that is developmentally appropriate, because cash is limited and people may trade services and help instead of buying them (see Stack, 1974). By offering them opportunities to do small jobs, such as being a "spotter," the drug dealer takes advantage of children's eagerness to participate in the adult world of work.

As children begin to engage in a wider social world, the need for money to facilitate their burgeoning autonomy becomes more salient (Williams & Kornblum, 1985). Affluent White youth work in legitimate jobs in order to purchase popular consumer goods (Greenberger & Steinberg, 1986). In the inner cities, adults compete with adolescents for scarce employment opportunities, whether it be making beds or making hamburgers (Williams & Kornblum, 1985), so that teenagers with financial disadvantages and African American and Hispanic teenagers have substantially lower rates of employment and higher rates of unemployment than White or teenagers with financial advantages (GAO, 1991; Wescott, 1981). The promise of material rewards, including the ability to buy gifts, appears to be an important factor in boys' (and adolescents') drug trafficking and intention to traffick (Black & Ricardo, 1994; Dembo et al., 1993; Feigelman et al., 1993; Li & Feigelman, 1994). Self-worth also may be associated with material possessions (Feigelman et al., 1993). Thus, children and young adolescents—males in particular—become targets for exploitation by drug dealers. Drug trafficking is not necessarily viewed as immoral, but rather as a normal work activity. As one 15-year-old stated, "Even though it might be illegal in the government, it's not illegal on the street. If you live in the neighborhood, it's just like getting a job at McDonald's" (Ricardo, 1994, p. 1056).

Outdated standards regarding hazardous working conditions and lack of enforcement of child labor laws also contribute to child labor abuses (Ahmed, 1991; Beyer, 1994; Goold, 1994). For example, in the United States, the provisions of the FLSA have not been systemically updated to incorporate information about new technologies and hazards (Golodner, 1994; Goold, 1994), and domestic service and agriculture are exempted in many countries. Although most countries have legislation establishing the minimum age of employment and regulating working conditions for children (ILO, 264th Session, 1995),[8] these regulations are sometimes inconsistent and are rarely enforced (Siddiqi & Patrinos, 1995). Many countries are giving no more than lip service to the legal protections available to child laborers (Harvey, 1993). Some countries are even eroding legal protections. Moreover, since many child laborers are essentially "invisible," they are afforded no protection at all.

CONCLUSION

Child labor can result in heightened exposures to environmental toxins, risk of serious injury, premature death, and psychological damage. Child laborers are too young to understand the physical and psychological hazards they face and are too powerless to escape them. Children with limited economic resources and ethnic minorities are particularly at risk for exploitation. At minimum, the gross abuses associated with child labor need to be addressed by governments and advocacy groups.

As attention to the serious problem of child labor abuses in developing countries grows, we should not ignore child labor practices of wealthy countries. There is heightened interest in preventing child labor abuses, particularly injuries, among adolescents in the United States (NIOSH, 1995). But the plight of our youngest workers remains largely unnoticed. Little systematic research exists on migrant farmworker children, on children trafficking drugs in our inner-city neighborhoods, on immigrant children in sweatshops, or on child prostitutes. Therefore, it

---

[8]Typically, the minimum age is 14 or 15 years old, but there are about 30 countries where it is 12 or 13 years old (Grootaert & Kanbur, 1995; Siddiqi & Patrinos, 1995).

is critical that we gather systematic data on the prevalence of child labor for those under 15 years old and on its physical, mental health, psychosocial, and educational consequences, including its long-term effects (see also Richter & Jacobs, 1991). An especially challenging but important effort is to include the largely invisible children working in the informal economy.

The focus on poverty, lack of educational and occupational opportunities, outdated standards, and lax enforcement of child labor laws as determinants of child labor makes it all too easy to ignore the role played by those who benefit from child labor. Included are factory and plantation owners, families that use domestic workers, village loan sharks who procure children for city brothels, men who exploit children for sex, and adult drug dealers who use juveniles because they are cheap and because children are not subject to the harsh criminal penalties for adult offenders (Dembo et al., 1993; Leviton et al., 1994; UNICEF, 1997).

The economic exploitation and maltreatment of defenseless young children are violations of their basic human rights. Even when permitted by law, child labor may be harmful. Insofar as child labor abuses are tied to family poverty, they cannot be tackled alone, without regard for the economic needs of these families. The idea that children are primarily of sentimental value, rather than of economic value, is a fairly recent historical development (Zelizer, 1985). Parents may not understand the harms associated with child labor, believing instead that they have a right to make use of all their human resources (Ahmed, 1991). Although child labor may help individual families in their day-to-day efforts to survive, ultimately it perpetuates the cycle of poverty. As such, it has enormous social costs. In depriving children of their rights and subjecting them to harm, exploitive child labor has enormous human costs.

REFERENCES

Ahmed, M. A. (1991). Child labor in Pakistan: A study of the Lahore area. *Child Welfare, 70*(2), 261–267.

Baker, B. (1990, July/August). Kids at work. *Common Cause Magazine*, 11–14.

Becker-Lausen, E., Sanders, B., & Chinsky, J. M. (1995). Mediation of abusive childhood experiences: Depression, dissociation and negative life outcomes. *American Journal of Orthopsychiatry, 65*(4), 560–573.

Belville, R., Pollack, S. H., Godbold, J. H., & Landrigan, P. J. (1993). Occupational injuries among working adolescents in New York State. *Journal of American Medical Association, 269,* 2754–2759.

Bequele, A. (1991). Combating child labour: Contrasting views and strategies for very poor countries. *Conditions of Work Digest, 10*(1), 7–15.

Bequele, A., & Myers, W. E. (1995). *First things in child labour: Eliminating work detrimental to children.* Geneva, Switzerland: International Labour Office.

Beyer, D. (1994). Child labor in the 90's: Trouble spots and timely solutions. In National Child Labor Committee (Ed.), *Essay in child labor in the 90's: How far have we come?* (pp. 26–30). New York: National Child Labor Committee.

Black, M. M., & Ricardo, I. B. (1994). Drug use, drug trafficking, and weapon carrying among low-income, African-American, early adolescent boys. *Pediatrics, 93*(6), 1065–1072.

Buirski, N. (1994). *Earth angels: Migrant children in America.* San Francisco: Pomegranate Artbooks.

Child miners: No simple way out. (1994, February 26). *The Economist, 330*(7852), 46.

Cogbill, T. H., Busch, H. M., & Stiers, G. R. (1985). Farm accidents in children. *Pediatrics, 76*(4), 562–573.

Committee on Environmental Health. (1995). The hazards of child labor. *Pediatrics, 95*(2), 311–313.

DeFleur, M. L. (1963). Children's knowledge of occupational roles and prestige: Preliminary report. *Psychological Reports, 13,* 760.

Dembo, R., Hughes, P., Jackson, L., & Mieczkowski, T. (1993). Crack cocaine dealing by adolescents in two public housing projects: A pilot study. *Human Organization, 52*(1), 89–96.

Department of Health and Human Services (Announcement No. 725). (1997, March 10). National Institute for Occupational Safety and Health; Childhood Agricultural Safety and Health Research, Notice of Availability of Funds for Fiscal Year 1997. *Federal Register, 62*(46), 10863–10867.

152

Doek, J. E. (1991). Management of child abuse and neglect at the international level: Trends and perspectives. *Child Abuse and Neglect, 15*(1), 51–56.

Eckenrode, J., Laird, M., & Doris, J. (1993). School performance and disciplinary problems among abused and neglected children. *Developmental Psychology, 29*(1), 53–62.

Erikson, E. H. (1968). *Identity, youth and crisis.* New York: Norton.

Feigelman, S., Stanton, B. F., Ricardo, I. (1993). Perceptions of drug selling and drug use among urban youths. *Journal of Early Adolescence, 13,* 267–284.

Finkelhor, D., & Browne, A. (1986). Initial and long-term effects: A conceptual framework. In D. Finkelhor & Associates (Eds.), *A sourcebook on child sexual abuse* (pp. 180–198). Thousand Oaks, CA: Sage.

General Accounting Office. (1990). *Child labor: Increases in detected child labor violations throughout the United States* (GAO/HRD Publication No. 90-116). Washington, DC: Author.

General Accounting Office. (1991). *Child labor characteristics of working children: Briefing report to congressional requestors* (GAO/HRD Publication No. 91-83BR). Washington, DC: Author.

Golodner, L. (1994). Child labor in 1994: An old problem that hasn't gone away. In National Child Labor Committee (Ed.), *Essay in child labor in the 90's: How far have we come?* (pp. 9–11). New York: National Child Labor Committee.

Goold, B. (1994). The scourge of child labor in America: Back to the future. In National Child Labor Committee (Ed.), *Essay in child labor in the 90's: How far have we come?* (pp. 17–19). New York: National Child Labor Committee.

Greenberger, E., & Steinberg, L. D. (1986). *When teenagers work: The psychological and social costs of adolescent employment.* New York: Basic Books.

Grootaert, C., & Kanbur, R. (1995). Child labor: An economic perspective. *International Labour Review, 134*(2), 187–203. Geneva, Switzerland: International Labour Organization.

Halperin, W. E. (1993). Epidemiologic studies of occupational fatality in children. In *Children who work—Challenges for the 21st century* (Capitol Hill briefing). (Available from Child Labor Coalition of the National Consumers League, 1701 K St. NW, Suite 1200, Washington, DC 20006)

Hart, S. N., & Brassard, M. R. (1987). A major threat to children's mental health: Psychological maltreatment. *American Psychologist, 42*(2), 160–165.

Harvey, P. J. (1993). International child labor: A global crisis. In *Children who work—Challenges for the 21st century* (Capitol Hill briefing). (Available from Child Labor Coalition of the National Consumers League, 1701 K St. NW, Suite 1200, Washington, DC 20006)

Inciardi, J. A., & Pottieger, A. E. (1991). Kids, crack and crime. *Journal of Drug Issues, 21*(2), 257–270.

International Labour Organization. (1991). Child labor: Law and practice. *Conditions of Work Digest, 10*(1), 209–210.

International Labour Organization. (1995, November, 264th session). Governing Body Document on Child Labour, Committee on Employment and Social Policy.

Kendall-Tackett, K. A., Williams, L. M., & Finkelhor, D. (1993). Impact of sexual abuse on children. A review and synthesis of recent studies. *Psychological Bulletin, 113,* 164–180.

Kruse, D. (1997, November). Illegal child labor in the United States. *Research Report,* Associated Press [On-line]. Available: Internet, http://wire.ap.org/APpa. . .study1/study1

Lamphear, V. S. (1985). The impact of maltreatment on children's psychosocial adjustment: A review of the research. *Child Abuse and Neglect, 9,* 251–263.

Landrigan, P. J., & Belville, R. (1993). The dangers of illegal child labor. *American Journal of Diseases of Children, 147,* 1029–1030.

Landrigan, P. J., & Carlson, J. E. (1995). Environmental policy and children's health. *The Future of Children, 5*(2), 34–52.

Lantos, T. (1992, February). The silence of the kids: Children at risk in the workplace. *Labor Law Journal, 13*(2), 67–70.

Leipziger, D., & Sibharwal, P. (1995, November). Child labor: The cutting edge of human rights. Research Report, Council on Economic Priorities [On-line]. Available from: Internet, http://www-2.realaudio.com/CEP/1195news/bodycopy.htm

Leviton, S., Schindler, M. A., & Orleans, R. S. (1994). African-American youth and the justice system. *Pediatrics, 93*(6), 1078–1084.

Li, X., & Feigelman, S. (1994). Recent and intended drug trafficking among male and female urban African-American early adolescents. *Pediatrics, 93*(6), 1045–1049.

Li, X., Stanton, B. F., Feigelman, S., & Black, M. M. (1994). Drug trafficking and drug use among urban African American early adolescents. *Journal of Early Adolescence, 14,* 491–509.

The little match girls. (1994, January 15). *The Economist, 330*(7846), 38.

Malinosky-Rummell, R., & Hansen, D. J. (1993). Long-term consequences of childhood physical abuse. *Psychological Bulletin, 114,* 68–79.

Martin, P. (1994). *Migrant farmworkers and their children.* (ERIC Document Reproduction Service No. ED 376 997) Charleston, WV: Clearinghouse on Rural Education and Small Schools.

Martinez, Y. G., & Cranston-Gingras, A. (1996). Migrant farmworker students and the educational process: Barriers to high school completion. *The High School Journal,* Oct./Nov., 29–38.

Miller, M. (1995). *Occupational injuries among adolescents in Washington state, 1988–1991: A review of workers' compensation data* (Tech. Rep. No. 35-1-1995). Olympia, WA: Washington State Department of Labor and Industries, Safety and Health Assessment and Research for Prevention.

Moore, S. E. (1995). Adolescent black males' drug trafficking and addiction: Three theoretical perspectives. *Journal of Black Studies, 26*(2), 99–116.

Mull, L. D. (1993, February 26). Broken covenant: The future of migrant farmworker children and families in the United States. In *Children who work —Challenges for the 21st century* (Capitol Hill briefing). (Available from Child Labor Coalition of the National Consumers League, 1701 K St. NW, Suite 1200, Washington, DC 20006)

Mullen, P. E., Martin, J. L., Anderson, J. C., Romans, S. E., & Herbison, G. P. (1996). The long-term impact of the physical, emotional and sexual abuse of children: A community study. *Child Abuse and Neglect, 20*(1), 7–21.

NIOSH. (1997). *Child labor research needs* (DHHS, NIOSH Publication No. 97-143). Cincinnati, OH: U.S. DHHS; Public Health Service; CDC; NIOSH.

NIOSH. (1995). *Alert: Request for assistance in preventing deaths and injuries of adolescent workers* (DHHS, NIOSH Publication No. 95-25). Cincinnati, OH: U.S. DHHS; Public Health Service; CDC; NIOSH.

Patterson, G. R., DeBaryshe, B. D., & Ramsey, E. (1989). A developmental perspective on antisocial behavior. *American Psychologist, 44*(2), 329–335.

Pogrebin, R. (1995, September 24). A family on the run. *The New York Times,* pp. 1, 11.

Pollack, S. H., Landrigan, P. J., & Mallino, D. L. (1990). Child labor in 1990: Prevalence and health hazards. *Annual Review of Public Health, 11,* 359–375.

Ricardo, I. B. (1994). Life choices of African-American youth living in public housing: Perspectives on drug trafficking. *Pediatrics, 93*(6), 1055–1059.

Richter, E. D., & Jacobs, J. A. (1991). Work injuries and exposures in children and young adults: Review and recommendations for action. *American Journal of Industrial Medicine, 19,* 747–769.

Siddiqi, F., & Patrinos, H. A. (1995, June). *Child labor: Issues, causes and interventions* (HRO Working Paper No. HROWP 56, Human Resources Development and Operations Policy Working Paper Series).

Sinclair, V., & Trah, G. (1991). Child labour: National legislation on the minimum age for admission to employment or work. *Conditions of Work Digest, 10*(1), 17–27.

Stack, C. B. (1974). *All our kin.* New York: Harper & Row.

Stanton, B. F., & Galbraith, J. (1994). Drug trafficking among African-American early adolescents: Prevalence, consequences, and associated behaviors. *Pediatrics, 93*(6), 1039–1043.

Suruda, A., & Halperin, W. E. (1991). Work-related deaths in children. *American Journal of Industrial Medicine, 19,* 739–745.

Swanson, J. A., Sachs, M. I., Dahlgren, K. A., & Tinguely, S. J. (1987). Accidental farm injuries in children. *American Journal of Diseases of Children, 141,* 1276–1279.

Tittle, C. K. (1981). *Careers and family: Sex roles and adolescent life plans.* Beverly Hills, CA: Sage.

Toscano, G. (1995, August). National census of fatal occupational injuries, 1994. *Research Report.* Bureau of Labor Statistics [On-line]. Available from: Internet, http://stats.bls.gov/osh/cfnr0001.txt

U.N. sharply increases estimate of youngsters at work full time. (1996, November 12). *The New York Times.*

UNICEF. (1997). *The state of the world's children.* New York: Oxford University Press.

U.S. Department of Labor. (1994a). *By the sweat and toil of children: The use of child labor in U.S. manufactured and mined imports.* Washington, DC: Author.

U.S. Department of Labor. (1994b). *Migrant farmworkers: Pursuing security in an unstable labor market.* Washington, DC: Author.

U.S. Department of Labor. (1995). *By the sweat and toil of children: The use of child labor in U.S. agricultural imports and forced and bonded child labor.* Washington, DC: Author.

Wescott, D. (1981). The youngest workers: 14- and 15-year-olds. *Monthly Labor Review, 104*(2), 65–69.

Whitehead, T. L., Peterson, J, & Kaljee, L. (1994). The "hustle:" Socioeconomic deprivation, urban drug trafficking, and low-income, African-American male gender identity. *Pediatrics, 93*(6), 1050–1054.

Williams, T. (1989). *The cocaine kids: The inside story of a teenage drug ring.* Reading, MA: Addison-Wesley.

Williams, T., & Kornblum, W. (1985). *Growing up poor.* Lexington, MA: Lexington Books.

Winters-Smith, C., & Larner, M. (1992). The Fair Start program: Outreach to migrant farmworker families. In M. Larner, R. Halpern, & O. Harkavy (Eds.), *Fair Start for children: Lessons learned from seven demonstration projects* (pp. 46–67). New Haven, CT: Yale University Press.

Wodarski, J. S., Kurtz, P. D., Gaudin, J. M., & Howing, P. T. (1990). Maltreatment and the school-age child: Major academic, socioemotional, and adaptive outcomes. *Social Work, 35*(6), 506–513.

Work safe this summer. (1996, June). *Child Labor Monitor, 1*(6), 1.

World Health Organization. (1987). *Children at work: Special health risks.* Geneva: Author.

Zelizer, V. A. (1985). *Pricing the priceless child.* New York: Basic Books.

Zigler, E. F., & Finn-Stevenson, M. (1987). *Children.* Lexington, MA: D. C. Heath.

7

Occupational Safety and Health in Young People

Dawn N. Castillo

On September 24, 1996, a 17-year-old youth was seriously injured while working the night shift at a municipal industrial recycling center in the United States. His job was to tear cardboard into pieces and throw them into a hopper of a conveyor. The conveyor discharged the cardboard pieces into a chute that fed into the baling chamber of a continuously operating baler. The cardboard jammed in the chute. The foreperson and five coworkers were off in other parts of the plant. Even though it was not part of the youth's duties, he decided he would unjam the baler. He emulated what he had seen his coworkers do in the past. He turned off the conveyor and climbed to the chute. While holding on to the top of the chute, he kicked the jam free. When the jam cleared, he fell into the baling chamber. While he was trying to climb out of the baling chamber, the baler, which had not been turned

---

Data and discussions in this chapter focus on the youngest working youth, those less than 18 years old. Labor laws and school attendance frequently differentiate this group from older working youth. Many occupational safety and health issues are similar, however, specifically, rates, patterns, and contributors to injury and illness, and prevention strategies. Data on youth through 24 years old are available from other published sources (Bureau of Labor Statistics [BLS], 1996; Castillo & Malit, 1997; Coleman & Sanderson, 1983; NIOSH, 1993; Toscano & Windau, 1997).

off, automatically cycled, and the baling ram amputated both of the youth's lower legs (National Institute for Occupational Safety and Health [NIOSH], 1997a).

This adolescent was just one of thousands of youth hurt at work in 1996. Work-related injuries and illnesses are a very real concern of youth employment. Although the safety and health of working young people have been addressed in the public health and medical fields (American Academy of Pediatrics, Committee on Environmental Health, 1995; American Public Health Association, 1995; Children's Safety Network & Massachusetts Occupational Health Surveillance Program, 1995; NIOSH, 1996a; U.S. Department of Health & Human Services, 1994), it has largely been ignored in the psychological fields.

Safety and health concerns for working youth are relevant to psychologists. Psychological and psychosocial factors undoubtedly contribute to the relatively high incidence of youth work-related injuries. Efforts to prevent injuries and illnesses include components that address behaviors of youth, employers, parents, teachers, and other parties interested in the well-being of youth. Knowledge and research from the psychological disciplines can inform efforts that seek to better understand the contributors to young people's work-related injuries and illnesses and to develop effective strategies for fostering safe and healthful alternatives. Finally, a holistic approach to youth well-being will address physical as well as mental health. Promotion of high-quality youth employment should recognize and address health and safety concerns to ensure that youth work experiences do not result in needless pain and suffering.

The goal of this chapter is to provide an overview of the occurrence and prevention of youth work injuries, with the hope that readers will consider ways to address occupational safety and health in their work or in their roles as parents or guardians. The epidemiology of young people's occupational injuries and illnesses, and various strategies for fostering safe and healthful work, are described. Areas in which psychologists could contribute to the understanding of the etiology and prevention of youth occupational injuries and illnesses are noted.

EPIDEMIOLOGIC DATA

Substantial amounts of epidemiologic research on occupational injuries among youth less than 18 years old have been conducted in the United States. There are undoubtedly differences in injury patterns among youth of the United States, Mexico, and Canada because of differences in regulatory safeguards, social conditions, patterns of youth employment, and school-based work education. However, data from the United States are illustrative of circumstances that too commonly result in injuries of young people at work, and the relatively high risk for such injuries.

Fatal Injuries

An injury is considered *work-related* if the victim was employed (working for pay, compensation, or profit) in a work activity at the time of the injury event, or present at the site of the event as a requirement of his or her job (Association for Vital Records and Health Statistics et al., 1992). Deaths occurring while commuting to or from work are not considered *work-related*.

Data on work-related fatalities of youth less than 18 years old are available from various sources in the United States. A surveillance system was established in 1992 in which multiple sources of data (death certificates, workers' compensation reports, reports to regulatory agencies, medical examiner reports, police reports, and newspaper reports) are used to record all work-related injury deaths across the country (Abraham, Weber, & Personick, 1996). A system using death certificates only, which capture approximately 80% of work-related injury deaths, has records dating from 1980 (NIOSH, 1993). Data are available from programs that investigate certain types of work-related injury deaths. And, data are available and have been examined from sources within individual states, such as death certificates, medial examiner's reports, and workers' compensation reports (Belville, Pollack, Godbold, & Landrigan, 1993; Cooper & Rothstein, 1995; Dunn & Runyan, 1993; Miller, 1995).

Each year, nearly 70 young people less than 18 years old die from injuries at work in the United States alone (Derstine, 1997). The majority of deaths are of youth 16 and 17 years old, although deaths in younger age groups are substantial (see Table 1). Approximately 90% of youth work-related injury deaths are of males (Castillo, Landen, & Layne, 1994; Castillo & Malit, 1997; Cooper & Rothstein, 1995; Derstine, 1997; Dunn & Runyan, 1993). For the 3-year period 1990–1992, the rate of work-related injury deaths for 16- and 17-year-old males was 5.6/100,000 full-time employee equivalents, and the rate for females was 1.0/100,000 full-time employee equivalents, based on data from death certificates only (Castillo & Malit, 1997). Higher fatality rates among males compared to females are found among all age groups of workers (NIOSH, 1993).

The majority of fatally injured young people work in agricultural industries, with over half working in a family business (Derstine, 1997;

Table 1
Work-Related Injury Deaths of Youth by Industry and Age Group, U.S., 1992–1995

Industry	Total youth	<14 Years	14- to 15-year-olds	16- to 17-year-olds
Agriculture, forestry, fishing	108	40 (31)	26 (16)	42 (11)
Retail trades	59	4	10	45 (5)
Construction	25	—	—	25
Services	19	—	—	19
Manufacturing	16	3	4	9
Public administration	4	—	—	4
Other/Nonclassifiable	18	—	—	18
Total	269	51	56	162

Note. Adapted from Derstine (1997). Fatality data are from the Census of Fatal Occupational Injuries, U.S. Bureau of Labor Statistics. Industry is categorized according to the Standard Industrial Classification Manual, 1987 (U.S. Office of Management & Budget, 1987). Numbers in parentheses indicate the number of youths working in family businesses. Dashes indicate that data are not available or do not meet the publication criteria of the U.S. Bureau of Labor Statistics.

Table 1). Among fatally injured youth younger than 16 years old, employment in family agricultural businesses predominates. Among older adolescents, 16–17 years old, there are slightly more deaths in retail trades than in agriculture, and employment in family businesses was less common. The term *retail trades* includes restaurants, grocery stores, department stores, and similar settings where products are sold to the consumer. Deaths in the construction industry are also relatively frequent among older adolescents (Castillo et al., 1994; Derstine, 1997; Suruda & Halperin, 1991).

Leading causes of deaths of youths by work-related injury in the United States are motor vehicle-related, homicide, machine-related, and electrocutions (Belville et al., 1993; Castillo, Landen, & Layne, 1994; Castillo & Malit, 1997; Cooper & Rothstein, 1995; Derstine, 1997; Dunn & Runyan, 1993; Suruda & Halperin, 1991). Motor vehicle-related events are the leading cause of death for males; homicide is the leading cause for females (Castillo & Malit, 1997; Derstine, 1997). These patterns are similar to those of adults (NIOSH, 1993).

Although federal child labor laws prohibit all but occasional driving by young people under 18 years old (U.S. Department of Labor, 1990a), the majority of motor vehicle-related work injury deaths involve youth driving the motor vehicle (Castillo et al., 1994; Castillo & Malit, 1997). Work-related driving is frequently required for purposes of delivery of passengers or goods, or in travel to provide services on location, such as appliance repair or landscaping services (NIOSH, 1995a). Motor vehicle-related deaths of working youth also include youth as passengers in motor vehicles, and pedestrians and bicyclists involved in crashes with motor vehicles. Motor vehicle-related pedestrian and bicycling deaths occur when work is conducted in areas of motor vehicle traffic, such as at road construction sites and in door-to-door sales and delivery. Pedestrian–motor vehicle crashes were the leading cause of work-related injury death for construction laborers under 20 years old for the years 1992–1995 (Derstine, 1997).

Firearms were used in 21 of 24 homicides of 16- and 17-year-old workers for the years 1990–1992 (Castillo & Malit, 1997). Half of the homicides occurred between the hours of 10:00 p.m. and 6:00 a.m. For the years 1992–1995, homicide was the leading cause of work-related death of youth less than 20 years old in the following occupations: sales workers, food preparation and service workers, and stock handlers (Derstine, 1997). Data from work-related homicides among workers of all ages demonstrate that work-related homicides are typically associated with robberies (NIOSH, 1996b).

Tractors and forklifts account for the most machine-related deaths of working youth (Castillo et al., 1994; Castillo & Malit, 1997; Dunn & Runyan, 1993; Suruda & Halperin, 1991). These and similar machines pose hazards of rolling over, of bystanders or operators being run over (operators after dismounting or falling off a running machine), or of being caught in running equipment such as power take-offs or lift mechanisms (Jenkins & Hard, 1992; NIOSH, 1994a; Stout-Wiegand, 1987).

Work-related electrocutions most frequently involve conductive equipment (such as poles, pipes, or ladders) contacting an energized power line (Castillo et al., 1994). Electrocutions also occur as a result of improperly wired equipment. Electrocution was the leading cause of death of construction trade workers under 20 years old for the years 1992–1995 (Derstine, 1997).

Violations of both occupational safety and health regulations and child labor laws have been associated with work-related deaths of youth less than 18 years old. Occupational safety and health regulations are designed to ensure safe and healthful working conditions for all workers, regardless of age. Of 104 deaths of youth less than 18 years old investigated by the U.S. Occupational Safety and Health Administration (OSHA) between 1984 and 1987, citations for safety violations were issued for 70% (Suruda & Halperin, 1991). Federal child labor laws include prohibitions against youth work in activities that are considered especially dangerous (U.S. Department of Labor, 1990a, 1990b). Research on work-related deaths of youth have found that 38–86% of the deaths are associated with prohibited activities (Castillo et al., 1994; Dunn & Runyan, 1993; Suruda & Halperin, 1991; U.S. General Accounting Office, 1990). These deaths may or may not have been covered by child labor laws, which include numerous conditions for, and exemptions from, coverage.

164

Rates of work-related injury deaths for youth 16 and 17 years old are displayed for years 1980–1992 in Figure 1. Although rates decreased dramatically in the early 1980s, the decreasing trend attenuated in later years. Rates of work-related injury deaths are moderately lower for 16- and 17-year-olds compared with workers ages 18–44 (see Table 2). That older workers tend to succumb to their injuries has been suggested as a reason for the relatively greater fatality rates among workers 45 years and older (Castillo & Rodriguez, 1997; Jenkins, Layne, & Kisner, 1992; Personick & Windau, 1995).

The relative comparability of work-related injury death rates for both youth and young *and* middle-aged adults is cause for concern. Although violations of child labor laws and resultant injury and death occur, employment data suggest that in general, young people work fewer hours than adults in particularly hazardous job settings. Data for

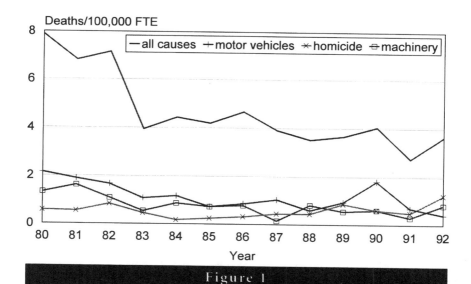

Figure 1

Rates for all leading causes of work-related injury deaths, 16- and 17-year-olds, U.S., 1980–1992. Fatality data are from the National Traumatic Occupational Fatality Surveillance System, NIOSH. Employment data, adjusted for hours of work, are from the Current Population Survey, U.S. Bureau of Labor Statistics. FTE = full-time employee equivalents.

Table 2

Frequency and Rates of Work-Related Injury Deaths per 100,000 Full-Time Employee Equivalents, Overall and for Leading Causes of Death, by Age Group, U.S., 1990–1992

Age group (Yrs)	Overall		Motor vehicles		Homicide		Machinery	
	No.	Rate	No.	Rate	No.	Rate	No.	Rate
16–17	111	3.51	32	1.01	24	0.76	18	0.57
18–19	325	3.91	71	0.85	56	0.67	43	0.52
20–24	1,389	3.87	309	0.86	243	0.68	151	0.42
25–34	3,975	3.95	870	0.86	610	0.61	424	0.42
35–44	3,762	3.93	789	0.82	618	0.65	402	0.42
45–54	2,786	4.56	710	1.16	404	0.66	309	0.51
55–64	1,996	6.39	470	1.50	257	0.82	310	0.99
65+	1,227	17.48	234	3.33	153	2.18	349	4.97

Note. Fatality data are from the National Traumatic Occupational Fatalities Surveillance System, National Institute for Occupational Safety and Health Employment data, adjusted for hours of work, are from the Current Population Survey, U.S. Bureau of Labor Statistics. Causes of death are classified according to the International Classification of Diseases, 9th Revision (WHO, 1977).

workers of all ages demonstrate that four industry sectors consistently have the highest rates of occupational injury death: mining, construction, transportation, and agriculture (NIOSH, 1993). Rates in these four industries are over twice the average for all industries. Data for 1991, not adjusted for hours of work, demonstrate that 8% of 16- and 17-year-olds worked in these industry sectors, compared with 17% of workers 18–44 years old (Stinson, 1996; see Figure 2). Youth may actually have a higher risk for work-related injury death than adults for similar work.

Nonfatal Injuries

Nonfatal work injuries of youth in the United States have been examined using workers' compensation data (Banco, Lapidus, & Braddock,

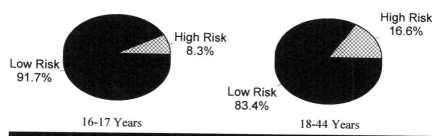

Figure 2

Youth and adult employment in industries with high and low risk for work-related injury death, U.S., 1991. Employment data, not adjusted for hours of work, are from the Current Population Survey, U.S. Bureau of Labor Statistics. High fatality risk industries (mining, construction, transportation, agriculture) ranged from 18–32 deaths/100,000 workers for 1980–1989; low-risk industries (finance, whole-sale and retail trades, service, manufacturing, public administration) ranged from 1–7 deaths/100,000 workers for the same period (NIOSH, 1993).

1992; Belville et al., 1993; Brooks & Davis, 1996; Bush & Baker, 1994; Cooper & Rothstein, 1995; Heyer, Franklin, Rivara, Parker, & Haug, 1992; Miller, 1995; Parker, Carl, French, & Martin, 1994a; Schober, Handke, Halperin, Moll, & Thun, 1988; State of Wyoming, 1984), data from an annual national survey of employers (Centers for Disease Control and Prevention [CDC], 1996), emergency department samples (Brooks, Davis, & Gallagher, 1993; Knight, Castillo, & Layne, 1995; Layne, Castillo, Stout, & Cutlip, 1994), and youth surveys (Cohen, Runyan, Dunn, & Schulman, 1996; Parker, Carl, French, & Martin, 1994b). Data from these different sources overlap; pieced together, they provide a picture, albeit incomplete, of work-related injuries experienced by youth in the United States. The picture is incomplete because there are gaps in the data (NIOSH, 1997b); for instance, data are not available for less serious injuries, and there are certain types of youth work which likely are not well represented by the data, such as work in agriculture, small businesses, and informal employment (e.g., baby-sitting and mowing lawns). Data are needed on the risks for specific types of work and how youth risks compare with those of adults doing similar work. In addition, data on economic and social consequences of youth work injuries are lacking. Available data do demonstrate, however, that youth work injuries are common, that the injuries can have a substantial impact on youths' lives, and that youth appear to be at greater risk for work injuries than adults. Information associated with work injuries about workplaces, jobs, circumstances, and characteristics of youth can be used to identify mechanisms to reduce the incidence of injuries and foster safe and healthful work experiences for them.

All 50 states in the United States have separate workers' compensation systems to provide income and medical benefits to victims of work-related injuries and illnesses (U.S. Chambers of Commerce, 1991). Analyses of work-related injuries of adolescents have been conducted in eight states, with annual averages ranging from 448 in Wyoming (State of Wyoming, 1984) to 4,450 in Washington (Miller, 1995). A study that pooled data from 24 states for 1980 found nearly 24,000 claims for work-related injuries among youth less than 18 years old (Schober et al., 1988). The analysis in Washington contrasted rates for youth to those of adults. The crude injury rate (not adjusted for hours of work) for 16- and 17-year-olds was 9.0/100 workers compared to a rate of 10.4/100 adult workers (Miller, 1995). Miller suggests that if the rates were adjusted for hours of work, the rates for 16- and 17-year-olds would be more than 3 times higher than those for adults, since most youth work part-time for only part of the year. The analysis in New York, which had an annual average of 1,200 compensated injuries to youth, found that 44% of the injuries resulted in permanent disability (Belville et al., 1993). Examples of permanent disability are partial or complete loss of vision or hearing, and injuries resulting in the loss or use of any limb or appendage. Although the objective of workers' compensation is to provide coverage for all workers, for various reasons no state law covers all forms of employment. Groups of workers frequently not covered under workers' compensation laws include employees working for small businesses, farm labor, domestic servants, and casual employees (U.S. Chambers of Commerce, 1991). Additionally, there is some data suggesting that youth are less likely than adults to be captured in workers' compensation systems (Brooks & Davis, 1996). An analysis in Minnesota, a state that requires reporting of injuries resulting in at least 3 days of disability, estimated that about one third of youth work injuries were captured in the workers' compensation system (Parker et al., 1994a).

Young people under 18 years old sustained an estimated 21,620 work-related injuries and illnesses serious enough to require at least one day away from work in the United States in 1993, based on a survey of approximately 250,000 businesses (CDC, 1996). The median days away from work was three. This estimate is conservative, as the survey excludes several types of employers: self-employed workers, farmers with fewer than 11 employees, private households, and government employees (Bureau of Labor Statistics [BLS], 1996). The injured youth in the case description at the beginning of the chapter would not have been represented by this survey because he worked for a city government. Employment data for 16- and 17-year-olds suggest that 11% of working youth are not represented by the survey (CDC, 1996).

Injuries treated in emergency departments include those serious enough to require time away from work, as well as less disabling injuries. An estimated 64,000 youth 14–17 years of age were seen in hospital emergency departments for work-related injuries in 1992, with hundreds hospitalized for their injuries (Layne et al., 1994). This estimate is based on a sample of 91 hospital emergency departments across the United States. The rate of work-related injuries was 5.8/100 full-time equivalent employees. A similar study conducted in the early 1980s, in which data were collected and analyzed for workers of all ages, demonstrated that the injury rates for 16- and 17-year-olds were exceeded only by the rates for 18- and 19-year-olds (Coleman & Sanderson, 1983). Telephone interviews were conducted with 14- to 16-year-olds identified in the first three months of surveillance in 1992 (Knight et al., 1995). A supervisor was present at the time of injury in only about 20% of the cases. More than half of the youth reported that they had not received any training in how to prevent the injury they sustained. Sixty-eight percent of the youths experienced limitations in their normal activities (including work, school, and play) for at least one day, and 25% experienced limitations for more than a week. A study in Massachusetts in the early 1980s suggested that work contributes substantially to injuries of adolescents treated at emergency departments.

Seven to thirteen percent of all such injuries of youth 14–17 years old were work-related (Brooks et al., 1993).

Not all work-related injuries are treated in emergency departments; some are treated in physicians' offices or clinics, and others are treated at the workplace or home. Research in 1975 suggested that only about one third of work-related injuries are treated in hospital emergency departments (Ries, 1978). Emergency departments tend to capture acute injuries, while chronic injuries, such as sprains and strains are more likely to be treated in physicians' offices or clinics (Fingar, Hopkins, & Nelson, 1992). A survey in Minnesota suggested that 17% of employed youths experienced a work-related injury during a 10-month period (Parker et al., 1994b). A study of students in Saskatchewan, Canada found that 18% of students working during the summer months sustained an injury (Glor, 1989).

Multiple studies have found that the incidence and rates of work-related injuries increase with age through adolescence, with the greatest numbers and rates among 17-year-olds (Banco et al., 1992; Belville et al., 1993; Brooks & Davis, 1996; Brooks et al., 1993; Cooper & Rothstein, 1995; Heyer et al., 1992; Layne et al., 1994; Miller, 1995; Schober et al., 1988; State of Wyoming, 1984). Although not as extreme as for fatal work injuries, greater numbers and rates of work injuries are reported for males than for females (Banco et al., 1992; Belville et al., 1993; Brooks & Davis, 1996; Brooks et al., 1993; CDC, 1996; Cooper & Rothstein, 1995; Layne et al., 1994; Miller, 1995; Parker et al., 1994a, 1994b; Schober et al., 1988). In 1992, the rate of work injuries treated at emergency departments for male adolescents was 7.0/100 full-time employee equivalents compared with 4.4/100 among females (Layne et al., 1994).

Retail trades have large numbers and relatively high rates of injury nationally, as well as in analyses within individual states (Banco et al., 1992; Belville et al., 1993; Brooks & Davis, 1996; Bush & Baker, 1994; CDC, 1996; Layne et al., 1994; Miller, 1995; Schober et al., 1988; State of Wyoming, 1984). Restaurants and food stores account for the most injuries among retail trades, and across all industry sectors. Nationally, nearly 40% of youth work injuries occur in restaurants and from 8–14% occur in food stores (CDC, 1996; Layne et al., 1994). Other industries that experience relatively high numbers of youth work injuries include general merchandise stores, nursing homes, and agriculture (CDC, 1996; Layne et al., 1994). Within individual states, other industries may account for a substantial number of work-related injuries. For example, in 1993, hotels and motels were the most common site of work-related injuries in Vermont and second most common in Utah (CDC, 1996). Among youths less than 16 years of age, agriculture is frequently among the industries accounting for the most work-related injuries (Belville et al., 1993; Hard & Layne, 1995; Heyer et al., 1992; Miller, 1995; Schober et al., 1988). The nature of injury and lost work time payments suggest that agricultural injuries may be more severe than injuries incurred in other industrial sectors (Belville et al., 1993; Hard & Layne, 1995; Heyer et al., 1992). Besides retail trades, high rates of injuries are generally seen in manufacturing and construction (Belville et al., 1993; Brooks & Davis, 1996; Layne et al., 1994; Miller, 1995). Occupations that are most frequently represented among injured youth workers include food service employees, cashiers, stock handlers, and laborers (Banco et al., 1992; CDC, 1996; Miller, 1995; Parker et al., 1994b; State of Wyoming, 1984).

Lacerations, sprains and strains, contusions, and burns are among the most common nonfatal work injuries (Banco et al., 1992; Belville et al., 1993; Brooks & Davis, 1996; Brooks et al., 1993; Bush & Baker, 1994; CDC, 1996; Layne et al., 1994; Miller, 1995; Parker et al., 1994a, 1994b; Schober et al., 1988; State of Wyoming, 1984). Emergency department data demonstrate that the nature of injury differs by industry (Figure 3). Among retail trades, lacerations are the leading cause of injury, accounting for nearly 40% of the injuries, followed by contusions, sprains and strains, burns, and fractures and dislocations. Burns account for a greater proportion of injuries in retail trades than in any other industry. Within restaurants, burns account for 23% of all injuries. Burns can be severe. Although burns represented 13% of youth work injuries in Minnesota, they represented 36% of all hospitalizations (Parker et al., 1994a, 1994b). Contusions and abrasions are the leading cause of injury in the service sector, accounting for 30% of those reported. Industries in the service sector that account for the most youth

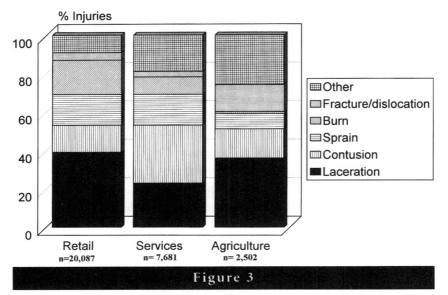

Figure 3

Nature of work-related injuries treated in hospital emergency departments for select industry sectors, 14- to 17-year-olds, U.S., July–December, 1992. Emergency
department data are from the National Electronic Injury Surveillance System
(NEISS), NIOSH.

work injuries are health services, such as nursing homes, amusement
and other types of parks, and schools (Layne et al., 1994). Although
lacerations and contusions or abrasions are the most common types of
injuries in agriculture, fractures are more prevalent in agriculture than
in other industries.

Common events resulting in youth work injury include falls on the
same level (i.e., falls to floors and falls onto or against objects), overexertion (i.e., from lifting, pulling, pushing, turning, wielding, holding,
carrying, or throwing objects), striking against objects (i.e., bumping
into, stepping on, kicking, and being pushed or thrown into or against
objects), contact with hot objects or substances, being struck by falling
objects, and being struck by a slipping hand-held object (Banco et al.,
1992; CDC, 1996; Miller, 1995; Parker et al., 1994b; State of Wyoming,
1984). One fifth of all agricultural injuries treated in emergency departments result from being caught in running machinery or equip-

Table 3

Common Circumstances of Nonfatal Youth Work Injuries in Select Industries

Industry	Injury	Common circumstances
Restaurants	Cut fingers	Knife slips while cutting vegetables
		Finger contacts blade while using or cleaning powered meat suppliers
	Burns	Grease splatters onto worker from grill or deep fryer
		Hand contacts grill while cleaning
		Youth slips on a slick surface, contacts grills or fryer when trying to break fall
		Grease spills on youth when draining or transporting hot grease from a fryer
		Hot liquid or food spills on youth
	Strains	Youth slips on a slick surface—strains muscles trying to avoid fall
	Bruises	Youth slips on a slick surface—is bruised in fall
Grocery stores	Cut arms or legs	Case-cutter slips while opening cardboard boxes
	Torso strains	Overexertion while lifting or moving inventory
		Overexertion in lifting customer bags
		Overexertion in retrieving carts from parking lot
Farms	Cuts, bruises, fractures, amputations	Body parts or clothing caught in running equipment, such as tractor driveshafts
		Pinned by overturned equipment or between equipment and structures
		Kicked or knocked down by farm animals or pinned between animals and structures
		Falls from equipment
	Musculoskeletal injuries	Strains from awkward postures and repetitive motions in harvesting

ment (Layne et al., 1994). Table 3 lists common injuries and associated circumstances for select industries.

Violations of child labor laws have been associated with nonfatal work-related injuries of youth (CDC, 1996; Knight et al., 1995). An estimated 1,475 youths in the United States incurred serious injuries as a result of illegal employment between 1983 and 1990 (U.S. General Accounting Office, 1991). Serious injuries were most commonly found in restaurants, followed by manufacturing, grocery stores, and construction industries.

Illnesses

Exposures to hazardous substances or conditions may result in an immediate illness; however, illness might not be detected for months or years after exposure, and the association with work may not be recognized. Workers' compensation data and the U.S. annual survey of employers include illnesses; however, their incidence is dwarfed by injuries. Illnesses identified in these systems tend to have short latencies (time from exposure to manifestation of disease) and fairly obvious associations with workplace exposures. Youth work-related illnesses identified in the annual survey of employers include dermatitis, tendinitis, and carpal tunnel syndrome (BLS, 1995). Work-related dermatitis can result from irritations or allergic reactions to chemicals and other contaminants in the workplace. Tendinitis and carpal tunnel syndrome can result from repetitive or strenuous motions in work processes.

Illnesses resulting from exposures to hazardous substances at work can have long latency periods. And, the association of an illness with a workplace exposure can be difficult because few occupational diseases have a single causative agent that is confined to exposures in the workplace. For example, lung cancer, which has a latency period of at least 10–20 years, can be caused by cigarette smoke (Office of Smoking and Health, 1982) or a number of occupational carcinogens, including asbestos, beryllium, chromium, coal tars, coke oven emissions, and nickel compounds (Frumkin, 1995). Although brief and transitory work patterns (BLS, 1992) may limit youth exposures to specific hazardous substances, such patterns will also undoubtedly complicate recognition of occupational diseases resulting from youth work exposures.

Young people are potentially exposed to a number of hazardous substances or conditions at work which have been documented or hypothesized to contribute to illness. Audiometric testing of vocational agricultural students in Wisconsin found that 57% of those who lived and worked on a farm had noise-induced hearing loss compared with 33% of students with little or no farm exposure (Broste, Hansen, Strand, & Stueland, 1989). Risks to hearing may also occur in other youth workplaces, such as manufacturing and construction. In a survey of 4-H students in North Carolina, 38% of the respondents who worked on farms reported using pesticides or other farm chemicals (Cohen et al., 1996). Pesticide exposures have been associated with various types of cancer, neurologic and behavioral abnormalities, reproductive hazards, and liver damage (Shaver & Tong, 1991). A couple of studies have documented that some working youth are exposed to gasoline (Cohen et al., 1996; Morse, 1996). Benzene in unleaded gasoline could potentially contribute to some leukemias or lymphomas (American Academy of Pediatrics, Committee on Environmental Health, 1995; Pollack, Landrigan, & Mallino, 1990). And, exposures to dusts, formaldehyde, and asbestos could contribute to respiratory diseases.

CONTRIBUTORS TO WORK INJURIES AND ILLNESSES

Identification of factors that contribute to work injuries and illnesses lays the groundwork for effective prevention efforts. Contributory factors include characteristics of and interactions between the work, work environment, and the worker. For example, in the case described at the beginning of this chapter, characteristics of the youth's work that placed him in close proximity to the baler, characteristics of the work environment in which the baler lacked safety features that would facilitate the safe clearing of jams, and characteristics of the youth who believed that he could solve the problem of the jammed baler without going to his supervisor or older coworkers all played a role in the injury event.

Inadequate training and lack of company adherence to written safety policies may have contributed to the youth attempting to clear the jam; written policies for clearing jams were not followed.

Although many contributory factors affect workers of all ages (e.g., hazards associated with machinery), physical and psychosocial development may introduce unique risks for youth. Research to elucidate the role of cognition, psychosocial factors, and work organization factors in the incidence of youth work injuries is needed (NIOSH, 1997b).

Work Tasks and Environment

The nature of work and the work environment can pose substantial risks for injury and illness. Machinery, equipment, tools, and chemicals used in work processes; substances and materials that workers handle or come into contact with; the general work environment; and physical demands of job tasks can lead to injury and illness. The work climate, such as company commitment to safety, can also influence the incidence of youth work injuries.

Youth work can involve interactions with heavy equipment and powerful machinery, such as motor vehicles, tractors and associated implements, forklifts, skid-steer and front-end loaders, augers, dump trucks, balers, road grading and surfacing machinery, powered conveyors, all-terrain-vehicles, drills, chain saws, compressed air or pneumatic tools, and meat grinders and slicers (Belville et al., 1993; Boyle et al., 1995; Castillo et al., 1994; Castillo & Malit, 1997; Cohen et al., 1996; Cooper & Rothstein, 1995; Derstine, 1997; Dunn & Runyan, 1993; Knight et al., 1995; Miller, 1995; Minnesota Fatality Assessment & Control Evaluation (FACE) Program, 1992, 1995; NIOSH, 1994b, 1995b, 1997a; Perry, 1995; Schenker, Lopez, & Wintemute, 1995; State of Wyoming, 1984; Suruda & Halperin, 1991). There are a multitude of ways in which injury can result. Injuries can occur to operators as well as to bystanders and are not limited to operating the equipment, but can be associated with feeding materials into machinery and performing maintenance on equipment. In the case of transport and industrial vehicles, injury can result from crashes into other vehicles or objects, overturns, and crashes into pedestrians. Injuries with heavy equipment and machinery also result when body parts are caught or struck by moving parts. Other types of equipment can contribute to injuries, such as cooking grills causing burn injuries (Hayes-Lundy et al., 1991). Although the dangers are not as great, youth can also be injured by nonpowered tools, such as knives and case-cutters (Banco et al., 1992; Brooks & Davis, 1996; CDC, 1996; Knight et al., 1995; Miller, 1995; Schober et al., 1988; State of Wyoming, 1984). Injuries result when these hand-held tools slip, contacting hands or other body parts.

Substances and materials used at work can lead to work injuries and illnesses. Injury or illness can result from contact with the skin, absorption through the skin, inhalation, and ingestion. Heat burns, a common youth injury in restaurants, can result from contact with hot grease, food, and liquids (Hayes-Lundy et al., 1991; Heinzman et al., 1993; Inansci & Guidotti, 1987; Knight et al., 1995; Parker et al., 1994a; Personick, 1991). Workers come into contact with hot grease when adding, filtering, or removing grease from hot fryers, from splattering during cooking, and when workers slip on a slick floor and inadvertently put their hands and arms into fryers while trying to break their falls (Hayes-Lundy et al., 1991; Heinzman et al., 1993). Cooking and serving food and beverages can also result in contact with hot foods and liquids. Chemical burns can result from contact with caustic chemicals, such as cleaning solutions (Layne et al., 1994; Miller, 1995).

Green tobacco sickness is an example of illness resulting from the absorption of hazardous substances through the skin. Harvesting and handling wet tobacco leaves can result in absorption of nicotine, leading to illness characterized by nausea, vomiting, weakness, and dizziness, and sometimes fluctuation in blood pressure or heart rate (Boylan et al., 1993). A 1992 outbreak in Kentucky included young people. The hospitalization of a youth from carbon monoxide poisoning resulting from operating a forklift in an enclosed space (NIOSH, 1994b), and a fatal poisoning of a youth using tetrachloroethylene to clean the inside of a metal mold used to form plastic containers (Colorado FACE Program, 1994) are examples of illness and injury resulting from inhalation of hazardous substances at work. Pesticides can lead to injury and illness through skin absorption, inhalation, and ingestion (Fenske & Simcox, 1995). Workers can be exposed to pesticides during application, in agricultural as well as nonagricultural settings (such as retail settings and schools), harvesting and handling of crops treated with pesticides, and contact with residue pesticides on surfaces. Pesticide dusts and sprays can be inhaled. Pesticide residues can be absorbed through the skin and ingested when workers eat unwashed crops or put their unwashed hands into their mouths. Work-related pesticide poisonings of youth have been documented (NIOSH, 1994b).

Other factors in the work environment can contribute to work injuries. For example, work-related assaults may be more likely in retail settings which are attractive to robbers because of a perception that they can get away with the crime (NIOSH, 1996b). Work environments can also include many electrical hazards. Energized power lines pose risks for workers working outside with equipment that can conduct electricity, such as ladders, poles, pipes, and boomed vehicles; and for employees working at heights, such as on roofs and in tree trimming (Casini, 1993). Improperly installed or damaged equipment can also lead to electricity-related injuries. Slippery floors, loose electrical cords and cables on floors, and working at heights can contribute to falling injuries. Working at heights can include working from a ladder or scaffold, working on roofs, and working on structures or near openings in building construction (NIOSH, 1995a). The hazards of falling from heights are not limited to work in construction, however.

The physical demands of work tasks can lead to injury and illness. Overexertion and cumulative trauma to the musculoskeletal system are leading causes of youth work injuries and illnesses. Task-related factors which contribute to overexertion injuries include weight and physical dimensions of the load, how the worker grips or holds the load, characteristics related to the height and distance that the load is moved, twisting and turning of the body, and the frequency of the task (Waters, Putz-Anderson, & Garg, 1994). Tasks that require repetitive motions or involve awkward body postures can lead to musculoskeletal disorders. For example, an ergonomic analysis of a blueberry raking task identified forceful and repetitive motions of the wrist which could explain the high prevalence of tendinitis (Tanaka, Estill, & Shannon, 1994).

How work is organized can also influence the occurrence of youth work injuries. The scheduling of work, including the number of hours, the time of day, rest schedules, and staffing can influence the occurrence of injuries. The need to work quickly during peak periods of production and service, which is impacted by levels of staffing, could cause workers to forget safety hazards and safe work practices. Working late at night and alone or in small numbers have been suggested as risk factors for workers' assaults (NIOSH, 1996b). Fatigue, resulting from young people trying to balance school, work, and a social life could increase the likelihood of injuries (Miller, 1995; Rosa, 1995).

Company commitment to safety can also impact the occurrence of injuries and illnesses (Shannon et al., 1996; Zohar, 1980). Examples of commitment to safety include written safety policies of which workers are aware, comprehensive and routine training in safety and health, provision of personal protective equipment, safety and health committees, investigations of injuries and illnesses with subsequent corrective measures, positive reinforcement for safe work practices, corrective actions for unsafe work practices, and worker rewards for good safety records. The workplace in the case described at the beginning of the chapter had written safety policies stating that only workers classified as machine operators were allowed to work on machinery, and that prior to working on machinery, power to the machinery had to be disengaged and the controls tagged so that other workers would not inadvertently activate the machinery (NIOSH, 1997a). The youth was classified as a laborer, and based on his job title, should not have attempted to unjam the baler. Further, the youth reported that he had emulated what he had seen other coworkers do when the baler became jammed, suggesting that unsafe work practices were not corrected by management.

Worker Characteristics

Physical, cognitive, and behavioral characteristics of workers can influence the occurrence of work injuries and illnesses. Some work tasks, such as operating equipment and manual handling of materials, require strength, agility, and height and weight restrictions. Skills in operating complex machinery, knowledge about workplace hazards and safe work practices, experience in addressing workplace hazards, and behavioral characteristics can influence the occurrence of work injuries and hazardous exposures.

It is a maxim of pediatrics that children are not "little adults." Although adolescents, who comprise the majority of working young people, are more like adults than younger children, their bodies are still growing and maturing (National Research Council [NRC], 1993). There are differences in anthropometry, physiology, and psychology that distinguish them from adults, and may translate into unique or increased risks for occupational injuries and illnesses.

Anthropometric characteristics are particularly relevant for young adolescents. In addition to age, height of 60 in. (152.4 cm) or less and weight less than 125 lbs (56.7 kg) were implicated in injuries involving ride-on mowers (U.S. Consumer Product Safety Commission, 1993). An investigation of a tractor fatality of a 12-year-old boy provides one example where a lack of fit between the youth and the machine may have contributed to the injury (Iowa FACE Program, 1995). The youth lost control and overturned a tractor in a roadside ditch. Among the potential contributors to the injury event were (a) the distance from the seat to the brakes, which was too long for the youth's legs; and (b) the youth's view of the wheel and the edge of the road may have been obstructed by the frame of the tractor.

Differences between children and adults may manifest in unique risk factors for occupational illness. Data covering youth through 17 years old demonstrate changes in body weight, surface area, and fat composition between younger and older adolescents who approximate adults (NRC, 1993). These physiological differences may result in differential effects of work exposures during different periods of adolescence, as well as in comparison to adults. Growth and maturation are not constant across organ systems. For example, although the brain approaches full adult size at about 4 years of age, the kidneys, spleen, ovaries, testes, and uterus reach adult weight at about 17 years of age.

The testes and uterus begin rapid growth at about 8 and 13 years of age, respectively. Prior to full maturation, damage to an organ or organ system could permanently prevent normal physical maturation, and organ systems may be more susceptible during rapid periods of growth. Exposure to hazardous substances and materials during youth increases the likelihood that illnesses with long latent periods will be experienced in one's lifetime. An example of increased susceptibility to a hazardous exposure during adolescence is found in studies of atomic bomb survivors. Breast cancer was more likely in those people exposed when they were younger than 20 years old compared with those exposed when they were 40 years old or older (Merke & Miller, 1992). Research on potential illness and disease resulting from youth work exposures is needed (NIOSH, 1997b).

Psychological development issues are thought to contribute to the high incidence of serious injuries among adolescents generally, not just in the workplace (Zuckerman & Duby, 1985). Psychological attributes of adolescence which may contribute to the occurrence of work injuries and hazardous exposures include poor judgment, sensation-seeking, poor risk assessment, vulnerability to peer pressure, incomplete self-image, pressure to excel, proving one's independence and maturity, desire to conform, and conversely, a need to rebel (NIOSH, 1997b). Psychological attributes likely contributed to the injury event in the case described at the beginning of the chapter.

As described previously, there are inherent hazards associated with industrial machinery and equipment, work environments, and work tasks. The operation of complex machinery requires skill, both in standard operation and maintenance, as well as quick responses to dangerous situations. Worker knowledge and skills in recognizing hazards, remediating hazards, and working safely can accrue through training and experience. Available data suggest that youth do not routinely receive training on hazards in their work environment or on safe work practices (Bush & Baker, 1994; Cohen et al., 1996; Human Resources Development Canada, 1997; Knight et al., 1995). Risk for injury appears to decrease with time spent on a job among workers of all ages (Leigh, 1986; Root, 1981; Van Zelst, 1954), presumably because workers become familiar with hazards in the work environment and safe work practices. Brief and transitory patterns of youth employment (BLS, 1992) may work against young people's gaining knowledge and skills specific to individual work sites, contributing to the high incidence of youth work injuries. In the injury event described at the beginning of the chapter, the youth had worked at the work site for 3 months, and had recently started a new shift with new tasks (NIOSH, 1997a).

PREVENTION OF WORK INJURIES AND ILLNESSES

Prevention of work-related injuries and illnesses requires a multifaceted approach, including regulations to protect against inappropriate and unsafe work by youth, engineering approaches which reduce the risks for hazardous exposures, and concerted efforts to foster safe and healthful work environments and adequate preparation of youth for work. In addition to efforts focused in the workplace, there is the potential for broadbased contributions involving numerous stakeholders who have an interest in the well-being and preparation of youth for adulthood. Groups that can play a role in preventing youth work injuries and illnesses include industry and labor groups, policy makers, standards-setting groups, equipment manufacturers, occupational safety and health practitioners, researchers, parents, educators, health care providers, and community groups.

Regulations

Working youth are protected by a patchwork of regulations, including occupational safety and health laws that mandate safe working conditions for workers of all ages, labor laws that provide a minimum age for employment and put limits on the types of work that youth can perform, workers' compensation laws to cover expenses related to work injury and illness, and mandatory school attendance laws. As described previously, violations of occupational safety and health laws and child labor laws have been associated with youth injury and death in the United States. The injury event described at the beginning of the chapter involved work in violation of a federal child labor law which prohibits youth from loading, operating, or unloading paper processing machines, including this type of baler (U.S. Department of Labor, 1990a).

One mechanism for preventing youth work injuries and illnesses is to improve compliance with existing regulations, which were enacted to preserve the health and welfare of workers in general, and youth specifically. Potential reasons for noncompliance include a lack of awareness about regulations or how to obtain information on the specifics of laws; difficulty on the part of employers and others interpreting the regulations; belief that the regulations are burdensome and unnecessary; and belief that violations will not have significant adverse consequences, whether it be injured workers or regulatory fines. Within the United States, there have been recommendations to increase the number of personnel for enforcement of child labor laws and to increase monetary penalties for violations (Child Labor Coalition, 1993; National Committee for Childhood Agricultural Injury Prevention, 1996; National Safe Workplace Institute, 1992; Pollack et al., 1990; U.S. GAO, 1990). Campaigns to improve voluntary compliance through outreach and education may also be worthwhile. Research into the reasons for noncompliance could be informative.

The workplace is dynamic (NIOSH, 1996a). Jobs shift across industrial sectors; there are changes in how work is organized; and there are new chemicals, materials, processes, and equipment used in the workplace. These changes may result in new hazards for workers, and in some cases, may even result in previously hazardous work becoming safer. Knowledge about occupational safety and health hazards and prevention is also dynamic, with information about the causes and prevention of work injuries accruing over time. Labor laws dictating the types of work that youth can perform should be periodically reviewed to ensure that the laws reflect prevailing knowledge about safety and health hazards (American Public Health Association, 1995; Child Labor Coalition, 1993; NIOSH, 1994b). Research assessing the appropriateness of specific work for youth from a developmental perspective would enhance the body of scientific data that should be used to inform policy decisions (NIOSH, 1997b).

Note that not all working youth are covered by laws regulating employment. For example, in the United States, federal child labor laws do not apply to youth working for their parents in agriculture, youth employed as actors or performers, youth engaged in the delivery of newspapers to the consumer, and youth engaged in the making of wreaths (U.S. Department of Labor, 1990a, 1990b). In the United States, recommendations have been made for both expanded coverage of child labor laws (Child Labor Coalition, 1993; NIOSH, 1994b), and the development and dissemination of voluntary standards based on a consensus-building process (National Committee for Childhood Agricultural Injury Prevention, 1996).

Engineering Approaches

Industrial machinery, equipment, and tools can be designed to reduce the risk of injury or hazardous exposures. Hazardous substances and tools used in work processes can be replaced with less hazardous materials. When hazardous exposures cannot be eliminated, personal protective equipment (e.g., hard hats and safety goggles) can be used to minimize or remove the risk of injury or illness. Finally, principles of ergonomics can be used to redesign work processes to be more compatible with the human body.

By evaluating the circumstances under which injuries occur, safety features can be incorporated into machinery or tools. For example, in the baler described in the chapter opening case, providing an access door on the side of the feed chute large enough to facilitate clearing of jams would eliminate the need, perceived or otherwise, for a worker to climb up on the conveyor to clear the jam (NIOSH, 1997a). Access doors should be interlocked with the baler's control circuitry so that the baler cannot operate once the access door is opened (American National Standards Institute, 1990). Other examples of safety features that can be incorporated into machinery to reduce injury are found on tractors and fat fryers. Rollover protective structures, or cabs, on tractors, when used in conjunction with seat belts, are very effective in preventing crushing injuries during an overturn (Thelin, 1990). Newer models of deep fat fryers include safety features to reduce the risk of grease burns, such as built-in grease filters, improved grease disposal systems, automatic food-lowering devices, and vat covers (Hayes-Lundy et al., 1991; Heinzman et al., 1993).

In the asphyxiation death of the 17-year-old using tetrachloroethylene to clean a plastics mold, the use of a less hazardous substance could have possibly prevented the death (Colorado FACE Program, 1994). A study in Connecticut found that replacing a standard case-cutter with one featuring a built-in safety guard, in combination with an education program in safe work practices, resulted in a marked decrease in associated lacerations (Banco, Lapidus, Monopoli, & Zavoski, 1997). In order to prevent youth sprains and strains from manual lifting tasks at work, training in proper lifting techniques should be provided, and the appropriateness of the lifting task for this age group considered (NIOSH, 1994b).

Personal protective equipment can be used to minimize the risk for injury or hazardous exposure when hazards cannot be removed. For example, gloves can protect workers from injuries and illnesses resulting from skin contact or absorption of hazardous substances or materials used or encountered at work. Earplugs can protect workers from damaging levels of noise. Safety belts, harnesses, lanyards, and lifelines can reduce the risk of severe injuries and fatalities when workers fall from heights, and respirators can protect workers from inhalation of hazardous substances. The effective use of personal protective equipment frequently requires proper fitting of the equipment, training on its proper use, and a maintenance program to ensure its integrity (Wegman & Levy, 1995).

Engineering strategies are generally preferred by occupational safety and health professionals because they are passive and don't rely wholly on human behavior (National Committee for Injury Prevention and Control, 1989). Behavioral considerations are rarely absent, however. For example, rollover protection on tractors is highly effective *when* seat belts are used. Workers sometimes resist the use of personal protective equipment because they consider it cumbersome (Wegman & Levy, 1995). Research on barriers and aids to acceptance and routine use of safer work machines, processes, and practices is needed (NIOSH,

1997b) to ensure that the maximum potential of engineering solutions is realized.

Work Environments and Tasks

Responsibilities and accountability for safety and health should be delegated throughout all levels of management (Keyserling, 1995; Shannon et al., 1996). Safety and health committees, comprised of managers, supervisors, and employees are considered an effective tool for creating and maintaining safe workplaces (Keyserling, 1995). The work environment and work tasks need to be periodically assessed from a safety and health perspective. Compliance with safety, health, and labor laws should be evaluated. Potential hazards should be identified, and strategies for removing or minimizing the hazard developed and implemented. These strategies can include engineering approaches, changes in how work is organized, or changes in how work is conducted. For example, in a fast-food restaurant, the installation of vat covers over deep fat fryers would be an engineering approach to reduce injuries associated with grease splatters and slick floors. Waiting for grease to cool before draining from fryers (for purposes of filtering or disposal) would be a change in how work is organized to prevent injuries from hot grease. And, instructing employees on cutting techniques to reduce the risk of injuries from slipping knives would be a change in how work is conducted. When injuries and illnesses occur, an investigation to identify the contributors to the injury or illness should be conducted and corrective actions taken to prevent future injuries and illnesses from similar circumstances (Keyserling, 1995).

Training

The hazards in the work environment need to be clearly explained to all workers, and training on safe work practices needs to be provided (Keyserling, 1995). Employers should recognize that young people bring little experience to the workplace and may require additional time, attention, and different approaches from adults. In general, training is most effective when

1. It is based on the specific knowledge and skills required for the work task,
2. the goals of the training are clear (e.g., recognition of hazards or safe work practices),
3. the mechanisms of training match the goals (e.g., although media and classroom training would be appropriate for recognizing hazards, training on the safe operation of equipment should include simulation or practice), and,
4. the knowledge and skills of workers are evaluated following training and feedback is provided to the worker (Johnston, Cattledge, & Collins, 1994).

Research into the specific training needs of young people, and training methods which are most likely to result in retention and application of knowledge and skills could advance efforts to safely introduce youth into the workplace. The skills and knowledge of youth, maturity, and hazards in the workplace should be taken into consideration in the assignment of work tasks and in determining appropriate levels of supervision. Managers and supervisors need to ensure that safety and health practices are followed. This includes discipline of workers who engage in unsafe behavior and of supervisors who encourage and permit unsafe activities (Keyserling, 1995).

Broad-Based Efforts to Ensure Safe and Healthful Work for Youth

Youth are an unique worker population in that parents still have many social and legal responsibilities. Parents can play a role in fostering safe and healthful youth employment by taking an active role in the employment decisions of their children and by discussing the types of work involved, training, and supervision provided by the employer (Bush & Baker, 1994; Massachusetts Department of Public Health and Education Development Center, Inc., 1997a; NIOSH, 1995a; We Will Not Forget SAJE Inc., 1996).

Educators play a role in occupational safety and health of young people in approving work permits, providing or facilitating work experience, and preparing students for the world of work. School staff who sign work permits and are involved in coordinating work experience programs should be knowledgeable about legislation to ensure that job placements are appropriate (Bush & Baker, 1994; NIOSH, 1995a; Province of British Columbia Ministry of Education, 1995; U.S. Departments of Education & Labor's Office of School-to-Work Opportunities, 1995). Interactions with students on work issues provide opportunities for school staff to give materials on worker safety and health to students and to discuss the rights and responsibilities of working (Bush & Baker, 1994).

Vocational education courses are included in many secondary schools as a means of providing students with marketable job skills. A safe and healthful environment for the development of vocational skills, and knowledge and skills in hazard recognition and safe work practices, should be an integral component of school vocational programs (Bush & Baker, 1994; Gregson, 1996; NIOSH/OSHA, 1981). Anecdotal cases in the United States have pointed to injuries and unhealthful conditions in some vocational programs (Wallace, Lentz, Fajen, & Palassis, 1997; Massachusetts Sentinel Event Notification System of Occupational Risks, 1993, 1995). A survey of state departments of education in the United States found that 19% of high school agricultural classes had no requirements related to safety and health (Ehlers, 1992).

Education in hazard recognition and methods of removing or reducing hazardous conditions is relevant for all students, not just those in vocational programs. Work is a reality for many students, and the majority of students will work at some point in their lives. The workplace frequently poses serious hazards to health and safety, yet existing data suggest that workplace safety training is not commonplace (Johnston et al., 1994). Providing training and information on occupational safety and health through general education in schools has been recommended (American Public Health Association, 1995; Bush & Baker, 1994; Massachusetts Department of Public Health and Education Development Center, 1997b).

Every community sees the protection of its youth as a high priority, which presents unique opportunities for preventing work-related injuries and illnesses of our young people. Community groups, such as parent–teacher organizations, chambers of commerce, 4-H groups, Future Farmers of America, scouts, and health care provider groups can provide information on youth worker safety and health to their constituencies. Community-based approaches to young worker safety and health, based on the needs, resources, and capacity of individual communities, hold promise. Demonstration projects to evaluate the feasibility and effectiveness of community-based approaches are underway in three communities in the United States (NIOSH, 1997b). Project activities include development of health and safety learning activities for integration in high school curricula, peer leadership programs, and development and dissemination of materials to parents, employers, and health care providers. Similar activities are being pursued by a Safe Community project in Ontario, Canada, which is supported through a private foundation (Kells & Conrad, 1997).

CONCLUSION

Data, primarily from the United States, demonstrate that work poses substantial risks for injury and illness to young workers. Although the magnitude and patterns of youth occupational injury may differ between the United States, Mexico, and Canada, contributory factors and prevention strategies, for the most part, will be generalizable. In addition to the hazards that are inherent in work machinery, processes, and environments, there are a number of characteristics of young people which may increase their risk for work injuries and hazardous exposures. These include inexperience, lack of safety and health training, and factors related to their physical and psychological development. Research into the role of cognition, psychosocial, and work organizational factors in the incidence of youth work injury and illness could provide guidance on appropriate work and levels of supervision for youth.

Injuries and illnesses should not be considered a cost of gaining work experience. There are concrete steps that can be taken to protect workers' health. These include modifications to industrial machinery, work processes, and environments, as well as training workers in the hazards in their environment and safe work practices. Research to identify mechanisms for encouraging adoption of safe work practices could provide additional tools in the prevention of work injuries.

Although it is important that youths have the opportunity to work as they develop and grow up, it is equally important that their lives and futures not be jeopardized by these early work experiences. Efforts to increase youth employment for developmental, social, and economic purposes should recognize and address occupational safety and health hazards. Systems are needed to prepare youth to effectively deal with work hazards, and to safely transition them into the world of work.

REFERENCES

Abraham, K. G., Weber, W. L., & Personick, M. E. (1996, April). Improvements in the BLS safety and health statistical system. *Monthly Labor Review,* 3–12.

American Academy of Pediatrics, Committee on Environmental Health. (1995). The hazards of child labor. *Pediatrics, 95,* 311–313.

American National Standards Institute. (1990). *American National Standard for Refuse Collection, Processing, and Disposal—Baling Equipment—Safety Requirements* (ANSI No. Z245.5-1990). New York: Author.

American Public Health Association. (1995). Protection of child and adolescent workers—Policy statement adopted by the governing council of the American Public Health Association, November 2, 1994. *American Journal of Public Health, 85,* 440–442.

Association for Vital Records and Health Statistics, NIOSH, National Center for Health Statistics, and National Center for Environmental Health and Injury Control. (1992). *Operational guidelines for determination of injury at work.* (Available from State Vital Statistics Offices)

Banco, L., Lapidus, G., & Braddock, M. (1992). Work-related injury among Connecticut minors. *Pediatrics, 89,* 957–960.

Banco, L., Lapidus, G., Monopoli, J., & Zavoski, R. (1997). The safe teen work project: A study to reduce cutting injuries among young and inexperienced workers. *American Journal of Industrial Medicine, 31,* 691–622.

Belville, R., Pollack, S. H., Godbold, J. H., & Landrigan, P. J. (1993). Occupational injuries among working adolescents in New York State. *Journal of the American Medical Association, 269,* 2754–2759.

Boylan, B., Brandt, V., Muehlbauer, J., Auslander, M., Spurlock, C., Finger, R., & the CDC. (1993). Green tobacco sickness in tobacco harvesters— Kentucky, 1992. *Morbidity & Mortality Weekly Report, 42,* 237–240.

Boyle, D. J., Parker, D. L., Lexau, C., Wahl, M. S., Shutske, J., & the CDC. (1995). Agricultural auger-related injuries and fatalities—Minnesota, 1992–1994. *Morbidity & Mortality Weekly Report, 44,* 660–663.

Brooks, D. R., & Davis, L. K. (1996). Work-related injuries to Massachusetts teens, 1987–1990. *American Journal of Industrial Medicine, 29,* 153–160.

Brooks, D. R., Davis, L. K., & Gallagher, S. S. (1993). Work-related injuries among Massachusetts children: A study based on emergency department data. *American Journal of Industrial Medicine, 24,* 313–324.

Broste, S. K., Hansen, D. A., Strand, R. L., & Stueland, D. T. (1989). Hearing loss among high school farm students. *American Journal of Public Health, 79,* 619–622.

Bureau of Labor Statistics. (1992). *Work and family: Jobs held and weeks worked by young adults.* Report No. 827. Washington, DC: U.S. Department of Labor.

Bureau of Labor Statistics. (1995). *Survey of occupational injuries and illnesses, Bureau of Labor Statistics.* (Unpublished data, by personal communication, June, 1995.)

Bureau of Labor Statistics. (1996). Occupational injuries and illnesses: Counts, rates, and characteristics, 1993 (Bulletin No. 2478). Washington, DC: U.S. Department of Labor.

Bush, D., & Baker, R. (1994). Young workers at risk: Health and safety education and the schools. Berkeley, CA: University of California, Berkeley.

Casini, V. J. (1993). Occupational electrocutions: Investigation and prevention. *Professional Safety, 38,* 34–39.

Castillo, D. N., Landen, D. D., & Layne, L. A. (1994). Occupational injury deaths of 16- and 17-year-olds in the United States. *American Journal of Public Health, 84,* 646–649.

Castillo, D. N., & Malit, B. D. (1997). Occupational injury deaths of 16- and 17-year-olds in the United States: Trends and comparisons to older workers. *Injury Prevention, 3,* 277–281.

Castillo, D. N., & Rodriguez, R. L. (1997). Follow-back study of oldest workers with emergency department treated injuries. *American Journal of Industrial Medicine, 31,* 609–618.

Centers for Disease Control and Prevention (CDC). (1996). Work injuries and illnesses associated with child labor—United States, 1993. *Morbidity & Mortality Weekly Report, 45,* 464–468.

Child Labor Coalition. (1993). *Child labor update and recommendations for action.* Washington, DC: National Consumers' League.

Children's Safety Network at Education Development Center, Inc., & Massachusetts Occupational Health Surveillance Program. (1995). *Protecting working teens: A public health resource guide.* Newton, MA: Education Development Center.

Cohen, L. R., Runyan, C. W., Dunn, K. A., & Schulman, M. D. (1996). Work patterns and occupational hazard exposures of North Carolina adolescents in 4-H clubs. *Injury Prevention, 2,* 274–277.

Coleman, P. J., & Sanderson, L. M. (1983). Surveillance of occupational injuries treated in hospital emergency rooms—United States, 1982. *Morbidity & Mortality Weekly Report, 32,* 31SS–37SS.

Colorado FACE Program. (1994). 17-year-old worker at a plastics manufacturing plant died as a result of an overexposure to tetrachloroethylene (also known as perchloroethylene) (Colorado FACE Investigation 94CO006A). Denver: Colorado Department of Health.

Cooper, S. P., & Rothstein, M. A. (1995). Health hazards among working children in Texas. *Southern Medical Journal, 88,* 550–554.

Derstine, B. (1997). *Job-related fatalities involving youths, 1992–1995. Fatal workplace injuries in 1995: A collection of data and analysis* (U.S. DOL Rep. No. 913). Washington, DC: U.S. Department of Labor.

Dunn, K. A., & Runyan, C. W. (1993). Deaths at work among children and adolescents. *American Journal of Diseases of Children, 147,* 1044–1047.

Ehlers, J. (1992). *Occupational health and safety education in high school agricultural education.* Unpublished master's thesis, University of Cincinnati.

Fenske, R., & Simcox, N. J. (1995). Agricultural workers. In B. S. Levy & D. H. Wegman (Eds.), *Occupational health: Recognizing and preventing work-related disease* (3rd ed., pp. 665–683). Boston: Little, Brown.

Fingar, A. R., Hopkins, R. S., & Nelson, M. (1992). Work-related injuries in Athens County 1982 to 1986: A comparison of emergency department and workers' compensation data. *Journal of Occupational Medicine, 34,* 779–787.

Frumkin, H. (1995). Carcinogens. In B. S. Levy & D. H. Wegman (Eds.), *Occupational health: Recognizing and preventing work-related disease* (3rd ed., pp. 287–304). Boston: Little, Brown.

Glor, E. D. (1989). Survey of comprehensive accident and injury experience of high school students in Saskatchewan. *Canadian Journal of Public Health, 80,* 435–440.

Gregson, J. A. (1996). A critical examination of safety texts: Implications for trade and industrial education. *Journal of Industrial Teacher Education, 33,* 29–46.

Hard, D. L., & Layne, L. A. (1995, March 8–9). *A national sample of nonfatal occupational injuries incurred by youth presenting to hospital emergency departments: Agriculture compared to other industries.* Poster session presented at Child & Adolescent Rural Injury Control Conference, Madison, WI.

Hayes-Lundy, C., Ward, R. S., Saffle, J. R., Reddy, R., Warden, G., Schnebly, W. A. (1991). Grease burns at fast-food restaurants: Adolescents at risk. *Journal of Burn Care and Rehabilitation, 12,* 203–208.

Heinzman, M., Thoreson, S., McKenzie, L., Cook, M., Hoffman, R. E., Parker, D., Carl, W. R., & the CDC. (1993). Occupational burns among restaurant workers—Colorado and Minnesota. *Morbidity & Mortality Weekly Report, 42,* 713–716.

Heyer, N. J., Franklin, G., Rivara, F. P., Parker, P., & Haug, J. A. (1992). Occupational injuries among minors doing farm work in Washington State: 1986 to 1989. *American Journal of Public Health, 82,* 557–560.

Human Resources Development Canada. (1997). *Occupational safety and health: A factor of productivity/healthy workplace . . . Healthy business!— Article No. 23.2.* (Text available on the Internet: http://gala.ccohs.ca/naosh/wk23-2en.htm)

Inansci, W., & Guidotti, T. L. (1987). Occupation-related burns: Five-year experience of an urban burn center. *Journal of Occupational Medicine, 29,* 730–733.

Iowa FACE Program. (1995). *12-year-old boy dies from a tractor rollover in a roadside ditch* (Report No. 95IA009). Iowa City: University of Iowa, Iowa FACE Program.

Jenkins, E. L., & Hard, D. L. (1992). Implications for the use of E-codes of the international classification of diseases and narrative data in identifying tractor-related deaths in agriculture, United States, 1980–1986. *Scandinavian Journal of Work & Environmental Health, 18*(Suppl. No. 2), 49–50.

Jenkins, E. L., Layne, L. A., & Kisner, S. M. (1992). Homicide in the workplace: The U.S. experience, 1980–1988. *American Association of Occupational Health Nurses Journal, 40*, 215–218.

Johnston, J. J., Cattledge, G. T. H., & Collins, J. W. (1994). The efficacy of training for occupational injury control. *Occupational Medicine: State of the Art Reviews, 9*, 147–158.

Kells, P., & Conrad, B. (1997, February 24–25). *Focus on innovation: Reducing health and safety risks.* Paper presented at Improving Children's Lives: Child and Youth Labor in North America, San Diego, CA.

Keyserling, W. M. (1995). Occupational safety: Prevention of accidents and overt trauma. In B. S. Levy & D. H. Wegman (Eds.), *Occupational health: Recognizing and preventing work-related disease* (3rd ed., pp. 145–159). Boston: Little, Brown.

Knight, E. B., Castillo, D. N., & Layne, L. A. (1995). A detailed analysis of work-related injury among youth treated in emergency departments. *American Journal of Industrial Medicine, 27*, 793–805.

Layne, L. A., Castillo, D. N., Stout, N., & Cutlip, P. (1994). Adolescent occupational injuries requiring hospital emergency department treatment: A nationally representative sample. *American Journal of Public Health, 84*, 657–660.

Leigh, J. P. (1986). Individual and job characteristics as predictors of industrial accidents. *Accident Analysis & Prevention, 18*, 209–216.

Massachusetts Department of Public Health and Education Development Center. (1997a). *A guide for parents: Protecting your working teen.* Newton, MA: Education Development Center.

Massachusetts Department of Public Health and Education Development Center. (1997b). Safe work/safe workers: A guide for teaching high school students about occupational safety and health. Newton, MA: Education Development Center.

Massachusetts Sentinel Event Notification System of Occupational Risks Program. (1993). *Quarterly progress report: April 1, 1993–June 30, 1993.* Boston: Massachusetts Department of Public Health, Occupational Health Surveillance Program.

Massachusetts Sentinel Event Notification System of Occupational Risks Program. (1995). *Quarterly progress report: October 1, 1994–December 31, 1994.* Boston: Massachusetts Department of Public Health, Occupational Health Surveillance Program.

Merke, D. P., & Miller, R. W. (1992). Age differences in the effects of ionizing radiation. In P. S. Guzelian, C. J. Henry, & S. S. Olin (Eds.), *Similarities and differences between children and adults.* Washington, DC: ILSI Press.

Miller, M. (1995). *Occupational injuries among adolescents in Washington State, 1988–1991: A review of workers' compensation data* (Tech. Rep. No. 35-1-1995). Olympia: Washington State Department of Labor and Industries, Safety and Health Assessment and Research for Prevention.

Minnesota FACE Program. (1992). *Landscape laborer dies after being struck by the bucket of a case skid steer loader* (Minnesota Face Investigation No. MN9209). Minneapolis: Minnesota Department of Health, Minnesota FACE Program.

Minnesota FACE Program. (1995). *Farmer youth dies after being struck by a loader bucket* (Minnesota Face Investigation No. 95MN04601). Minneapolis: Minnesota Department of Health, Minnesota FACE Program.

Morse, E. P. (1996, November 17–21). *Teenagers at work: Health hazard evaluations: Implications for research and policy development.* Abstract presented at American Public Health Association 124th Annual Meeting and Exposition, New York, NY.

National Committee for Childhood Agricultural Injury Prevention. (1996). *Children and agriculture: Opportunities for safety and health.* Marshfield, WI: Marshfield Clinic.

National Committee for Injury Prevention and Control. (1989). *Injury prevention: Meeting the challenge.* Oxford, England: Oxford University Press.

National Institute for Occupational Safety and Health. (1993). *Fatal injuries to workers in the United States, 1980–1989: A decade of surveillance: National profile* (DHHS NIOSH Publication No. 93-108). Washington, DC: U.S. Government Printing Office.

National Institute for Occupational Safety and Health. (1994a). *NIOSH alert: Preventing scalping and other severe injuries from farm machinery* (DHHS NIOSH Publication No. 94-105). Cincinnati, OH: U.S. Department of Health and Human Services, Public Health Service, Centers for Disease Control and Prevention, NIOSH.

National Institute for Occupational Safety and Health. (1994b, October 25). *Comments of the National Institute for Occupational Safety and Health on the Department of Labor/wage and hour division advance notice of proposed rulemaking on child labor regulations, orders and statements of interpretation.* Cincinnati, OH: U.S. Department of Health and Human Services, Public Health Service, Centers for Disease Control and Prevention, NIOSH.

National Institute for Occupational Safety and Health. (1995a). *NIOSH alert: Preventing deaths and injuries of adolescent workers* (DHHS NIOSH Publication No. 95-125). Cincinnati, OH: U.S. Department of Health and Human Services, Public Health Service, Centers for Disease Control and Prevention, NIOSH.

National Institute for Occupational Safety and Health. (1995b). *Review of safeguarding technology used on paper balers.* Morgantown, WV: U.S. Department of Health and Human Services, Public Health Service, Centers for Disease Control and Prevention, NIOSH, Division of Safety Research.

National Institute for Occupational Safety and Health. (1996a). *National occupational research agenda* (DHHS NIOSH Publication No. 96-115). Cincinnati, OH: U.S. Department of Health and Human Services, Public Health Service, Centers for Disease Control and Prevention, NIOSH.

National Institute for Occupational Safety and Health. (1996b). *NIOSH current intelligence bulletin 57: Violence in the workplace: Risk factors and prevention strategies* (DHHS NIOSH Publication No. 96-100). Cincinnati, OH: U.S. Department of Health and Human Services, Public Health Service, Centers for Disease Control and Prevention, NIOSH.

National Institute for Occupational Safety and Health. (1997a). *Laborer's legs amputated inside paper baler at resource recovery center* (FACE Publication No. 97-02). Morgantown, WV: U.S. Department of Health and Human

Services, Public Health Service, Centers for Disease Control and Prevention, National Institute for Occupational Safety and Health, Division of Safety Research.

National Institute for Occupational Safety and Health. (1997b). *NIOSH special hazard review: Child labor research needs: Recommendations from the NIOSH child labor working team* (NIOSH Publication No. 97-143). Cincinnati, OH: U.S. Department of Health and Human Services, Public Health Service, Centers for Disease Control and Prevention.

National Institute for Occupational Safety and Health, Occupational Safety and Health Administration. (1981). *Safety and health for industrial/vocational education: For supervisors and instructors.* Cincinnati, OH: U.S. Department of Health and Human Services, Public Health Service, Centers for Disease Control and Prevention, NIOSH, Division of Training and Manpower Development.

National Research Council. (1993). *Pesticides in the diets of infants and children.* Washington, DC: National Academy Press.

National Safe Workplace Institute. (1992). *Sacrificing America's youth: The problem of child labor and the response of government.* Chicago: National Safe Workplace Institute.

Office of Smoking and Health. (1982). *The health consequences of smoking: Cancer—A report of the Surgeon General* [DHHS Publication No. (PHS)82-50179]. Rockville, MD: U.S. Department of Health and Human Services, Public Health Service.

Parker, D. L., Carl, W. R., French, L. R., & Martin, F. B. (1994a). Characteristics of adolescent work injuries reported to the Minnesota Department of Labor and Industry. *American Journal of Public Health, 84,* 606–611.

Parker, D. L., Carl, W. R., French, L. R., & Martin, F. B. (1994b). Nature and incidence of self-reported adolescent work injury in Minnesota. *American Journal of Industrial Medicine, 26,* 529–541.

Perry, K. (1995, July 28). For many teens, jobs mean danger. *The Cincinnati Post,* p. 1.

Personick, M. E. (1991). Profiles in safety and health: Eating and drinking places. *Monthly Labor Review, 114,* 19–26.

Personick, M. E., & Windau, J. A. (1995). Characteristics of older workers' injuries. In U.S. DOL, BLS, *Fatal workplace injuries in 1993: A collection of data and analysis* (Rep. No. 891). Washington, DC: U.S. Department of Labor, Bureau of Labor Statistics.

Pollack, S. H., Landrigan, P. J., & Mallino, D. L. (1990). Child labor in 1990: Prevalence and health hazards. *Annual Review of Public Health, 11*, 359–375.

Province of British Columbia Ministry of Education. (1995). *Work experience handbook: Policy, guidelines and best practices.* Victoria, British Columbia, Canada: Ministry of Education, Skills Branch.

Ries, P. W. (1978). Episodes of persons injured: United States, 1975. *Advance Data, 18*, 1–12.

Root, N. (1981). Injuries at work are fewer among older employees. *Monthly Labor Review, 104*, 30–34.

Rosa, R. R. (1995). Extended workshifts and excessive fatigue. *Journal of Sleep Research, 4*, 51–56.

Schenker, M. B., Lopez, R., & Wintemute, G. (1995). Farm-related fatalities among children in California, 1980–1989. *American Journal of Public Health, 85*, 89–92.

Schober, S. E., Handke, J. L., Halperin, W. E., Moll, M. B., & Thun, M. J. (1988). Work-related injuries to minors. *American Journal of Industrial Medicine, 14*, 585–595.

Shannon, H. S., Walters, V., Lewchuck, W., Richardson, J., Moran, L. A., Haines, T., & Verma, D. (1996). Workplace organizational correlates of lost-time accident rates in manufacturing. *American Journal of Industrial Medicine, 29*, 258–268.

Shaver, C. S., & Tong, T. (1991). Chemical hazards to agricultural workers. Health hazards of farming. *Occupational Medicine, State of the Art Reviews, 6*, 391–413.

State of Wyoming. (1984). *Characteristics of youth occupational injuries & illnesses, 1979–1983.* Cheyenne: Wyoming Department of Labor and Statistics.

Stinson, J. (personal communication, September 13, 1996). [Current population survey, Bureau of Labor Statistics]. Unpublished data.

Stout-Wiegand, N. (1987). Characteristics of work-related injuries involving forklift trucks. *Journal of Safety Research, 18*, 179–190.

Suruda, A., & Halperin, W. E. (1991). Work-related deaths in children. *American Journal of Industrial Medicine, 19*, 739–745.

Tanaka, S., Estill, C. F., & Shannon, S. C. (1994). Blueberry rakers' tendinitis. *New England Journal of Medicine, 331*, 552.

Thelin, A. (1990). Epilogue: Agricultural occupational and environmental health policy strategies for the future. *American Journal of Industrial Medicine, 18*, 523–526.

Toscano, G., & Windau, J. A. (1997). *National census of fatal occupational injuries, 1995. Fatal workplace injuries in 1995: A collection of data and analysis* (Report No. 913). Washington, DC: U.S. Department of Labor.

U.S. Chambers of Commerce. (1991). *Analysis of workers' compensation—1991 edition.* Washington, DC: Author.

U.S. Consumer Product Safety Commission. (1993). [Ride-on mower hazard analysis (1987–1990)]. Unpublished data of the U.S. Consumer Product Safety Commission, Directorate for Epidemiology, National Injury Information Clearinghouse.

U.S. Departments of Education and Labor's Office of School-to-Work Opportunities. (1995). *School-to-work opportunities and the Fair Labor Standards Act: A guide to work-based learning, federal child labor laws, and minimum wage provisions.* Washington, DC: Author.

U.S. Department of Health and Human Services. (1994). *Healthy people 2000: National health promotion and disease prevention objectives* (DHHS Publication No. PHS 94-1232-1). Washington, DC: U.S. Government Printing Office.

U.S. Department of Labor. (1990a). *Child labor requirements in nonagricultural occupations under the Fair Labor Standards Act* (WH 1330). Washington, DC: U.S. Department of Labor, Employment Standards Administration, Wage and Hour Division.

U.S. Department of Labor. (1990b). *Child labor requirements in agriculture under the Fair Labor Standards Act* (Child Labor Bulletin No. 102). Washington, DC: U.S. Department of Labor, Employment Standards Administration, Wage and Hour Division.

U.S. General Accounting Office. (1990). *Child labor: Characteristics of working children* (GAO Publication No. HRD-91-83BR). Washington, DC: Author.

U.S. General Accounting Office. (1991). *Child labor: Increases in detected child* labor violation throughout the United States (GAO Publication No. HRD-90-116). Washington, DC: Author.

U.S. Office of Management and Budget. (1987). *Standard industrial classification manual, 1987*. Washington, DC: U.S. Government Printing Office.

Van Zelst, R. H. (1954). The effect of age and experience upon accident rate. *Journal of Applied Psychology, 5*, 313–317.

Wallace, M. J., Lentz, T. J., Fajen, J. M., & Palassis, J. (1997). Assessment of students' exposure to welding fumes in a vocational school welding shop. *Applied Occupational & Environmental Hygiene, 12*, 712–715.

Waters, T. R., Putz-Anderson, W., & Garg, A. (1994). *Applications manual for the revised NIOSH lifting equation* (DHHS/NIOSH Publication No. 94-110). Cincinnati, OH: U.S. Department of Health and Human Services, Public Health Service, Centers for Disease Control and Prevention, NIOSH.

We Will Not Forget SAJE Inc. (1996). *How to survive and thrive at work: A guide for teenagers (and parents, employers, and other concerned adults)*. Austin, TX: Author.

Wegman, D. H., & Levy, B. S. (1995). Preventing occupational disease. In B. S. Levy & D. H. Wegman (Eds.), *Occupational health: Recognizing and preventing work-related disease* (3rd ed., pp. 83–101). Boston: Little, Brown.

World Health Organization. (1977). *International classification of diseases: Manual on the international statistical classification of diseases, injuries, and causes of death* (9th rev.). Geneva, Switzerland: Author.

Zohar, D. (1980). Safety climate in industrial organizations: Theoretical and applied implications. *Journal of Applied Psychology, 65*, 96–102.

Zuckerman, B. S., & Duby, J. C. (1985). Developmental approach to injury prevention. *Pediatric Clinics of North America, 32*, 17–29.

8

Reconceptualizing Youth Unemployment

Graham S. Lowe and Harvey Krahn

The past two decades have been marked by jarring economic, labor market, and workplace transformations on a global scale. Public and academic discussions about these changes are dominated by themes such as the end of work, downsizing, and economic insecurity. Clearly, unemployment is the leading economic and social problem of the late 20th century. As a result, there is mounting concern about the marginalization of central groups in the labor market and how economic polarization is threatening the social cohesion of many nations. Making this point, the International Labour Organization's 1996/1997 *World Employment* report states: "The world employment situation remains grim. Unemployment remains stubbornly high in many industrialized countries ... there has been growing concern over the social exclusion that this is breeding" (International Labour Organization, 1996, p. xiii).

Echoing this with an emphasis on youth, the Organization for Economic Cooperation and Development (OECD) observed in its July

This chapter draws on research supported by the Social Sciences and Humanities Research Council of Canada. We thank Sandra Rastin for assisting with the literature review and Trish McOrmond for helping to prepare the bibliography.

1996 Employment Outlook that "the current economic and social state of many young people falls far short of what is desirable. . . . As long as total unemployment remains high, it is unrealistic to expect a significant improvement in youth job prospects . . ." (OECD, 1996, p. x). There is no doubt that 15- to 24-year-olds have faced the highest risk of unemployment in many industrialized countries, even though unemployment is far from being strictly a "youth problem." But we cannot simply generalize from our understanding of adult unemployment to the experiences of youth. To fully comprehend the nature of the current unemployment crisis, especially its implications for individuals and society in the early 21st century, one must focus on what it means now for young people starting out in a labor market.

These points are not new; indeed, they are recurrent in the literature on unemployment. Nevertheless, there have been notable shifts in emphasis. Policy research in the United States in the 1960s and 1970s identified the problem of youth unemployment, especially among Black teenagers, as requiring active policy intervention (Adams, Mangum, Stevenson, Seninger, & Mangum, 1978; Herman et al., 1968). Viewing emergent trends in the late 1970s, the OECD (1980) concluded that most youth make the transition from school to work without major difficulties. However, a hard core of disadvantaged youth experienced serious problems, and a larger and growing group encountered unemployment as a normal feature of this transition. The economic recession of the early 1980s greatly exacerbated employment problems for youth in many nations (Commonwealth Secretariat, 1988; Fiddy, 1985). In the late 1980s, the International Labour Organization observed that the concept of a "career" for youth was being threatened (International Labour Organization, 1988). Writing at the same time, Coffield (1987) noted: "In a little more than ten years the economic crisis in western societies has transformed the golden age of youth into a massive social problem" (p. 87). In the 1990s, chronically high unemployment has become a structural feature of many economies. Research today is focusing not only on individual social–psychological correlates of youth unemployment, but also on how youth as a period of life has become more risky and prolonged (Petersen & Mortimer, 1994).

Thus, over the past two decades, a huge research and policy literature has emerged on youth unemployment. It is not our intention to replicate the many thorough reviews of this literature (see Banks & Ullah, 1988; Feather, 1990; Garonna & Ryan, 1991; Hammarstrom, 1994; Petersen & Mortimer, 1994). Rather, we focus on the changing socioeconomic context in which youth unemployment arises. By integrating two major research perspectives—one on school-to-work transitions, the other on the life course—we offer a way of reconceptualizing the nature of youth unemployment at the end of the 20th century. There are two main reasons why this theoretical convergence provides a more thorough understanding of contemporary patterns of youth employment. First, it embeds youth labor market activities and experiences in the complex developmental processes of attaining economic independence and becoming integrated into society as adults. Second, it integrates individual developmental issues within the profound structural changes that recently have transformed labor markets.

The fundamental changes in youth labor markets and the institutions governing the school-to-work transition process in the past two decades are pushing the explanatory limits of existing scholarly approaches to studying youth unemployment. The personal and social consequences of unemployment among young people go beyond an extended period of dependence or diminished well-being. Indeed, transition and life course researchers are reinterpreting the problem of youth unemployment. For example, it has been framed as a "moral" issue, reflecting the social valuation of different groups and the claims and obligations they make on everyday resources (Irwin, 1995, p. 181), and as a "citizenship" issue related to young people's rights, identities, and social participation (Coles, 1995; Jones & Wallace, 1992). This kind of reconceptualization is only possible if we integrate the structural insights of school-to-work transitions and youth labor markets with the life course emphasis on how individuals personally navigate within these structures. Moving in this direction, we argue, raises new questions about the nature, meaning, and possible consequences of youth unemployment, and provides a research agenda that holds considerable promise for theoretical and policy developments.

Furnham (1994, p. 219) has questioned whether "economic conditions shape how researchers view young people. . . . Are researchers' hypotheses, and indeed methods, influenced by the prevailing economic conditions?" The answer, it would seem is *yes*—but with a considerable lag between scholarly innovations and changes in the environment being studied. In the next section, we argue that unemployment in the 1990s reflects a radically new set of economic conditions, signs of which were evident in the 1980s. However, youth unemployment research, most of which was launched in response to conditions prevailing 10 or more years ago, is only now beginning to adapt its theoretical perspectives accordingly.

This chapter is organized as follows: We begin with an overview of youth labor market trends, of which unemployment is but one. We highlight how labor markets' restructuring has especially affected youth. The next section provides a theoretical perspective on youth unemployment that draws together strands from psychology, sociology, and labor market research. We argue that youth unemployment is both multidimensional and sociohistorically based. The third section of the chapter builds on this by documenting how school-to-work transition and life course perspectives can enrich a social–psychological understanding of youth unemployment.

TRENDS IN YOUTH UNEMPLOYMENT

Although research on adult unemployment goes back to the 1930s, youth unemployment emerged as a concern among policy analysts and social science researchers in the mid 1970s. Despite a relative diminishment in the size of the youth cohort, and rising educational participation by individuals in their late teens and early twenties, youth employment conditions generally have worsened. Indeed, as unemployment has emerged as a global economic crisis it has affected youth more than any other age group (OECD, 1994). Following the recession in 1974–1975, unemployment among 15- to 24-year-olds jumped to double-digit levels in Canada, the United States, the United Kingdom, and Australia, and these levels have not receded (OECD, 1980, 1996).[1] But the gap between youth and adult unemployment rates has narrowed in OECD countries since 1980, reflecting the increase in structural unemployment in these economies. In other words, adult unemployment rates have risen, while youth rates have remained high, although young people's spells of unemployment typically are shorter than those experienced by adults (OECD, 1994). Even in the U.S. labor market, where strong employment growth has lowered overall unemployment, joblessness still remains a problem for youth.

In 1980, the OECD warned of the "twilight existence" facing growing numbers of young people in the labor market, as bouts of unemployment were interspersed with marginal employment. Some initial joblessness—or what has been referred to as "periods of foundering" between school and stable employment (Klerman & Karoly, 1994, p. 31) has long been a feature of youth labor markets. In the 1970s, viewing some of this activity as voluntary, Osterman (1980) labeled it a "moratorium." But during the 1980s the element of choice was diminished by a tightening labor market with reduced opportunities. In North America, the changing transition mechanisms connecting school and work for teenagers have redefined the experience of adolescence (Hess, Petersen, & Mortimer, 1994). In Britain, some 56% of 16-year-olds directly entered employment from school in 1976, but this had declined to 15% by 1986 (Wallace & Cross, 1990, p. 4).

Figure 1 presents youth unemployment and labor force participation rates for selected OECD countries in 1995. Both trends are key indicators of the economic activity of youth. They document the diversity of youth labor market conditions cross-nationally, within the broad context of generally high unemployment. Only 2 of the 12 countries have youth unemployment rates below 10%. Japan is the lowest, at 6%. Canada, the United States, Australia, and New Zealand are in the 12–16% range, while in Europe the rate ranges from a low of 8.5%

---

[1]Generally, *youth* refers to 15- to 24-year-olds, and this is reflected in official labor market statistics as in Figure 1. However, some countries, such as Spain, Sweden, the United Kingdom, and the United States define youth as 16- to 24-year-olds. Direct cross-national comparisons in unemployment and labor force participation rates are imperfect, given different measures used.

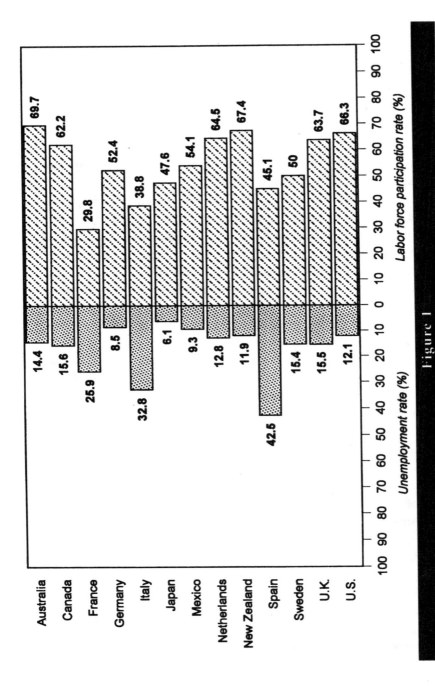

Youth unemployment rates and labor force participation rates, from selected OECD countries, 1995. *Youth* refers to 15- to 24-year-olds in all countries except Spain, Sweden, the United Kingdom (U.K.), and the United States (U.S.), where it is defined as 16- to 24-year-olds. Data derived from *Employment Outlook, July 1996* (p. 187), by the Organization for Economic Cooperation and Development (OECD), 1996, Paris: OECD. Copyright 1996 by OECD. Used with permission.

Figure 1

in Germany to over 40% in Spain. There is even greater variance in youth labor force participation, ranging from a low of 30% in France to two thirds or more in the United States, Australia, and New Zealand.

Several further points are relevant. First, although not apparent from Figure 1, in all these countries the youth labor force participation rates have declined since the late 1970s. As growing numbers of youth have faced barriers to employment, and have responded by withdrawing from the formal labor market (usually returning to school, although some may work for pay in the informal or "grey" economy, a phenomenon that is difficult to measure), they would not be counted as officially unemployed. In countries with well-developed student labor markets, such as Canada and the United States, these jobs have shrunk in relative terms. Second, when youth unemployment is disaggregated, we find higher rates among teenagers (15- to 19-year-olds) than young adults (20- to 25-year-olds), and slightly higher rates among females than males, especially for teenagers (OECD, 1996, p. 114). As Desmarais and Curtis suggest (see chap. 4, this volume), it is important to look beyond this minor gender difference in unemployment in order to understand that gender inequalities emerge during the early years in the labor market. Still, the highest unemployment rates are observed for out-of-school teenaged males (OECD, 1996, p. 146). Third, age of labor market entry also varies considerably cross-nationally, as does the extent to which students combine work and school. For example, Canada and the United States are unique in having well-developed labor markets for high school and college students, mainly in lower-level retail and personal service industries (Krahn & Lowe, 1992). Fourth, because Figure 1 shows only annual averages, smoothing out monthly fluctuations in the youth labor market, it does not capture the initial unemployment experienced by school leavers. In Australia, for example, the 1991 and 1992 unemployment rates for 15- to 19-year-olds in February (the month that school leavers would be searching for work) stood at 23% and 26%, respectively (Winefield, Tiggemann, Winefield, & Goldney, 1993). Fifth, most youth who are unemployed reside in family settings. In the European Community, only 8% of youth unemployment occurs outside families (OECD, 1994). During the past decade, a growing proportion of unemployed youth were in households where no one had a job (OECD, 1996; Payne, 1987). This situation could further reduce the employment prospects of these youth through the multiple disadvantages of poverty and a lack of social networks that could lead to a job.

Educational attainment is a strong negative correlate of youth unemployment. Our own panel study (1985–1992) of high school and university graduates in Edmonton, Canada shows, for example, that the more years of fill-time education a young person acquires, the lower their probability of being unemployed and the shorter their unemployment spells (Krahn & Lowe, 1993). The trend toward higher educational attainment in OECD countries can be interpreted positively as increased investment in human capital that should reduce the chances of unemployment for most youth. But there is also a negative side to this trend. In a more competitive labor market in which youth on average have more credentials, those with the least education face increased marginalization. Thus in 1995, Canada's employment:population ratio for university educated youth (15–24 years) was three times greater than for high school dropouts. Similarly, compared with university graduates, unemployment rates among high school dropouts are almost three times higher among 15- to 24-year-olds and four times higher among 25- to 29-year-olds (Betcherman & Leckie, 1997). Cross-nationally, this dilemma can be seen in the rising proportion of youth who are not in education, training, or employment. In the United Kingdom in 1994, for example, more than one third of 18-year-olds (31% of 22-year-old males, and 37% of females the same age) were neither employed nor in school (OECD, 1996). The OECD calls this "a worrying trend" that requires further research before effective policy interventions can be developed (OECD, 1996, p. 128). The longer term implications of this social marginalization require close monitoring (Tanner, Krahn, & Hartnagel, 1995).

In many of the industrialized countries, training and education programs have proliferated, with the overall effect of keeping youth out of the labor market for longer time periods (OECD, 1996). As a result, the official youth unemployment rate often appears to underestimate the extent of the problem. Furthermore, it is now recognized that standard measures of unemployment—being out of work and seeking employ-ment—may not be adequate. Some youth would be counted as "dis-couraged workers," because they have given up the search for work, believing none is available. In Canada, for example, the number of dis-couraged workers peaked after the 1981–1982 recession and has fallen since. Young workers have been overrepresented among discouraged workers, comprising 37% of this group in 1980, and declining to 22% in 1995. To help interpret these numbers, we should note that the youth share of the total labor force declined during this period from 27% to 16.4%. Over the same period, the proportion of youth in part-time jobs (averaging less than 30 hours weekly) who wanted full-time jobs in-creased from 20% to 27% (Betcherman & Leckie, 1997). This "invol-untary" part-time work is considered a form of underemployment.

Although youth unemployment has remained high, the majority of young labor force participants do find work. But the spread of part-time, temporary, contract, and other "nonstandard" forms of work has fundamentally altered youth labor markets (OECD, 1996). One major consequence, seen in all OECD countries except Sweden, has been de-clining youth wage levels relative to those of adults (OECD, 1996). In Canada, real annual earnings of 17- to 24-year-old males dropped 33% between 1981 and 1993, while the comparable decline for women in this age cohort was 23% (Betcherman & Morissette, 1994; Morissette, Myles, & Picot, 1994; see also Ryscavage, 1995 for the United States, & Westergaard, 1995 for Britain).

Observing these youth employment and unemployment trends in Canada, Statistics Canada (1997) concluded that

> a growing proportion of those who manage to secure jobs may do so on a temporary basis, earn low wages, and have little access to promotion opportunities. Under such conditions, these young workers may be quickly sidelined by any reorga-nization or downsizing, and today's difficulties may affect future prospects throughout their working careers. (p. 5)

Much the same could be said about any OECD nation. Indeed, there are growing concerns about "scarring," whereby early unemployment experiences increase the probability of future unemployment, although there is no consensus on this issue among labor economists (Betcherman & Morissette, 1994, p. 9). Panel studies, which track individuals from adolescence into adulthood, lend support to this hypothesis (Adams et al., 1978; Ward, Dale, & Joshi, 1993). Thus, compared with previous generations, the current generation of youth may be less likely to achieve or surpass its parents' living standards (Krymkowski & Krauze, 1992). Canadian surveys suggest that even among university graduates, for whom investments in higher education still "pay off" in relative terms, successive cohorts are facing increased difficulties finding the "good" jobs to which they aspire (Davies, Mosher, & O'Grady, 1994; Little, 1995).

At a time when national economic policies are acknowledging the "competitive advantages" of investing in human resources through higher education and training of the labor force (Economic Council of Canada, 1992; Reich, 1991), it is ironic that underemployment among the well educated is often overlooked. There is a tendency in contemporary school-to-work transition research to focus on disadvantaged youth with the most immediate problems, such as early school leavers or the unemployed. However, there is an equally large group of educated youth, who on the surface appear to have made the transition into the labor market, but for whom finding a job that uses their education and abilities is very difficult.

Although the term *underemployment* commonly is used to indicate a shortage of work (e.g., the involuntary part-time noted above), it also can describe a mismatch between acquired skills and educational credentials and the demands of a job (see chap. 2, this volume). From this perspective, underemployment is obviously a concern for better-educated labor market participants, particularly university graduates. Mismatch underemployment can be measured by comparing the educational attainment of job-holders with the educational requirements of their jobs, or by asking workers to assess the extent to which they are overqualified for their jobs. These objective and subjective measures of mismatch underemployment produce similar findings (Redpath, 1994).

Canada's 1989 national General Social Survey found that 23% of all employed Canadians (ages 15–64) felt they were overqualified for their jobs (Krahn, 1992). Comparisons by educational attainment (for all ages combined) showed the same level (23%) of self-reported un-deremployment among those with postsecondary qualifications, but a higher level (27%) among high school graduates, and a lower level (18%) among those who had not completed high school. Comparisons by age (all education levels combined) showed that underemployment was highest among 15- to 24-year-olds (35%) and lowest (16%) among the oldest cohort of employed Canadians. More recently, Canadian data from the 1994 International Adult Literacy Survey clearly show that young workers, despite very high levels of literacy, have higher than average rates of literacy skills underutilization in the workplace (Krahn & Lowe, 1998; see also Boothby, 1993).

Although these data suggest higher levels of mismatch underem-ployment among well-educated youth compared with older workers possessing similar credentials, the independent effects of age and edu-cation on underemployment remain unclear. Anecdotal accounts imply that higher proportions of well-educated youth are underemployed to-day (the stereotypical taxi driver with a PhD), compared to a generation ago, as postsecondary graduates are forced by labor market restructur-ing to accept jobs previously filled by workers with fewer educational credentials. However, we have little information on changes over time in underemployment among youth. Although several national studies in Canada offer some support for this hypothesis (Davies et al., 1994; Grayson & Hall, 1992; Little, 1995), U.S. research shows that the prob-lem also existed before the labor market upheavals of the 1980s (Collins, 1979; Rumberger, 1981), reflecting an earlier increase in postsecondary enrollments compared with other OECD countries (OECD, 1996).

What has changed dramatically in the past decade, however, is the youth labor market, which has been evolving toward temporary, part-time, and other forms of "nonstandard" work as the norm. Almost half of employed Canadian youth are working in either a part-time or tem-porary job, although most are still students (Krahn, 1995). In light of these trends, it is important not to set up a false dichotomy between employed and unemployed youth. Given rising educational attainment in many countries (OECD, 1996), researchers must also address job quality and possible mismatch problems, even among those youth who report full-time employment.

CONTEXT AND PROCESS IN YOUTH UNEMPLOYMENT RESEARCH

The experiences of youth in today's labor market are best understood, in our view, from a perspective that synthesizes elements of the distinct literatures in psychology, sociology, and labor market analysis. Because issues central to school-to-work transitions and life course research have at least been acknowledged in the social–psychological youth unemployment literature for over a decade, a theoretical convergence is quite feasible. In particular, two central themes in this literature provide potential bridges: the importance of the immediate context in shaping experiences of, and responses to, unemployment, and the dynamic nature of young people's experiences in the labor market, which makes it difficult to treat unemployment as a single overriding status. These themes have been peripheral in the literature until recently, when attempts have been made to explicitly incorporate them into a more theoretically grounded research agenda.

What distinguishes youth from adult unemployment is that the former affects individuals at a time of crucial life transitions and psychosocial development. Recognition of this in the youth unemployment literature may have led to the dominance of an "individual pathology" model, which emphasizes the negative effects of unemployment for individuals (Banks & Ullah, 1988, p. 4). Thus concerns about the negative longer term impact of unemployment on youth tend to be developmental in perspective, raising concerns about delayed, truncated, or unsuccessful passages into adulthood.

There are three such approaches found in the literature. The first and most prevalent comes out of developmental psychology, examining the effects of joblessness on the psychological well-being and development of youth (Feather, 1990; Winefield et al., 1993). The second em-

212

phasizes the squandering of human resources if the talents of the youth generation are lost, through failure to develop a strong work ethic, occupational identity, or work skills and experience (Burman, 1988; Furnham & Lewis, 1986; Jehoel-Gijsbers, & Groot, 1989). As Deaton (1983, p. 16) states, "Today's unemployed youth become tomorrow's unemployables." The third approach is more concerned with the negative behavioral consequences of unemployment, and what this may mean for society. Crime, drug abuse, violence, and political agitation are the main antisocial reactions to blocked employment opportunities that this literature has portrayed (Cote & Allahar, 1994; OECD, 1980; Roberts, Clark, & Wallace, 1984), although some researchers have labeled this approach as somewhat of a "moral panic" (Tanner, Lowe, & Krahn, 1984; Tanner et al., 1995).

Cross-sectional studies cannot untangle the complex causal relationships among personal characteristics, labor market experiences, and the possible negative consequences of unemployment. However, findings from a number of longitudinal studies permit generalizations about some of the effects of unemployment on young people. Research conducted in a variety of countries documents minor and inconsistent negative effects of unemployment and underemployment on mental health (Banks & Jackson, 1982; Feather, 1990; Feather & O'Brien, 1986; Hammarstrom, 1994; Morrell, Taylor, Quine, Kerr, & Western, 1994; Warr, Jackson, & Banks, 1982; Winefield et al., 1993). Overall, unemployment diminishes well-being, but the evidence linking labor market difficulties to mental health problems has not been nearly as consistent among youth as among adults (Hammarstrom, 1994; Hartnagel & Krahn, 1995; Horowitz, 1984).

In other words, an individual's stage in the life course influences the impact of unemployment. This is entirely consistent with the basic proposition that psychological well-being is a function of how individuals' resources interact with their immediate environment (Hamilton, Broman, Hoffman, & Renner, 1990). As Warr (1987) explains, in general terms an unemployed young person's environment presents fewer difficulties than the middle-aged unemployed person would face, particularly regarding the consequences of unemployment for income, family, physical security, social relationships, and social status. Compared with older workers, young people's resilience and optimism, the options of returning to school and continuing to live with parents, and not having dependents make unemployment less psychologically distressing.

Turning to specific studies, a longitudinal (1985–1989) analysis of the labor market experiences of high school and university graduates in three Canadian cities observed only weak effects (Hartnagel & Krahn, 1995). High school graduates who had experienced more unemployment over the 4-year period tended to report increased feelings of depression and powerlessness, and reduced feelings of self-esteem. But similar findings were not observed among university graduates, a group further along in the school-to-work transition and hence more likely to be concerned about unemployment. Similarly, a longitudinal study of South Australian school leavers during the 1980s found negative psychological consequences of unemployment. But this was due to the psychological benefits of employment rather than the negative consequences of unemployment (Winefield et al., 1993). Being satisfied with one's job was the key determinant of psychological well-being. This suggests that the presence of satisfying work is essential for a healthy transition to adulthood.

By viewing the youth unemployment problem as one of finding quality employment, we necessarily must expand our scope of enquiry to encompass a wide range of labor market experiences and employment conditions. This extends Jahoda's (1982) functional theory of the manifest and latent functions of employment, raising questions about how the nature and quality of young people's activities in employment, unemployment, training programs, and on the fringes of the labor market affect the transition process itself. Recent literature on the quality of activities engaged in by unemployed youth (O'Brien, Feather, & Kabanoff, 1994), on changes over time in the self-esteem of high school students (Dooley & Prause, 1995), and on unemployment as a cause of psychological disturbance (Morrell et al., 1994) provides further support for this enlarged focus. As one group of researchers concluded, after examining two youth cohorts from the Australian Longitudinal Survey over 4-year periods, the best antidote for any psychological morbidity arising from unemployment is a job (Morrell et al., 1994).

In the interest of demonstrating the utility of a more contextualized, process-oriented perspective on youth unemployment, our overview of youth unemployment literature has been selective. Clearly other factors, especially gender and race, shape school-to-work transitions, the risk of unemployment, and individual responses to unemployment. Research on both topics tends to lend additional support to our proposition that youth unemployment must be studied from a life course perspective that takes into account labor market variations. For example, like many aspects of employment (see chap. 4, this volume), youth unemployment is a gendered phenomenon in terms of precursors, experiences, and outcomes (Banks & Ullah, 1988; Hammarstrom, 1994; Hutchens, 1994; Liem & Rayman, 1984; Mortimer, 1994; Taylor, 1986; Winefield et al., 1993). For some young women, traditional gender roles and attitudes may still provide a fall-back position in times of unemployment, although it is not clear to what extent recent cohorts are rejecting these traditional roles. Especially for adolescent girls, labor market or family difficulties can influence choices regarding household formation, marriage or cohabitation, and fertility—transitions that can be best understood in the context of the life course (Hagan & Wheaton, 1993).

Similarly, there is no question that race or ethnicity are determinants of labor market outcomes, although these personal characteristics have received less attention in the social-psychological literature than gender. Historically Black Americans have been more susceptible to unemployment than Whites (Bowman, 1984; Powers, 1994). Bowman (1990, p. 88) argues that chronic joblessness makes the school-to-work transition "a special challenge" for Black Americans. He advocates a life span approach to understanding the antecedents and long-term developmental consequences of job search problems encountered by Black youth. In his qualitative analysis of unemployment among Black youth in Britain, Ullah (1987) emphasized the importance of understanding how these young people organize their lives, their racial identities, and views of society, and how they experience racism. In short, he advocates focusing on how unemployment is rooted in the specific social environment inhabited by this group of visible minority youth.

We could, of course, extend our discussion to include other antecedents, moderators, and outcomes of youth unemployment, but will restrict our comments to one additional issue. Briefly, research on deviant and criminal behavior among youth underlines the necessity of examining the multiple problems that define the lives of disadvantaged youth. For example, high school dropouts report more criminal activity, including drug use, than do young people who complete high school (Gilbert, Barr, Clark, Blue, & Sunter, 1993; Tanner et al., 1995). Among dropouts, those who have experienced more labor market difficulties, particularly unemployment, tend to report more criminal behavior (Hartnagel & Krahn, 1989; Samuelson, Hartnagel, & Krahn, 1996). However, it is difficult to prove that unemployment is the primary cause. Similarly, although a longitudinal study of high school graduates in Toronto, Edmonton, and Sudbury (Ontario) showed somewhat more frequent drug use among individuals who had experienced labor market problems (Hartnagel, 1995, 1996), the contingent factors and causal mechanisms are far from clear. Thus, as researchers in Britain and the United States have argued, under some conditions and among some groups of youth there may be a relationship between school-to-work transition problems, broadly defined, and criminal behavior (Sampson & Laub, 1990). But more confident generalizations regarding a causal relationship between unemployment and crime are not supported by published research findings. One way that future research could explore this relationship is by investigating the social "embeddedness" of youth in social networks that either increase the chances of getting a job or of turning to crime (Hagan, 1993). This gives credence to our more general argument that youth unemployment is multidimensional and sociohistorically based.

LOOKING BEYOND THE SOCIAL PSYCHOLOGY OF YOUTH UNEMPLOYMENT

Although the literature we have reviewed on youth unemployment has the potential to move beyond a strictly social-psychological perspective on the topic, so far this potential has not been realized. Psychologists use the language of "transitions," but essentially apply a developmental perspective to youth unemployment. For example, in a longitudinal study of unemployed Australian school leavers in the 1980s, Winefield et al. (1993, p. 150) concluded: "Unemployment in the young, then, may be viewed as a transition problem. It occurs in the context of many other physical, political and social changes." These researchers do not pursue the theoretical possibilities of this statement, rather, they fall back to a developmental psychology perspective which treats the transition from school to work as one sequence of a multistage life cycle.

Erikson's influential model (1968, p. 132) of adolescent psychological development did acknowledge the importance of social structure: "Youth after youth, bewildered by the incapacity to assume a role forced on him [sic] by the inexorable standardization of American adolescence, runs away in one form or another, dropping out of school, leaving jobs, staying out all night, or withdrawing into bizarre and inaccessible moods." Dooley and Prause (1995, p. 77) cite Erikson regarding the need for youth to develop a "meaningful occupational identity," arguing that due to economic conditions "the young person may be denied the opportunity to negotiate a successful school-to-work transition. Thwarted in this transition, young people may experience self-doubt that can put them at elevated risk of persistent occupational and psychological disfunction." At issue, then, is how young people respond to rapidly changing social and economic structures. Under what circumstances do some youth acquiesce to a constraining social environment, whereas others redefine structured roles? Moreover, what are the longer term implications for individuals and society of some youth encountering adversities in attempting to enter adult work, family, and community roles? We now consider the insights offered into these and related questions by school-to-work transition and life course research.

YOUTH UNEMPLOYMENT, SCHOOL-TO-WORK TRANSITIONS, AND THE LIFE COURSE

The voluminous research on youth transitions provides not so much an alternative to social–psychological studies, but rather a complementary basis from which to examine youth unemployment. Embedded in this literature is the assumption that unemployment must be viewed as part of the school-to-work transition process which, in turn, is situated within the institutional contexts of education, labor markets, peers, and family (Jones & Wallace, 1992). Moreover, youth labor markets are influenced by national differences in educational and training systems, formal linkages between schools and the labor market, industrial structures, and technologies (Ashton, 1988; Ashton & Lowe, 1991; Evans & Heinz, 1994). These national institutional arrangements create differences in attitudes and aspirations about education and work, age of labor market entry, and educational attainment and credentials.

School-to-work transition research illuminates the dynamic social processes and institutional frameworks within which unemployment occurs. Researchers have expanded the concept of transition, coming to view specific behavioral and psychological dimensions of youth from a longer range, more holistic life course perspective (Hogan & Astone, 1986). Theoretically, a life course perspective has the advantage of being able to document and explain the diversity of roles, events, and decisions that cumulatively determine an individual's "biography" (Heinz, 1992). For psychologists, it is axiomatic that adolescence and young adulthood are crucial stages of human development (Erikson, 1968; Hess et al., 1994). Life course models build on these insights, integrating developmental issues within relevant social contexts and institutional structures, recognizing that experiences in teenage and young adult years can have lasting implications for adult life course trajectories (Buchmann, 1989; Heinz, 1992; Hogan, 1989; Rossi, 1985). Increasingly, the individual focus of life-course studies is being integrated with the more structural focus on youth labor market research to more fully indicate how young people move from dependence to independence in the spheres of employment and family (Irwin, 1995).

Life course research has been criticized, however, for not addressing how the state plays a crucial rule in organizing and regulating the life course, which partly explains how transitions today differ from those in earlier eras, as well as cross-nationally (Mayer & Schoepflin, 1989). State labor market and educational policies bear directly on the magnitude of employment difficulties, as evidenced by wide national variations in spending on youth employment and training measures. In the early 1990s, for example, Japan had no measures and spent nothing, the United States had 13 active programs costing .003% of gross domestic product (GDP), while France, the United Kingdom, and Italy each had 30 or more measures costing between .24% and .37% of GDP (Garonna & Ryan, 1991). Britain's Youth Training Scheme, which provided job-related training for out-of-school 17- and 18-year-olds during the mid 1980s, essentially made official unemployment disappear—critics would say essentially delayed it—for 2 years by creating "surrogate labor markets" (Ashton, Maguire, & Spilsburg, 1990; Lee, Marsden, Hardey, Rickman, & Masters, 1987).

Life course researchers also examine generational differences. So how much has the transition to work and adulthood changed historically? Historical research suggests that in the United States, passage to adulthood during the late 19th century was "disorderly" and "capricious" in comparison to the 1970s (Modell, Furstenberg, & Hershberg, 1976, p. 8). Stevens' (1990) analysis of U.S. census data between 1910 and 1980 documents changes in key youth transitions: leaving school, entering the workforce, finding full-time employment, leaving their parents' household, first marriage, and establishment of own household. There is some continuity over the 7 decades, especially regarding the ordering of transition behaviors, suggesting that the more recent cohorts of youth "faced a much stricter and more age-determined passage to adulthood" (Stevens, 1990, p. 173).

This conclusion is supported by recent U.S. demographic research. Demographers view the young adult years (between ages 18 and 30) as defined by a large concentration of role transitions: school leaving, employment, migration, marriage, and fertility. Rindfuss (1991) suggests that the disorder and diversity in school-to-work transitions observed today is not as different from the past as many think. Rindfuss detects more diversity in the family sphere, given rising rates of marital dissolution, remarriage, and cohabitation. But in terms of education and work, the evidence is less clear. Although rising levels of educational attainment and labor market restructuring have led to a more extended and difficult school-to-work transition, wars and the Great Depression also disrupted the transition for previous generations of youth. The U.S. National Longitudinal Study of the high school class of 1972 shows that, 12 years later, only 10% had worked all 12 years—and this was the most common path followed (see also Rindfuss, Swicegood, & Rosenfeld, 1987). This point is underscored by Coleman (1984), whose analysis of the educational and employment histories of U.S. men born during the 1930s challenges the view of the transition involving a movement from full-time education to full-time employment.

Although this U.S. research displays broad historical patterns in the ordering of key role changes during adolescence and youth, it does not focus on unemployment. Katz's study of Hamilton in mid 19th-century Canada offers details of unemployment experiences in the preindustrial era. Large numbers of young males did not work or go to school. According to Katz (1975, p. 262), about half of 11- to 15-year-olds and 25% of 16- to 20-year-olds "remained in what must have been a state of partial idleness. Many adolescents must have roamed around the city with little or nothing to do, a situation which provides an objective underpinning for the desire felt by adults in this period to devise institutions that would take adolescents off the streets." Katz (1975) also comments that, compared with young men, "young women suffered even more than young men from a period of life in which they neither went to school or had a job" (p. 272). As a result of industrialization and educational reform, by the early 20th century in Canada "youth" was a prolonged and regulated phase of life.

Overall, 20th-century socioeconomic development has contributed to a more structured, or institutionalized, life course (Fend, 1994). The creation of adolescence as the stage for education and career preparation sets up conditions for personal and social crisis if individuals do not achieve economic independence. But new social and economic forces in the 1980s and 1990s may have eroded the basis on which a structured life course had developed. This changing context has affected all social groups, but particularly young people. Transitions to work and adulthood appear to have become more hazardous, fragmented, and disorderly. Again, national contexts matter in this regard. British researchers would dispute U.S. demographer's claims of continuity in life course patterns (e.g., Rindfuss et al., 1987), contending that transitions to employment were sequential and predictable in the 1970s. But with the "collapse" of the youth labor market in the 1980s, transitions were fraught with difficulties associated with widespread unemployment and underemployment and high levels of participation in education and training schemes to escape joblessness (Ashton et al., 1990; Furlong, 1992; Raffe, 1987; Willis, 1977).

National demographic trends also influence youth transitions. For example, in Europe, shrinking youth cohorts in the 1980s began to shift the focus of policy to potential labor scarcities (Garonna & Ryan, 1991), although this possible development would affect cohorts entering the labor market in the early 21st century. In Canada, the 1981–1982 Recession coincided with a large cohort of youth exiting high school. These combined economic and demographic trends pushed youth unemployment to the highest levels since the Depression of the 1930s, then abating somewhat later in the decade as this demographic pressure subsided (Foot & Li, 1986).

This discussion of demographic factors raises fundamental questions regarding the changing relationship between individuals, particularly youth, and society. Most theoretical perspectives on youth view this period as a developmental stage characterized by instabilities (Chisholm & du Bois-Reymond, 1993). However, postmodern interpretations draw our attention to the destructuring of labor markets, workplaces, and social institutions generally. Taken as a whole, these changes signal a deinstitutionalization, or "individualization," of school-to-work transitions. Lacking the guideposts that previous generations followed into adulthood, youth are scripting their own biographies (Beck, 1992; see also Hutchens, 1994; Jones & Wallace, 1992). This is a contentious point, of course. Researchers on both sides of the Atlantic present evidence that can be interpreted either as increased fragmentation and individualization of the school-to-work transition, or persistence of structural barriers and opportunities, depending on a youth's socioeconomic characteristics, in the face of increased risks and uncertainties (Banks et al., 1992; Evans & Heinz, 1994; Heinz, 1996; Irwin, 1995; Jones & Wallace,

1992; Krahn & Lowe, in press). Postmodern interpretations suggest that within postindustrial societies—typically, those in North America and Western Europe that have moved beyond mass industrial production, mass consumption and the welfare state as dominant forms of economic and social organization—the main alternative to unemployment has become diverse forms of insecure underemployment (Beck, 1992; Geissler & Krüger, 1992). Structuralist researchers (Ashton et al., 1990; Furlong, 1992; Roberts & Parsell, 1992) counter that opportunity structures for youth, including the risk of unemployment, still are largely determined, as they have been for decades, by social-class background, gender, educational attainment, and local labor market conditions.

Sociologists and psychologists have long debated the extent to which young people exercise choice in the school-to-work transition (Layder, Ashton, & Sung, 1991). Layder et al.'s research on British school leavers suggests that individual choice and social structure are interlinked. This captures the essence of the "youth debate" in the United Kingdom during the 1980s (Jones & Wallace, 1992). Indeed, there is growing convergence between micro and macro positions, in light of findings suggesting that there is greater individualization and diversity in youth transitions within the constraints imposed by location, socioeconomic status, education, and gender (Jones & Wallace, 1992; Roberts et al., 1994). But generally there is little support for the proposition that more individuals are "choosing" unemployment over other options, at least based on social surveys representative of the adult populations in the United States and Europe over the past two decades (International Labor Organization, 1996). We should acknowledge, though, that some school leavers—perhaps those with a well-developed career plan—may willingly prolong their unemployment in order to search more thoroughly for a job that meets their expectations. Yet to the extent that transitions are becoming more "individualized" within changing labor market structures, an integrated micro and macro perspective becomes all the more necessary. The interconnections between labor market experiences, on one hand, and the process of establishing independence in family and social spheres, on the other, remain opaque. Thus as Irwin (1995) pointed out, there is no general effect of unemployment on the life course trajectories of youth because of the diversity of individual experiences and characteristics that also influence the move to independence.

CONCLUSION

Youth unemployment research may well be at a theoretical crossroads. Persistently high youth unemployment has become a feature of most industrialized economies. Yet to understand how young people experience unemployment today, and its individual and social implications, researchers must take into account that the youth labor market has been fundamentally restructured in the past two decades. It is well documented that some groups of young people are more at risk of unemployment than are others. For example, males who have not completed secondary education experience considerable difficulties in the labor market, whereas young women face different challenges and dilemmas associated with household and family roles. But in a labor market that increasingly is characterized by insecurity and instability with the spread of nonstandard forms of employment, especially for young people, unemployment may have become part of typical school-to-work transitions for growing numbers of youth.

In light of this changing context, we have argued, it is timely to find ways of integrating the insights from social–psychological perspectives on youth unemployment with school-to-work transition and life course research. Theoretically, the core research problem is the relationship between the individual and society and how this may be in flux. Studying youth unemployment is an ideal way to probe this question, but only if researchers treat unemployment not as a discrete dependent or independent variable (Who becomes unemployed? What are the effects of unemployment?), but rather as one possible experience through which a young person may pass. As such, unemployment is embedded in less predictable and destructured school-to-work transition processes and, furthermore, can have implications for a young person's choices regarding future education, career plans, geographic mobility, marriage, and family. Studies of the minor negative social–

psychological effects of youth unemployment, although important from the perspective of current well-being and personal development, typically miss the ways in which the experiences of unemployment may shape the subsequent life course. At the same time, transition and life course researchers need to acknowledge that trajectories into employment, or personal biographical strategies, are themselves influenced by how at a social–psychological level unemployment affects a young person.

We also have suggested that unemployment is not the only labor market problem faced by youth, and that researchers should focus more attention on issues of employment quality, particularly underemployment. The turbulence of youth labor markets became very apparent in the 1980s. Throughout the industrialized world, educational attainment has risen since the 1970s and transitions into employment have been extended into young adulthood. In North America, acquiring further education has been the response of many young adults to a more competitive labor market, with direct implications for their movement into independent adult roles. Just as the incidence of unemployment has tended to decline among older cohorts of youth, so too has underemployment. Over the longer term, underemployment is more pervasive than unemployment. In a youth labor market where "good" jobs are scarce, it is especially important to examine the social–psychological effects on young people of prolonged exposure to unrewarding work, and in turn to examine how this may influence their life course.

Is it possible to integrate into a unified perspective on youth unemployment the analytic themes of class, gender, labor market structures and processes, expectations and aspirations, and behavioral and psychological responses? Ultimately, this is essential for understanding at the individual and societal level the implications of why some youth get good jobs while others remain underemployed or unemployed. But this integration has thus far been elusive. As Jahoda (1982) remarked some time ago, there is no coherent theory of work, employment, and unemployment. Our contribution to youth unemployment research is a modest prescription for how we could move in this direction.

REFERENCES

Adams, A. V., Mangum, G. L., Stevenson, W., Seninger, S. F., & Mangum, S. L. (1978). *The lingering crisis of youth unemployment.* Kalamazoo, MI: W. E. Upjohn Institute for Employment Research.

Ashton, D. N. (1988). Sources of variation in labor market segmentation: A comparison of youth labor markets in Canada and Britain. *Work, Employment & Society,* 1–24.

Ashton, D. N., & Lowe, G. S. (1991). *Making their way: Education, training and the labor market in Canada and Britain.* Toronto, Ontario, Canada: University of Toronto Press.

Ashton, D. N., Maguire, M. J., & Spilsburg, M. (1990). *Restructuring the labor market: The implications for youth.* London: Macmillan.

Banks, M. H., Bates, I., Breakwell, G., Byner, J., Emler, N., Jamieson, L., & Roberts, K. (1992). *Careers and identities.* Milton Keynes, England: Open University Press.

Banks, M. H., & Jackson, P. R. (1982). Unemployment and risk of minor psychiatric disorder in young people: Cross-sectional and longitudinal evidence. *Psychological Medicine, 12,* 789–798.

Banks, M. H., & Ullah, P. (1988). *Youth unemployment in the 1980s: Its psychological effects.* London: Croom Helm.

Beck, U. (1992). *Risk society: Towards a new modernity.* Thousand Oaks, CA: Sage.

Betcherman, G., & Leckie, N. (1997). *Youth employment and education trends in the 1980s and 1990s* (Working Paper No. W03). Ottawa, Ontario, Canada: Canadian Policy Research Networks.

Betcherman, G., & Morissette, R. (1994). *Recent youth labor market experiences in Canada.* Ottawa, Ontario, Canada: Analytic Studies Branch, Statistics Canada.

Boothby, D. (1993). Schooling, literacy and the labor market: Towards a 'literacy shortage'? *Canadian Public Policy, 24,* 29–35.

Bowman, P. J. (1984). A discouragement-centered approach to studying unemployment among black youth: Hopelessness, attributions, and psychological distress. *International Journal of Mental Health, 13*(1–2), 68–91.

Bowman, P. J. (1990). The adolescent-to-adult transition: Discouragement among jobless black youth. *New Directions for Child Development, 46,* 87–105.

Buchmann, M. (1989). *The script of life in modern society: Entry into adulthood in a changing world.* Chicago: University of Chicago Press.

Burman, P. (1988). *Killing time, losing ground: Experiences of unemployment.* Toronto, Ontario, Canada: Wall & Thompson.

Chisholm, L., & du Bois-Reymond, M. (1993). Youth transitions, gender and social change. *Sociology, 27,* 259–279.

Coffield, F. (1987). From the celebration to the marginalization of youth. In G. Cohen (Ed.), *Social change and the life course* (pp. 87–105). London: Tavistock.

Coleman, J. S. (1984). The transition from school to work. *Research in Social Stratification and Mobility, 3,* 493–512.

Coles, B. (1995). *Youth and social policy: Youth citizenship and young careers.* London: UCL Press.

Collins, R. (1979). *The credential society: An historical sociology of education and stratification.* New York: Academic Press.

Commonwealth Secretariat. (1988). *Jobs for young people: A way to a better future. Report of a commonwealth expert group.* London: Author.

Cote, J. E., & Allahar, A. L. (1994). *Generation on hold: Coming of age in the late twentieth century.* Toronto, Ontario, Canada: Stoddart.

Davies, S., Mosher, C., & O'Grady, B. (1994). Trends in labor market outcomes of Canadian post-secondary graduates, 1978–1988. In L. Erwin & D. Mac-Lennan (Eds.), *Sociology of education in Canada: Critical perspectives on theory, research and practice* (pp. 352–369). Toronto, Ontario, Canada: Copp Clark Longman.

Deaton, R. (1983). Unemployment: Canada's malignant social pathology. *Perception, 6*(5), 14–19.

Dooley, D., & Prause, J. (1995). Effect of unemployment of school leavers' self-esteem. *Journal of Occupational and Organizational Psychology, 68,* 177–192.

Economic Council of Canada. (1992). *A lot to learn: Education and training in Canada.* Ottawa, Ontario, Canada: Supply and Services Canada.

Erikson, E. H. (1968). *Identity, youth and crisis*. New York: Norton.

Evans, K., & Heinz, W. R. (1994). *Becoming adults in England and Germany*. London: Anglo-German Foundation.

Feather, N. T. (1990). *The psychological impact of unemployment*. New York: Springer-Verlag.

Feather, N. T., & O'Brien, G. E. (1986). A longitudinal analysis of the effects of different patterns of employment and unemployment on school-leavers. *British Journal of Psychology, 77,* 459–479.

Fend, H. (1994). The historical context of transition to work and youth unemployment. In A. C. Petersen & J. T. Mortimer (Eds.), *Youth unemployment and society* (pp. 77–94). Cambridge, England: Cambridge University Press.

Fiddy, R. (1985). *Youth, unemployment and training: A collection of national perspectives*. London: Falmer Press.

Foot, D. K., & Li, J. C. (1986). Youth employment in Canada: A misplaced priority? *Canadian Public Policy, 12,* 499–506.

Furlong, A. (1992). *Growing up in a classless society? School to work transitions*. Edinburgh, Scotland: University of Edinburgh Press.

Furnham, A. (1994). The psychosocial consequences of youth unemployment. In A. C. Petersen & J. T. Mortimer (Eds.), *Youth unemployment and society* (pp. 199–223). Cambridge, England: Cambridge University Press.

Furnham, A., & Lewis, A. (1986). *The economic mind: The social psychology of economic behavior*. Brighton, England: Wheatsheaf Books.

Garonna, P., & Ryan, P. (1991). The problems facing youth. In P. Ryan, P. Garonna, & R. C. Edwards (Eds.), *The problem of youth: The regulation of youth employment and training in advanced economies* (pp. 1–31). London: Macmillan.

Geissler, B., & Krüger, H. (1992). Balancing the life course in response to institutional requirements. In W. Heinz (Ed.), *Institutions and gatekeeping in the life course. Status passages and the life course* (Vol. III, pp. 151–167). Weinheim, Germany: Deutscher Studien Verlag.

Gilbert, S., Barr, L., Clark, W., Blue, M., & Sunter, D. (1993). *Leaving school: Results from a national survey comparing school leavers and high school graduates 18 to 20 years of age*. Ottawa, Ontario, Canada: Minister of Supply and Services.

Grayson, J. P., & Hall, M. H. (1992). *Transitions from school: Ontario's record.* Toronto, Ontario, Canada: Institute for Social Research, York University.

Hagan, J. (1993). The social embeddedness of crime and unemployment. *Criminology, 31,* 465–491.

Hagan, J., & Wheaton, B. (1993). The search for adolescent role exits and the transition to adulthood. *Social Forces, 71,* 955–980.

Hamilton, V. L., Broman, C. L., Hoffman, W. S., & Renner, D. S. (1990). Hard times and vulnerable people. *Journal of Health and Social Behavior, 31,* 123–140.

Hammarstrom, A. (1994). Health consequences of youth unemployment: Review from a gender perspective. *Social Science and Medicine, 38,* 699–709.

Hartnagel, T. F. (1995). Labor market problems in the transition from school to work and illegal drug use: A panel study of Canadian youth. *Current Perspectives on Aging and the Life Cycle, 4,* 61–90.

Hartnagel, T. F. (1996). Cannabis use and the transition to young adulthood. *Journal of Youth and Adolescence, 25,* 241–258.

Hartnagel, T. F., & Kralin, H. (1989). High school dropouts, labor market success and criminal behavior. *Youth and Society, 20,* 416–444.

Hartnagel, T. F., & Krahn, H. (1995). Labor market problems, and psychological well-being. A panel study of Canadian youth in transition from school to work. *British Journal of Education and Work, 8,* 33–53.

Heinz, W. R. (1992). *Institutions and gatekeeping in the life course. Status passages and the life course.* Weinheim, Germany: Deutscher Studien Verlag.

Heinz, W. R. (1996). *The transition from education to employment in a comparative perspective.* Toronto, Ontario, Canada: University of Toronto, Centre for International Studies.

Herman, M., Sadofsky, S., & Rosenberg, B. (1968). *Work, youth, and unemployment.* New York: Thomas Y. Crowell.

Hess, L. E., Petersen, A. C., & Mortimer, J. T. (1994). Youth, unemployment and marginality: The problem and the solution. In A. C. Petersen & J. T. Mortimer (Eds.), *Youth unemployment and society* (pp. 3–33). Cambridge, England: Cambridge University Press.

Hogan, D. P. (1989). Institutional perspectives on the life course: Challenges and strategies. In D. Kertzer & K. W. Schaie (Eds.), *Age structuring in comparative perspective.* Hillsdale, NJ: Erlbaum.

Hogan, D. P., & Astone, A. M. (1986). The transition to adulthood. *Annual Review of Sociology, 12,* 109–130.

Horowitz, A. V. (1984). The economy and social pathology. *Annual Review of Sociology, 10,* 95–119.

Hutchens, S. (1994). *Living a predicament: Young people surviving unemployment.* Aldershot, England: Avebury.

International Labour Organization. (1988). *World employment review.* Geneva, Switzerland: Author.

International Labour Organization. (1996). *World employment 1996/97: National policies in a global context.* Geneva, Switzerland: Author.

Irwin, S. (1995). *Rights of passage: Social change and the transition from youth to adulthood.* London: UCL Press.

Jahoda, M. (1982). *Employment and unemployment: A social–psychological analysis.* Cambridge, England: Cambridge University Press.

Jehoel-Gijsbers, G., & Groot, W. (1989). Unemployed youth: A lost generation? *Work, Employment and Society, 3,* 491–508.

Jones, G., & Wallace, C. (1992). *Youth, family and citizenship.* Buckingham, England: Open University Press.

Katz, M. B. (1975). *The people of Hamilton West: Family and class in a mid-nineteenth-century city.* Cambridge, MA: Harvard University Press.

Klerman, J. A., & Karoly, L. A. (1994). Young men and the transition to stable employment. *Monthly Labor Review, 117,* 31–48.

Krahn, H. (1992). *Quality of work in the service sector. General social survey analysis series no. 6.* Ottawa, Ontario, Canada: Statistics Canada.

Krahn, H. (1995). Non-standard work on the rise. *Perspectives on Labour and Income, 7,* 35–42.

Krahn, H., & Lowe, G. S. (1992). Do part-time jobs improve the labor market chances of high school graduates? In B. D. Warme, K. L. P. Lundy, & L. Lundy (Eds.), *Working part-time: Risks and opportunities* (pp. 131–148). New York: Praeger.

Krahn, H., & Lowe, G. S. (1993). *The school-to-work transition in Edmonton, 1985–1992* (Final research report prepared for Alberta Advanced Education and Career Development). Edmonton, Alberta, Canada: University of Alberta, Population Research Laboratory.

Krahn, H., & Lowe, G. S. (1998). *Literacy utilization in Canadian workplaces.*

Ottawa, Ontario, Canada: Statistics Canada and Human Resources Development Canada.

Krahn, H., & Lowe, G. S. (in press). School–work transitions and post-modern values: What's changing in Canada? In W. Heinz (Ed.), *From education to work: Cross national perspectives*. Cambridge, England: Cambridge University Press.

Krymkowski, D. H., & Krauze, T. K. (1992). Occupational mobility in the year 2000: Projections for American men and women. *Social Forces, 71,* 145–157.

Layder, D., Ashton, D. N., & Sung, J. (1991). The empirical correlates of action and structure: The transition from school to work. *Sociology, 25,* 447–464.

Lee, D., Marsden, D., Hardey, M., Rickman, P., & Masters, K. (1987). Youth training, life chances and orientations to work: A case study of the Youth Training Scheme. In P. Brown & D. N. Ashton (Eds.), *Education, unemployment and labour markets* (pp. 138–159). London: Falmer.

Liem, R., & Rayman, P. (1984). Perspectives on unemployment, mental health, and social policy. *International Journal of Mental Health, 13*(1–2), 3–17.

Little, D. (1995). Earnings and labor force status of 1990 graduates. *Education Quarterly Review, 2,* 10–20.

Mayer, K. U., & Schoepflin, U. (1989). The state and the life course. *Annual Review of Sociology, 15,* 187–209.

Modell, J., Furstenberg, F., Jr., & Hershberg, T. (1976). Social change and transitions to adulthood in historical perspective. *Journal of Family History, 1,* 7–32.

Morissette, R., Myles, J., & Picot, G. (1994). Earnings inequality and the distribution of working time in Canada. *Canadian Business Economics, 2,* 3–16.

Morrell, S., Taylor, R., Quine, S., Kerr, C., & Western, J. (1994). A cohort study of unemployment as a cause of psychological disturbance in Australian youth. *Social Science & Medicine, 38,* 1553–1564.

Mortimer, J. T. (1994). Individual differences as precursors of youth unemployment. In A. C. Petersen & J. T. Mortimer (Eds.), *Youth unemployment and society* (pp. 77–94). Cambridge, England: Cambridge University Press.

O'Brien, G. E., Feather, N. T., & Kabanoff, B. (1994). Quality of activities and the adjustment of unemployed youth. *Australian Journal of Psychology,* *46*(1), 29–34.

Organization for Economic Cooperation and Development. (1980). *Youth unemployment: The causes and consequences.* Paris: Author.

Organization for Economic Cooperation and Development. (1994). *The OECD jobs study: Evidence and explanations. Part I—Labour market trends and underlying forces of change.* Paris: Author.

Organization for Economic Cooperation and Development. (1996). *Employment outlook, July 1996.* Paris: Author.

Osterman, P. (1980). *Getting started: The youth labour market.* Cambridge, MA: MIT Press.

Payne, J. (1987). Does unemployment run in families? Some findings from the General Household Survey. *Sociology, 21,* 199–214.

Petersen, A. C., & Mortimer, J. T. (1994). *Youth unemployment and society.* Cambridge, England: Cambridge University Press.

Powers, D. A. (1994). Transitions into idleness among White, Black, and Hispanic youth: Some determinants and policy implications of weak labor force attachment. *Sociological Perspectives, 37,* 183–201.

Raffe, D. (1987). Youth unemployment in the United Kingdom 1979–1984. In P. Brown & D. Ashton (Eds.), *Education, unemployment and labour markets* (pp. 218–247). London: Falmer.

Redpath, L. (1994). Education-job mismatch among Canadian university graduates: Implications for employers and educators. *Canadian Journal of Higher Education, 24,* 89–114.

Reich, R. B. (1991). *The work of nations: Preparing ourselves for 21st-century capitalism.* New York: Alfred A. Knopf.

Rindfuss, R. R. (1991). The young adult years: Diversity, structural change, and fertility. *Demography, 28,* 493–512.

Rindfuss, R. R., Swicegood, C. G., & Rosenfeld, R. A. (1987). Disorder in the life course: How common and does it matter? *American Sociological Review, 52,* 785–801.

Roberts, K., Clark, S. C., & Wallace, C. (1994). Flexibility and individualization: A comparison of transitions into employment in England and Germany. *Sociology, 28,* 31–54.

Roberts, K., & Parsell, G. (1992). Entering the labour market in Britain: The survival of traditional opportunity structures. *Sociology Review, 40,* 726–753.

Rossi, A. (1985). *Gender and the life course.* New York: Aldine.

Rumberger, R. W. (1981). *Overeducation in the U.S. labor market.* New York: Praeger.

Ryscavage, P. (1995, August). A surge in growing income inequality? *Monthly Labour Review,* 51–61.

Sampson, R. J., & Laub, J. H. (1990). Crime and deviance over the life course: The salience of adult social bonds. *American Sociological Review, 55,* 609–627.

Samuelson, L., Hartnagel, T. F., & Krahn, H. (1996). Crime and social control among high school dropouts. *Journal of Crime and Justice, 18,* 129–166.

Statistics Canada. (1997). *Labour force update: Youths and the labor market.* Ottawa, Ontario, Canada: Author.

Stevens, D. A. (1990). New evidence on the timing of early life-course transitions: The United States 1900 to 1980. *Journal of Family History, 15,* 163–178.

Tanner, J., Krahn, H., & Hartnagel, T. F. (1995). *Fractured transitions from school to work: Revisiting the dropout problem.* Don Mills, Ontario, Canada: Oxford University Press.

Tanner, J., Lowe, G. S., & Krahn, H. (1984). Youth unemployment and moral panics. *Perception, 7,* 27–29.

Taylor, S. (1986). Teenage girls and economic recession in Australia: Some cultural and educational implications. *British Journal of Sociology of Education, 7,* 379–395.

Ullah, P. (1987). Unemployed black youths in a northern city. In D. Fryer & P. Ullah (Eds.), *Unemployed people: Social and psychological perspectives* (pp. 111–147). Milton Keynes, England: Open University Press.

Wallace, C., & Cross, M. (1990). Introduction: Youth in transition. In C. Wallace & M. Cross (Eds.), *Youth in transition: The sociology of youth and youth policy* (pp. 1–10). London: Falmer.

Ward, C., Dale, A., & Joshi, H. (1993). Participation in the labour market. In E. Ferri (Ed.), *Life at 33: The fifth follow-up of the national child development study* (pp. 60–91). London: National Children's Bureau.

Warr, P. (1987). *Work, unemployment and mental health.* Oxford, England: Clarendon Press.

Warr, P., Jackson, P. R., & Banks, M. H. (1982). Duration of unemployment and psychological well-being in young men and women. *Current Psychological Research, 2,* 207–214.

Westergaard, J. (1995). *Who gets what? The hardening of class inequality in the late twentieth century.* Cambridge, England: Polity Press.

Willis, P. (1977). *Learning to labour: How working class kids get working class jobs.* London: Saxon House.

Winefield, A. H., Tiggemann, M., Winefield, H. R., & Goldney, R. D. (1993). *Growing up with unemployment: A longitudinal study of its psychological impact.* London: Routledge.

9

Youth and Labor Representation

Daniel G. Gallagher

Labor unions have generally viewed themselves as agents for the enhancement and protection of the economic and procedural rights of employees in the workplace, as well as advocates for broader economic and social reforms that benefit society in general. The extent to which unions have succeeded in meeting these immediate and broader objectives is an ongoing subject of discussion (Strauss, Gallagher, & Fiorito, 1991; Sverke, 1997). In addition, the extent of union effectiveness may vary by country, industry, occupation, stage of economic development, and the ideological orientation of those offering the evaluation. It is also increasingly clear that, like most other organizations, unions have and must continue to undergo change to survive and prosper. Although the history of trade unionism varies from country to country, a similar pattern of union development generally appears (Frenkel, 1993; Olney, 1996). This development can take the form of unions serving as the advocates of workers' interests in specific skilled

The author appreciates the information and suggestions provided by Dr. Christina Cregan at the University of Melbourne, and by Mr. Chris Walton, Organising Works—Australian Council of Trade Unions (ACTU), Melbourne, Australia. The author also thanks Karen Bennington for her suggestions and assistance in the preparation of this chapter.

occupations or crafts, or of unions organizing and representing workers of the entire industry.

For many unions in developed economies, the transition of employment from a structured industrialized context to a more fluid post-Fordist environment, with increased emphasis on the service sector and organic or flexible organizational forms, has represented a threat to the traditional base of union membership. This transition has also presented a set of challenges for union organizations. Most notably, unions in many countries have witnessed not only declining rates of unionization among industry, but also have experienced actual declines in membership levels. Sectoral shifts from an industrial or manufacturing foundation to service-based economies in a number of countries have driven unions to focus on organizing and representing service sector industries (e.g., wholesale and retail trade, health care, financial services, and government). Within countries such as the United States, union representation in the post-Fordist environment is gradually shifting. Although these groups are not mutually exclusive, unions are generally shifting from the representation of middle-class and blue-collar workers toward increased representation of women, racial minorities, and the "new immigrants." Ironically, in contrast to the United States's declining membership rates, union membership in Canada has remained relatively stable, at twice the level of unionization found in the United States.

By virtue of the disproportionate percentage of young workers—especially teenagers—who are employed in the service sectors, youth have the potential of being exposed to unions during their employment. Not only are young workers beginning to be more actively sought out as members by some labor organizations, but many unions also are increasingly resurrecting an emphasis on young people as the future of the labor movement in terms of membership, organizing, and leadership.

Despite such expressions of union interest in young workers, exposure to union involvement is not uniform across the young population. For some, unions are an avenue through which inexperienced youth gain access to apprenticeship programs and entry into careers as skilled craft workers. Historically, such apprenticeship programs have not always provided equal access to interested youth but may have been available based on parental union membership, gender, or other demographic factors. Historic union opposition to alternative employment arrangements, such as part-time employment, may have indirectly limited the growth of jobs available to students on restricted work schedules (Barling & Gallagher, 1996). Although not generalizable to all unions and countries, in the past, union approaches toward youth may have been best characterized as neglectful or indifferent. Regardless of intentions or motivations (or lack thereof), the fact remains that workers in the 15- to 19-year age range are the most significantly underrepresented by unions in most developed countries.

The spirit of the "new unionism" may be associated with increased union interest in organizing young workers; however, a number of questions immediately surface. First, despite growing union interest in young people, are young people interested in unions? Most notably, when given an opportunity to organize or join an existing union, are youth likely to elect union affiliation? Second, to what extent are youth given the opportunity to make the decision to join an existing workplace union or to vote for or against union representation in the context of a union organizing effort? Cregan and Johnston (1990) noted that many of the preceding issues are tied to a broader debate of whether unionism among young people is a function of their "propensity" to join unions or a function of the presence or absence of an "opportunity" to join, or a combination of both propensity and opportunity.

Issues related to the union-joining propensities and opportunities among young people were embedded in the responses of Australian teenagers to a 1989 national opinion poll commissioned by the Australian Council of Trade Unions (ACTU) to identify young people's views toward labor unions. The results of the ACTU survey indicated that

1. Young people have little awareness of unions.
2. What they do know tends to be negative.
3. Young people do not view unions as taking a positive role in helping them enter the workforce.

4. Many have positive feelings toward unions as a way of protecting workers from exploitation.
5. Youth often view union officials as lazy, political, and remote.
6. A large share of young workers list among their major reasons for not joining a union (a) never been asked to join; or (b) a previous negative experience.

It is not immediately possible to determine the extent to which these survey results would be replicated in other countries. It is reasonable to suggest that, at a minimum, young people's awareness of unions may be more extensive in the limited number of countries with unionization levels greater than Australia's and considerably less in countries where unionization is less prevalent and declining. The ACTU survey is also interesting for another insight that it provides. The survey infers that young people might view unions as a means of helping others, but as being of limited personal value.

The primary objectives of this chapter are not only to better understand the relationship between youth and labor unions, but also to understand the extent to which unions could serve to improve the employment experiences of younger workers. Focus is directed toward understanding the motivation (or absence of motivation) for young workers to join unions or to seek union representation. Closely related to this issue of union-joining propensity is the identification of the most salient factors in shaping the attitudes of young people toward unions and union representation. Finally, the chapter closes with some general observations concerning the current and future relationship between young workers and labor unions.

THEORETICAL PERSPECTIVES ON JOINING UNIONS

The decision to join a union or to support labor union representation is an issue that confronts workers of all age groups and in a variety of different work settings. In an employment relationship where a union currently holds the right to represent specific jobs or occupations, membership in the union may be a mandatory condition of employment. A young high school student, starting to work as a stock clerk at a local supermarket, might discover that a "union shop" clause in the existing union–management contract requires joining the union within a specified period of time as a condition of continued employment. Under such circumstances, the student may become an "involuntary" dues paying member of the union. Conversely, the student may not focus on the issue of volition, but rather accept union membership as a benefit or a necessary condition of employment. In either case, the issues of union representation and membership are predetermined and outside the immediate control of the student.

In other contexts, the question of union membership or representation may involve more active decision making by the employee. It is entirely possible that although a young worker's job in an organization is represented by a union, union membership is totally voluntary. Under such an arrangement, the new hire retains the benefits of union representation but is not obligated to join the union while maintaining employment. A second type of "choice" is present in a non-unionized workplace where a union is seeking to gain representational rights. In this situation, young workers must choose to support or reject the union representation of their jobs through written authorization or a vote in a union certification election. Admittedly, the implications of a choice to join an existing union or to select representation in a previously non-union environment may have different implications for the newly hired young worker, the union, and the employer.

To date, a substantial amount of empirical and theoretical research has focused on identifying factors that influence the willingness or propensity of workers to vote or petition for union representation (see, Barling, Fullagar, & Kelloway, 1992; Premack & Hunter, 1988). To a lesser extent, a body of literature has examined unionization choice in the context of the *free-rider* phenomenon, or the decision not to voluntarily join the union that currently represents similar positions at the workplace (e.g., Chaison & Dhavale, 1992; Jermier, Cohen, & Gaines, 1988). Although empirical and theoretical investigations of pro-union voting (certification) and individual decisions to join a union are technically distinct and may be influenced by different factors, they can be characterized as decisions that are in support of a union.

The effort to better understand the willingness or propensity of young workers to support labor unions may benefit by considering the numerous theoretical perspectives used to model union support by workers of all age groups. From these theoretical perspectives, it may be reasonable to speculate over the relevance or relative weight that various determinants of union support may carry for younger workers. Based upon a review and synthesis of the literature by Wheeler and McClendon (1991), the following two broad theoretical frameworks are offered in an effort to understand the willingness of young workers to support unions in their workplace.

Dissatisfaction–Instrumentality Models

Dissatisfaction–instrumentality models of union joining suggest that the individual decision to support (or seek) union representation is a function of work-related experiences and beliefs about unionism. Operationalizing the model suggests that the initial motivation for taking an action (i.e., to vote, authorize, or join) is a function of individuals' perceptions of their existing work experiences. The theory posits that workers who are experiencing dissatisfaction or dissonance (i.e., expected vs. actual job experiences and outcomes) will seek mechanisms to resolve the dissonance.

The extent to which young or older workers are willing to turn to unions as a means to address employment-related dissatisfactions is further hypothesized to be a function of the perceived instrumentality of unions. Even if workers experience dissatisfaction or dissonance with the employment situation, they may be unlikely to seek union representation unless the involvement or support is perceived to lead to tangible results. Alternatively stated, unless there is a belief or feeling that having a union in the workplace will lead to constructive changes, then workers will forego unionization and potentially seek other mechanisms to resolve their job-related dissatisfactions.

Kochan, Katz, and McKersie (1986) modified this model by proposing that in addition to instrumentality considerations workers must be willing to overcome the general negative image or stereotypes of unions. Empirical support for this proposition was found by Deshpande and Fiorito (1989), who established that besides the general union image perceptions, the beliefs that workers hold about the specific impact of unions in the local workplace still explain pro-union intentions at the workplace even after controlling for general union image perceptions.

On the surface, it seems that dissatisfaction–instrumentality models are an intuitively appealing framework for understanding union support (or nonsupport) among young workers. Such models would argue that young people who are dissatisfied with their jobs and feel that a union can make improvements would be likely to support union representation if given an opportunity to do so. Although appealing, the applicability of the model to younger workers has some limitations.

Limitations

First and foremost is that the manner in which individual workers react to job-related dissatisfactions differs. Among younger workers, reactions to dissatisfaction and the degree of that dissatisfaction may be dependent on their attachment to the workforce or employer. For example, young workers who are employed part-time while attending school may be less attached to the employment relationship, viewing it as a transitory short-term arrangement. Under such circumstances, job-related dissatisfaction may be more easily addressed by so-called exit behavior (i.e., quitting) rather than evaluating the instrumentality of union representation. As an alternative to exiting, dissatisfied individuals may opt to stay on the job but make minimal contributions until they find other employment. Some authors have also suggested that younger workers may have a higher tolerance for unsatisfactory working environments due, in part, to overall lower job expectations (Cregan & Johnston, 1993). In contrast, the role and value of union representation in addressing job dissatisfactions may increase for recent high school graduates who move to full-time employment status with long-term expectations of attachment to the labor market and potential employers. Furthermore, as young workers increase their ties to an organization and job changing behavior decreases, it is reasonable to project that

241

issues of job satisfaction and union instrumentality may become increasingly relevant.

A second shortcoming of the explanatory strength of the model is that young workers may not have a well-developed or a realistic assessment of union instrumentality. It is reasonable to suggest that through observational learning from parents and other sources young workers probably have formulated general impressions or attitudes about unions. But in the absence of prior work experience in a unionized environment or an effective union informational campaign, it is highly unlikely that young workers have sufficient direct knowledge of the potential effect unions can have in the workplace. This observation is consistent with survey results suggesting that young people's opinions about unions more typically reflect a lack of knowledge about unions, rather than strongly rooted assessments of the benefits and drawbacks of union representation.

Finally, dissatisfaction–instrumentality models of union support offer only limited insight into how and what factors contribute to worker perceptions of union instrumentality. As suggested above, understanding the process by which instrumentality perceptions are formed by young workers with limited work experience may be as important as the perceptions themselves.

Ideological Models

Ideological, or political belief, models of union support are extremely generalized perspectives. These models posit that the motivation to support union activity is a function of the individual worker's political or ideological beliefs. Wheeler and McClendon (1991) suggested that the ideological and political models of union support have received considerably greater attention in countries outside North America, where class and class consciousness are hypothesized to be central determinants of union support (e.g., Guest & Dewe, 1988).

One variation on the ideological or political beliefs model is what Klandermans (1986) labeled the "interactionist theories." These theories suggest that union involvement is, in large part, reflective of group culture. If workers live in a social environment that is conscious of class distinction and supportive of union membership and participation, then individual workers are likely to develop similar attitudes. In many respects, the individual worker's orientation toward union support may reflect the need to retain solidarity or identification with other members of the community. Conversely, as communities become more ideologically and economically diversified or fragmented, the interactionist basis for union support may diminish and union identification may decline.

At first blush, it appears that such ideological considerations would not be major motivating factors to drive young workers to join a union. However, Cregan and Johnston's (1990) study of London 16-year-old school leavers found that the decision by young people to join a union was often stated as a desire "to support the union," or a collective instrumentality, rather than to seek a specific individual benefit. Further evidence of the potential relevance of broader ideological orientations to the understanding of union-related attitudes of younger workers was found in research conducted by Barling, Kelloway, and Bremermann (1991), who found that among a sample of high school and college students in Canada, Marxist and humanistic work beliefs were significantly related to a positive attitude toward unions and a subsequent willingness to join a union. These results appear consistent with opinion surveys of some young workers for whom unionism is an expression of a desire to be part of a broader collective organization (Australian Council of Trade Unions [ACTU], 1995).

Utility Models

In sharp contrast to ideological perspectives, utility models of union support can also be characterized as "calculative," "rational choice," or "cost–benefit" approaches to the decision of whether to support union involvement in the workplace. Research by Klandermans (1986) hypothesized that decisions made by individual workers to join, participate, and remain in a union were a multiplicative function of the so-called consequences of union support relative to the value of those consequences for the individual.

Utility models of union support can be extended to incorporate an

243

expectancy component. Not only are there outcomes or consequences but also the need to realize that workers may attach probabilities to the likelihood that a certain course of action will lead to a particular outcome. Utility models have also been expanded to consider the role of subjective norms. Fishbein and Ajzen's (1975) theory of reasoned action has been applied to the study of trade unions (e.g., Brief & Rude, 1981; Montgomery, 1989). These applications suggest that behavioral intentions are not only a function of an individual's beliefs that performing a behavior will result in an outcome and the value attached to that outcome but also that the intent is influenced by a normative component. The willingness of an individual to engage in a particular behavior is influenced by subjective norms, or opinions, about what other people think the individual should do and how much relative importance the individual places on complying with the various referents (e.g., coworkers, friends, parents). In many respects, the utility models of union support assume that individual decision making involves a complex cost–benefit calculus integrating individual perceptions of instrumentality and valence.

The utility or rational choice models of union joining, including Fishbein and Ajzen's theory of reasoned action, are significantly more complicated than dissatisfaction–instrumentality models. However, the former may be of particular value in understanding the union joining behavior of young workers.

One underlying assumption of utility models as applicable to young workers as to adults is that various aspects of the employment relationship carry differing weight or importance for each worker. For young workers, union joining may be attractive if they believe that unions can improve the overall quality of their jobs *and* feel that job quality is important. Among students in short-term employment arrangements, the importance of the quality of work may be less salient and, hence, less of a motivating force to seek union representation than among those young workers in employment relationships with longer term prospects.

In reality, utility models appear to be particularly relevant to the study of labor union joining among young people because they suggest that unless unions can identify work-related outcomes that are important to young workers—regardless of union effectiveness or instrumentality—union joining or support will not be viewed by young people as an important course of action.

A second critical component of utility models suggested by Fishbein and Ajzen (1975) and incorporated into a growing number of studies of union joining and support is the importance of subjective norms in the decision-making process. Decision-making or behavioral intentions are not only influenced by the beliefs of referent others (e.g., family, friends, and coworkers) but by the importance the individual attaches to complying with the expectations of the referent others. The desire to meet the expectations of others or to behave in a way that is consistent with the attitudes of significant others may be more influential for young workers than in later stages of personal development. At the very least, one would expect over time a narrowing or greater selectivity of the salient referent groups. In general, union joining among young people (as with older adults) will involve not only a personal cost–benefit calculus, but also consideration of how a particular course of action is perceived by others.

Finally, similar to other frameworks for determining union joining actions, a primary issue that still remains in the utility model approach is to identify the forces that are instrumental in shaping the attitudes of young workers toward both unions in general and the role of unions in the immediate workplace.

FORMATION OF ATTITUDES TOWARD UNIONS

The literature on union joining and support suggests a variety of factors that can influence the willingness of a worker to support union representation. These factors may include the individual's experiences in the workplace, past participation or involvement with unions, and attitudes not only toward unions in general but feelings about the extent to which a union can be instrumental in the current work environment. In many respects, support for unionization is both a function of the attitudes that an individual brings to the workplace and the experiences that are encountered once on the job.

The attitudes that young workers hold toward unions are less likely, compared with those of older workers, to have been shaped by immediate first-hand experiences and past union membership. The absence of direct union experiences may reflect the limited work life of young people but also that they are disproportionately more likely to work in occupations or industries without union representation. In the absence of extensive workplace interactions with unions, the question is how young people formulate attitudes toward unions and a subsequent willingness to join or support union representation. Although the research is limited, young workers' attitudes or impressions about unions may largely be a function of the influences of family, friends, and popular culture. In addition, any early work experiences with unions may shape young workers' future disposition toward union support in other employment situations.

Family and Friends

The literature examining predictors of union joining or voting behavior also examines the role of parents in influencing the disposition of young people toward unionization. In most of these studies, *parental influence* was defined as whether one or both parents were at any time a union member (e.g., Huszczo, 1983; Youngblood, DeNisi, Molleston, & Mobley, 1984). Although often left unexplained, the underlying expectation appears to be that workers from families with a history of union membership are more likely to support unions than workers without such parental exposure to labor unions. Interestingly, much of this research fails to confirm the presence of a significant relationship between parental union status and a worker's attitudes toward unions.

In contrast, a growing body of research suggests that workers' attitudes toward unions, especially young workers' attitudes, are more a function of parental attitudes than parental union membership (Barling et al., 1991; Gallagher & Jeong, 1989; Heshizer & Wilson, 1995; Kelloway & Watts, 1994). In homes where one or both parents hold favorable attitudes toward unions, young people are more likely to have similarly favorable attitudes. Barling et al. (1991) suggested that the formation of general union attitudes among young people reflects a social learning process between parent and child that impacts union attitudes as well as career orientations and work values. What is particularly interesting about the Barling et al. study is that although young people inferred their parents' attitudes to be a function of parental participation in union-related activities, parental participation demonstrated no direct effect on the children's own attitudes toward unions. Rather, the results confirm a strong link between the perception of parental attitudes and the young person's own attitudes toward unions in general and a related willingness to join a labor organization if given the opportunity. The Barling et al. (1991) research of high school and college students also confirmed an ancillary hypothesis that young people with Marxist and humanistic work beliefs are significantly more positive in their attitudes toward unions in general.

Subsequent replication and extension of the Barling et al. (1991) study by Kelloway and Watts (1994) strongly affirms the relationship between parental attitudes and student attitudes toward unions. The study established that student perceptions of parental attitudes and participation were, in fact, significantly related to parental self-reports of such attitudes and participation. However, contrary to expectations, student work beliefs (i.e., Marxist work beliefs), although influencing union attitudes, were not predicted by the corresponding beliefs of their parents. In essence, it appears that parents' union attitudes have a greater impact on their children than do work beliefs.

The role of normative influences on actual union-related attitudes and behaviors of young workers is impacted by the motivation to comply with parental attitudes or expectations. The motivation to comply with parental attitudes may, however, compete with the relative importance of complying with the perceived attitudes of other key referent groups, such as friends and coworkers.

Using a sample of undergraduate college students, Heshizer and Wilson (1995) reaffirmed the link between parental union attitudes and students' own attitudes toward unions. Heshizer and Wilson also established that this desire to comply with parental attitudes moderated the relationship between perceived parental union attitudes and the student's own attitudes, suggesting that a greater motivation to comply

DANIEL G. GALLAGHER

was associated with a stronger link between parent and child perceptions.

The Heshizer and Wilson (1995) study points to a number of other
findings relevant to the understanding of union attitudes among young
people. First, parental attitudes were more effective in explaining the
attitudes of young workers in general toward unions rather than students' attitudes toward the usefulness of a specific union. This tends to
confirm both the distinction between each type of attitude noted by
Deshpande and Fiorito (1989) and that instrumentality is more heavily
influenced by the context of the specific workplace and union. Second,
the Heshizer and Wilson results suggest that with increasing age and
work experience, the relationship between parental attitudes and
younger worker attitudes toward unions becomes weaker, implying that
other sources besides family may become increasingly more important
socialization agents. Finally, even among college age workers, the attitudes of friends and coworkers and the desire to comply with those
referent groups was related to the attitudes of students toward unions.
However, it is especially interesting to note that although the attitudes
of friends and coworkers toward unions and a desire to comply with
these referent groups is important to young people, parental influences
are still more influential (Amann & Silverblatt, 1987).

Popular Culture

Although there is increasing evidence that parents and other referent
groups play a role in formulating the attitudes of young people toward
unions in general, these sources of subjective norms still leave unexplained a sizeable portion of the variance in the attitudes of young
people toward unions. Perhaps young people's knowledge and perceptions of labor unions are a function of the image projected through the
media and the existing popular culture. In his study of the relationship
between the media and organized labor in the United States, William
Puette (1992) noted that

> In earlier times people were more likely to form their values
> and opinions as well as class and party allegiances under the

influence of family, neighbor, teacher, preacher, and co-worker, but the educational role of such diverse influences has been increasingly co-opted by the media at a rate that has, in fact, accelerated since 1975. (p. 4)

Puette's comment is interesting in several respects. In countries like the United States, where unionization levels are in the range of 15%, unions are becoming an increasingly remote experience for most people, while the media is simultaneously becoming a more immediate experience. Puette (1992) and others (e.g., Parenti, 1986; Rollings, 1983) have suggested that news coverage of unions by the print and electronic media tends to be biased toward selecting events about actual or impending strike actions. For most of the public then, union activity becomes closely associated with negative costs, such as the disruption of employment, services, and worker income. In addition, unions are often portrayed in the media as a political force, and limited attention is focused on the role of unions as catalysts for broader economic or social change (Puette, 1992). Although press coverage of union activities may be particularly influential on the attitudes or beliefs of individuals who have limited knowledge about labor organizations, the more likely situation is that regular exposure or interest in written and electronic news media may be limited among very young workers of high school and college age. In contrast, it is reasonable to suggest that the attitudes that young people develop about labor unions may be more influenced by the *images* that are displayed in movies and television, two media sources that are of particular appeal to adolescents and young adults.

Puette (1992) noted that with some isolated exceptions (e.g., *Hoffa* & *Norma Rae*) North American movies with broad public release have not focused on unions. In contrast Puette observed that instances in which casual or flippant remarks reflecting negatively on unions are numerous in film. It is not unusual to identify subplots within movies that imply or overtly express connections between labor unions and organized crime, or corrupt leadership (e.g., *On the Waterfront, The Godfather, F.I.S.T., & Ransom*). Despite the lack of conclusive evidence, most young people can probably describe the disappearance of Jimmy Hoffa and the role played by organized crime in his death as a result of watching the movie *Hoffa*. Even in comedies, union leaders are frequently portrayed as poorly educated and corrupt individuals who are more concerned about collecting dues than about representing the interests of rank-and-file workers (e.g., *Armed and Dangerous*). Made-for-television movies, such as *Teamster Boss: The Jackie Presser Story* or *Mother Trucker: The Diana Kilmury Story*, and even animated comedies such as *The Simpsons* reinforce popular themes of organized crime and corruption in the labor movement and the existence of union leaders who place personal interests ahead of those of the membership. Even fewer general release movies present a balanced perspective on unions and unionism (e.g., *The American Dream*).

Although no empirical research links the attitudes of young people toward unions with movies and television, it appears reasonable to hypothesize that young people, through the entertainment industry, are frequently exposed to negative images of unions. Such passive exposure may negatively impact on the "image" or beliefs that young workers formulate about unions. In the absence of any other countervailing exposure to images or experiences with unions, the popular culture image conveyed through movies and television may be a primary and prevailing initial source of union information for young people.

Direct Experiences With Labor Unions

Previous sections of this chapter have suggested that although the vast majority of young workers are unlikely to have first-hand experiences with labor unions, the probability of such interactions increases over time with more workforce experience. It is possible that for some young people the first encounter and interaction with unions comes through their part-time work experiences or full-time employment immediately after high school graduation. In most circumstances, this initial encounter with labor unions and union officials occurs on employment in an organization in which union representation is already present.

To date, there is a growing body of research suggesting that a worker's initial experiences with the union that represents them are of considerable importance in shaping the worker's long-term attitudes and commitment to the union (e.g., Fullagar & Barling, 1989; Fullagar,

Gallagher, Gordon, & Clark, 1995; Fullagar, McCoy, & Shull, 1992; Gordon, Philpot, Burt, Thompson, & Spiller, 1980). Experiences such as being personally invited by union officials to attend a union meeting; being informed of employee rights under the contract; or being introduced to the local union steward were significantly related to the worker's support of the union (Fullagar et al., 1995; Gordon et al., 1980). Fullagar et al. (1992) suggest that the relationship between early socialization experiences and a subsequent attachment to a union may be mediated by attitudes toward unions in general. However, it seems inherently reasonable to believe that workers who are made to feel welcomed by the union are likely to support it. In this vein, part of the socialization process for the union may be educating new hires about the instrumental value of union membership.

For young workers encountering their first experience with union representation, the presence or absence of meaningful communication with the union during the early stages of employment may be particularly important in shaping their limited understanding of the role of unions in the workplace. Active efforts to socialize new members can be particularly crucial where union membership is a contractual condition of employment. Under compulsory membership, providing new members with access to union leaders and an understanding of the purpose of the union can become particularly important. In contrast, union officials who neglect to orient new members (youth and adults) may cause long-term decreased loyalty and poor union support. Given young people's uncertain attitudes about unionization, a negative initial union experience characterized by mandatory dues deduction and neglect by union officials may create correspondingly negative long-term attitudes toward unions as well as reinforce negative union stereotypes portrayed through the media.

Finally, some preliminary evidence suggests that the characteristics of the socializing agents are important in shaping long-term attitudes of workers toward their representing unions. Fullagar et al. (1992) in a study of workers participating in a union apprenticeship program found that union representatives who conveyed individual consideration and charismatic leadership styles were particularly effective in developing union loyalty and support among new members. Given the relatively young age of union apprentices, these results suggest that not only is the union's message important for younger union members but also an appealing and comfortable leadership style.

In summary, it appears that the level of concern that unions convey to young people during their early or first experiences with union membership is critical. This may be particularly important for young workers whose first encounters with union membership may tend to support or contradict preexisting attitudes or dispositions toward unions. Like many other facets of professional and social encounters, first impressions may serve as lasting impressions.

CURRENT TRENDS AND FUTURE DIRECTIONS

The relationship between young people and labor unions suggests a number of broad observations. First, young workers, particularly those between the ages of 16 and 19, are disproportionately less likely to be union members than are workers in older age categories. This under-representation appears to be due, in part, to the large percentage of young workers employed in industries and relatively small workplaces (i.e., 20 or fewer employees) where unions have traditionally had low involvement or visibility. As suggested by Payne (1989), union joining may be more a function of opportunity than the personal characteristics of workers.

Second, both research studies and opinion surveys tend to indicate that young workers are not necessarily "anti-union." Rather, the data imply that young people are often very uninformed or indifferent about unions. Although considerable evidence suggests that young people's attitudes about unions are strongly influenced by their parent's attitudes, for many young people the role of unions is not well understood or of particular importance.

Finally, in light of some mixed evidence on the point, when young workers express positive attitudes toward unions or express a desire to join a union, the rationale offered is of ideological reasons rather than personal or instrumental gains (Cregan, 1991). Most notably, expressions of a desire to be part of the group, to protect the interests of working people from exploitation, and a general desire to support the union tend to prevail over issues of higher wages or employment security (Cregan & Johnston, 1990). Less clear is the extent to which age and work experience are associated with a movement away from ideological or social motives to a more calculative or self-interested assessment of union representation.

Unfortunately, there are few informative studies examining the reasons why young people decide to join, or not to join, unions. Except for research on the influence of parental attitudes, the reality is that we know very little about how young people formulate their opinions about union membership. In particular, the relative extent to which various factors, such as job satisfaction, past work history, coworker norms, friends' and family influences explain the attitudes of younger versus older workers toward unions is unknown. The question is this: Are models of union attitude formation a function of age or career stage? Young people's attitudes toward unions and union representation may dramatically shift during a short period of time. For example, among 16- to 18-year-olds working part-time jobs after school, union representation may have limited perceived importance. However, after high school graduation and with the search for more permanent employment, economic concerns may generate a greater propensity to support union representation. And, conceivably, young college graduates may have significantly different attitudes toward unions than cohorts of a similar age without college degrees but with 4–5 years of work experience.

As previously suggested, virtually no empirical evidence exists to identify the extent to which media and popular culture influence the attitudes of young workers toward unions. Of particular value would be research determining if popular images of unions shape young people's attitudes and the extent to which such positive and negative images decline in importance with the worker's own first-hand experiences with unionization.

An ancillary question centers on actions that unions themselves can take to gain the current and future support of young workers. Most importantly, what young people desire from union representation is unclear. Although broad ideological reasons may be given by high school and college aged students to support unions, the motivation for union joining may, in fact, change as young people begin full-time work careers. Unfortunately, little is known about what young people seek or expect from union representation.

Unions have begun to place greater emphasis on developing union organizers and local union officers who have gender and racial characteristics similar to the current or target membership. Along a similar line, more consideration might be given to the development of a younger cadre of union organizers. Such efforts at involving college age students in union organizing campaigns and political action was a central component of the Union Summer program organized in the United States by the AFL–CIO in 1996. The program's goal was to involve a new generation of unionists by reaching out to nontraditional union members and workers in low-wage industries. What is especially interesting about the Union Summer program is the involvement of young organizers under the theme, "Taking a Stand for Social Justice." This theme appears consistent with the previously noted ideological orientation of young union supporters (Chartrand, 1996). Furthermore, increased union efforts to rely on young workers to introduce other young workers to unionization appear entirely consistent with existing relational demography research. Such research suggests that young workers are more likely to identify with and respond to workers with similar demographic characteristics (Tsui & O'Reilly, 1989).

With the exception of reliable research findings which link early union socialization efforts and subsequent loyalty and union support (e.g., Fullagar et al., 1995; Gordon et al., 1980), very little can be said about strategies to involve young workers in the governance and activities of the union in which they may belong. If unions are serious about the importance of young people as the future of the labor movement, it seems that union efforts need to extend beyond organizing to include developing active union participation by young members. In environments where unions are experiencing decreased membership participation, it appears that research attention needs to identify the factors associated with the willingness of young members to take active roles in the unions that represent them.

CONCLUSION

Union representation among young people seems to be both a function of their propensity or willingness to join a union and the presence of an opportunity to join or to be represented by one. For young people in the industrialized nations, the propensity and opportunity to be represented by a labor union may differ dramatically. Among nations with dramatic declines in unionization, the visibility and benefits of union representation may be becoming more abstract for young workers. It is our hope that future investigations of the relationship between young workers and unions can better identify the factors that shape the attitudes of young people toward unions and also explore what tangible benefits associated with unionization are valued by young workers. By better understanding what young workers need, unions can become more effective in recruiting and maintaining the union members of the future.

REFERENCES

Amann, R. J., & Silverblatt, R. (1987). High school students' views on unionism. *Labor Studies Journal, 11,* 45–60.

Australian Council of Trade Unions. (1995, September). *Young people and unions* (Report to the ACTU Congress). Melbourne, Australia: Author

Barling, J., Fullagar, C., & Kelloway, E. K. (1992). *The union and its members.* Oxford, England: Oxford University Press.

Barling, J., & Gallagher, D. G. (1996). Part-time employment. In C. L. Cooper & I. T. Robertson (Eds.), *International review of industrial and organizational psychology* (Vol. 11, pp. 243–273). Chichester, England: Wiley.

Barling, J., Kelloway, E. K., & Bremermann, E. H. (1991). Pre-employment predictors of union attitudes: The role of family socialization and work beliefs. *Journal of Applied Psychology, 76,* 725–731.

Brief, A. P., & Rude, D. E. (1981). Voting in union certification elections: A conceptual analysis. *Academy of Management Review, 6,* 261–267.

Chaison, G. N., & Dhavale, D. G. (1992). The choice between union membership and free-rider status. *Journal of Labor Research, 13*, 355–369.

Chartrand, S. (1996, June 6). Labor adjusts strategies to digital era. *The New
York Times.*

Cregan, C. (1991). Young people and trade union membership: A longitudinal
analysis. *Applied Economics, 23*, 1511–1518.

Cregan, C., & Johnston, S. (1990). An industrial relations approach to the free
rider problem: Young people and trade union membership in the U.K.
British Journal of Industrial Relations, 28, 84–104.

Cregan, C., & Johnston, S. (1993). Young workers and quit behavior. *Applied
Economics, 25*, 25–33.

Deshpande, S. P., & Fiorito, J. (1989). Specific and general beliefs in union
voting models. *Academy of Management Journal, 32*, 883–897.

Fishbein, M., & Ajzen, I. (1975). *Belief, attitude, intention and behavior: An
introduction to theory and research.* Reading, MA: Addison-Wesley.

Frenkel, S. (Ed.). (1993). *Organized labor in the Asia-Pacific region.* Ithaca, NY:
ILR Press.

Fullagar, C., & Barling, J. (1989). A longitudinal test of a model of the antecedents and consequences of union loyalty. *Journal of Applied Psychology,
74*, 213–227.

Fullagar, C., Gallagher, D. G., Gordon, M. E., & Clark, P. (1995). Impact of
early socialization on union commitment and participation: A longitudinal study. *Journal of Applied Psychology, 80*, 147–157.

Fullagar, C., McCoy, D., & Shull, C. (1992). The socialization of union loyalty.
Journal of Organizational Psychology, 13, 13–26.

Gallagher, D. G., & Jeong, Y. A. (1989). *Methodological concerns with behavioral
studies of union memberships.* Paper presented at the 10th Annual Southern
Regional Industrial Relations Academic Seminar, West Virginia University,
Morgantown.

Gordon, M. E., Philpot, J. W., Burt, R. E., Thompson, C. A., & Spiller,
W. E. (1980). Commitment to the union: Development of a measure and
an examination of its correlates. *Journal of Applied Psychology, 65*, 479–
499.

Guest, D. E., & Dewe, P. (1988). Why do workers belong to a trade union? A social psychological study of the U.K. electronics industry. *British Journal of Industrial Relations, 26,* 178–193.

Heshizer, B. P., & Wilson, M. C. (1995). The role of referent beliefs in the socialization of union attitudes. *Journal of Social Behavior and Personality, 10,* 771–790.

Huszczo, G. E. (1983). Attitudinal and behavioral variables related to participation in union activities. *Journal of Labor Research, 4,* 287–297.

Jermier, J. M., Cohen, C. F., & Gaines, J. (1988). Paying dues to the union: A study of blue-collar workers in a right-to-work environment. *Journal of Labor Research, 9,* 168–181.

Kelloway, E. K., & Watts, L. (1994). Preemployment predictors of union attitudes: Replication and extension. *Journal of Applied Psychology, 79,* 631–634.

Klandermans, B. (1986). Psychology of trade union participation: Joining, acting, quitting. *Journal of Occupational Psychology, 59,* 189–204.

Kochan, T. A., Katz, H. C., & McKersie, R. B. (1986). *The transformation of American industrial relations.* New York: Basic Books.

Montgomery, R. B. (1989). The influence of attitudes and normative pressure on voting decisions in a union certification election. *Industrial and Labor Relations Review, 42,* 262–279.

Olney, S. L. (1996). *Unions in a changing world.* Geneva, Switzerland: ILO.

Parenti, M. (1986). *Inventing reality: The politics of mass media.* New York: St. Martin's Press.

Payne, C. (1989). Trade union membership and activism among young people in Britain. *British Journal of Industrial Relations, 27,* 111–132.

Premack, S. L., & Hunter, J. E. (1988). Individual unionization decisions. *Psychological Bulletin, 103,* 223–234.

Puette, W. J. (1992). *Through jaundiced eyes: How the media view organized labor.* Ithaca, NY: Cornell University Press.

Rollings, J. (1983). Mass communications and the American worker. In V. Mosco & J. Wasko (Eds.), *Labor, the working class, and the media* (pp. 129–152). Norwood, NJ: Ablex.

Strauss, G., Gallagher, D. G., & Fiorito, J. (Eds.). (1991). *The state of the unions.* Madison, WI: Industrial Relations Research Association.

Sverke, M. (Ed.). (1997). *The future of trade unionism.* Aldershot, England: Ashgate.

Tsui, A. S., & O'Reilly, C. A., III. (1989). Beyond simple demographic effects: The importance of relational demography in superior-subordinate dyads. *Academy of Management Journal, 32,* 402–423.

Wheeler, H. N., & McClendon, J. A. (1991). The individual decision to unionize. In G. Strauss, D. G. Gallagher, & J. Fiorito (Eds.), *The state of the unions* (pp. 47–83). Madison, WI: Industrial Relations Research Association.

Youngblood, S. A., DeNisi, A. A., Molleston, J. L., & Mobley, W. H. (1984). The impact of work environment, instrumentality, beliefs, perceived labor union image and subjective norms on union voting intentions. *Academy of Management Journal, 27,* 576–590.

Afterword: Implications for Policy and Research

The chapters in this volume have pointed to the fact that employed youth are neither a homogenous group, nor do they have homogenous work experiences. Several implications for further research and policy proceed from this observation. In general, all the findings of our contributors suggest a need for greater refinement of the variables of interest; that is, a more refined definition of *youth* and an elaborated consideration of the nature of youth employment.

Current practice defines *youth* as the life stage between the ages of 15 and 24 years (or in some countries 16 and 24 years; see chap. 8, this volume). However convenient this definition for statistical reporting of young people's employment and unemployment figures, it should be recognized that the use of arbitrary age boundaries for the category "youth" does not provide an adequate basis for either public policy or research. The problems with this definition have been previously reviewed as consisting of the exclusion of relevant members from the category and the obscuring of relevant differences within it.

Certainly, age is a relevant factor in policy formulation. For example, one would not argue for the abolition of child labor laws that exclude employment of children below a specified age. However, research and policy concerning youth and employment should also consider the timing and nature of such employment. For example, policies relevant to teenagers employed part-time during high school are probably not appropriately applied to school leavers who are full-time participants in the job market. Moreover, the research issues for each group differ substantially.

Policy makers and researchers should also consider both the context and content of employment. Policies that explicitly exclude certain types of occupations (e.g., agricultural work; see chap. 6, this volume) are not justified in light of the research evidence. For example, the physical risks involved in having a 12-year-old operate heavy machinery are similar whether the machinery consists of a forklift in a factory warehouse or farm tractor. Similarly, the physiological needs of children (i.e., for sleep, rest breaks, etc.) do not change because the child is employed in agricultural work. Policies or legislation dealing with youth employment that exempt, or make special provision for, specific industries are not justified in light of the developmental needs of the child.

Second, just as research on youth employment has ignored the informal economy, policy makers have (by definition) not considered the vast amount of youth employment that occurs outside the bounds of formal employment. Yet the tasks performed by workers in the informal economy may exactly parallel those performed by employees in more formal employment relationships. In this sense, the existence of the informal economy presents a challenge to policy makers.

One possible way of overcoming this challenge is to formulate policy addressing the nature of the tasks performed rather than the context in which these tasks are performed. To continue the preceding example about agricultural industry exemptions, if the intent of policy is to prohibit children of a certain age from operating heavy equipment, then the policy should be phrased in terms of the task (i.e., operating heavy equipment) rather than the employment relationship (i.e., as a formal job or as part of the social or irregular economy).

Such policies do not fit neatly into existing jurisdictions (e.g., child welfare, labor) but rather cut across jurisdictions to deal with a variety of contexts. However, the health and safety data (see chap. 7, this volume) and data on child labor (see chap. 6, this volume) suggest that policies and legislation regulating the nature of the activity, rather than the employment context in which the activity occurs, are clearly required.

Finally, and again following from the preceding discussion, policy makers should consider recent research evidence highlighting the importance of work quality in the experience of youth employment. Simply regulating whether young people can be employed, or for how many hours a week may not address the central determinants of individual well-being. Indeed, limiting the hours of employment in a high-quality job may be detrimental to the individual. Public policy on youth and employment should recognize that it is not whether an individual is employed or for how many hours a week that is of most importance. Rather, it is the nature of the tasks and relationships in the employment environment (i.e., the quality of the work) that makes the difference.

Throughout this discussion we have highlighted two central observations about youth and employment. First, youth are not a homogenous group. Second, employment is not a homogenous experience. Not surprisingly, the differences between high- and low-quality jobs have implications for the well-being and future of the individual.

To some extent, research on youth and employment has taken the worst of two fields: the worst of developmental psychology by using overly simplistic, convenience-based definitions of youth, and the worst of organizational psychology by treating employment as a dichotomous variable or a social address. As the chapters in this volume attest, researchers are now moving beyond these initial positions to adopt more sophisticated and appropriate definitions of both youth and employment. This movement requires a synthesis of data from both developmental and organizational psychology. We suggest that given the vulnerability of the population in question, such a synthesis is urgently required and hope that this volume assists researchers to move in that direction.

Author Index

Numbers in italics refer to listings in reference sections.

Subject Index

Work status, 92
  and academic attachment, 96–97
  and academic performance, 94–95
  and behavioral outcomes, 115–116
  and career development, 103–104
  and educational attainment, 101
  and family development, 109–110
  and health, 111–112

and occupational attainment, 107
and personality, 113–114

Young workers, 18
Youth, 5, 259
Youth employment, 31

Zimbabwe, 132

About the Editors

Julian Barling received his PhD in 1979 from the University of the Witwatersrand, in Johannesburg, South Africa. He joined the Department of Psychology at Queen's University in 1984 and moved to the School of Business in 1994, where he is now Professor of Organizational Behavior and Psychology. Since then, he has served as the Academic Director of the Executive MBA programs, and he is currently chair of the PhD and MSc programs.

He is the author of several books, including *Employment, Stress and Family Functioning* (1990), *The Union and Its Members: A Psychological Approach* (with C. Fullagar and E. K. Kelloway, 1992), and *Changing Employment Relations: Behavioral and Social Perspectives* (with L. Tetrick, 1995). Dr. Barling is coeditor (with E. K. Kelloway) of the Sage Publications series Advanced Topics in Organizational Behavior, and he is on the editorial boards of the *Journal of Organizational Behavior*, the *Journal of Occupational Health Psychology, Stress Medicine*, and the *Canadian Journal of Administrative Sciences*.

From 1989 to 1991, Dr. Barling was the chairperson of the Advisory Council on Occupational Health and Safety to the Ontario Minister of Labor. In 1995, he received the annual award for Excellence in Research from the School of Business, Queen's University. In 1997, Dr. Barling received the annual award for Excellence in Research from Queen's University.

E. Kevin Kelloway received his PhD in 1991 from Queen's University in Kingston, Ontario. He joined the Department of Psychology at the University of Guelph in 1991, where he is currently Professor of Organizational Psychology.

He is the author of several books, including *Using LISREL for Struc-*

tural Equation Modeling: A Researcher's Guide (1998), *Flexible Work Arrangements: Managing the Work-Family Boundary* (with B. Gottlieb and L. Barham, 1998), and *The Union and Its Members: A Psychological Approach* (with J. Barling and C. Fullagar, 1992). Dr. Kelloway is coeditor (with J. Barling) of the Sage Publications series Advanced Topics in Organizational Behavior.

Dr. Kelloway's research interests include unionization, occupational health psychology, leadership, and the development of work beliefs and work values.